Choose to Live Peacefully

SUSAN SMITH JONES, PH.D.

CELESTIAL ARTS
BERKELEY, CALIFORNIA

The health suggestions and recommendations in this book are based on the training, research and personal experiences of the author. Because each person and each situation is unique, the author and publisher encourage the reader to check with his or her holistic physician or other health professional before using any procedure outlined in this book. It is a sign of wisdom to seek a second or third opinion. Because there is some risk involved, neither the author nor the publisher is responsible for any adverse consequences resulting from a change in diet or from fasting or from the use of any other suggestions in this book. The publisher does not advocate the use of any particular diet, fasting or health program, but believes that the information in this book should be available to the public.

Note: *A person desiring to fast should do so only under proper hygienic or medical supervision. Be sure to discuss with your doctor the use of any drugs. (Please refer to the Resource Directory for Certified fasting supervision centers.)*

The consensus of medical opinion is that the use of drugs during a fast is highly dangerous and must be precisely regulated by an expert. Lengthy fasting is not recommended for those afflicted with diabetes, tuberculosis, or certain other advanced and debilitating diseases. Fasting during pregnancy and lactation should be avoided. Close supervision is strongly advised throughout the fast. Competent expertise is also necessary when breaking the fast, together with proper care during the post-adjustment period.

Cover design by Toni Good
Cover photo by Richard Thompson
Back cover photo by Mark Farrell
Text design and composition by Jeff Brandenburg, ImageComp

FIRST PRINTING 1992

Library of Congress Cataloging in Publication Data

Jones, Susan Smith
      Choose to live peacefully / Susan Smith Jones.
         p.   cm.
      Includes bibliographical references.
      ISBN 0-89087-615-0
      1. Conduct of life.   2. Peace of mind.   3. Health.   I. Title.
BJ1581.2.J657   1991
291.4'48—dc20   90-25583
                                                       CIP

---

5 6 7 8 9 — 00 99 98 97 96

Table of Contents

This book is lovingly dedicated:

To Jesus Christ, my prince of peace, who has shown me how to live peacefully and lovingly.

To Paramahansa Yogananda, without whose teachings and guidance in my spiritual unfoldment this book would not have been written.

To all seekers.

Peace I leave with you; my peace I give to you . . .

Jesus Christ
John 14:27

The greatest romance is with the Infinite. You have no idea how beautiful life can be. When you suddenly find God everywhere, when He comes and talks to you and guides you, the romance of divine love has begun.

Paramahansa Yogananda
Man's Eternal Quest

Acknowledgements

I want to express my gratitude to the following people:

June B. Smith, my best friend and mother, for teaching me about unconditional love, to believe in myself, and to go after my dreams;

Peace Pilgrim, who has inspired me to live my life more fully—by embracing simple living and high thinking, solitude and silence, joy and peace, and for showing me how to live in the presence of God;

Paramahansa Yogananda, my spiritual teacher, who, for the last twenty-five years, has been building my bridge of love and helping me to make it to the other side;

Lynn Carroll, Helen Guppy, Jimmy Langkop, Kathy Martelli, Rev. John Strickland, Mary and Wayne Bianchin, George Marks, Arch and Dee Wilkie, Brian D. Sievers, Ralph J. Rudser, Gloria and Wally Hill, Mary A. Tomlinson, Bill Carnahan and Dean Ornish, M.D., my special friends who have all been a steady source of support, inspiration, and love;

David Hinds, Sal Glynn, and Mary Ann Anderson at Celestial Arts, for supporting my vision with encouragement, kindness, and love;

My guardian angels, my constant celestial companions, who gently guide me every step of the way with their affectionate attention, wise counsel, sense of humor, loving patience and support and for enlivening my day-to-day activities.

Introduction

'Tis the good reader that makes the good book; in
every book he finds passages which seem
confidences or asides hidden from all else and
unmistakenly meant for his ear; the profit of all books
is according to the sensibility of the reader; the
profoundest thought or passion sleeps as in a mine,
until it is discovered by an equal mind and heart.

Ralph Waldo Emerson, "Success"

Hello,

This moment — right now — can be a new peaceful beginning.
No longer do you need to repeat the past, worry about the future,
or struggle through life as a victim of circumstances. For as long
as you live your life absorbed in the present moment, surrendered
to God, responsible and accountable for who you are and what
you want to become — you will come to experience a life more
splendid, more wondrous and more peaceful than you ever dreamed
possible. Unleash the peace within you now. There is simply
nothing in the world more valuable than peace, and it is within
each of us to choose as a conscious goal.

It is with great joy that I share with you this book and my
adventure — an adventure to realize and experience a deeper
peace within me and in all life. From my international travels, my
meeting and talking with people from all walks of life, I have
become acutely aware that we all want the same thing. Peace. We
all want more peace in our own lives and in our world. Peace
between nations must rest on a solid foundation of peace between
individuals. And to feel peaceful with others, we must first feel
peace within ourselves. What is peace to you? How peaceful are
you?

Can you remain peaceful regardless of the circumstances in
your life? If you have a quarrel with a family member or friend,

can you still be at peace? If the traffic is backed up for miles and you know you'll be an hour late for work and will miss an important meeting, does your peace fly out the window? If your bills far exceed your income, can you be peaceful? If you were fired, gained weight, came down with the flu, or if you blew two tires at once, could you feel peaceful? According to great spiritual teachers, no matter what befalls you, you always have a choice and can choose to be peaceful. *A Course in Miracles*, a three-volume text on spiritual matters and peaceful living, says, "I could see peace instead of this."

I wanted to write this book for two reasons. First, I wanted to share my feelings and ideas about peace — what it is and how we each can create more peace in our lives and in our world. Secondly, I wanted to take you along with me on a forty-day consecration fast, part of my personal spiritual program. Following inner guidance, I have decided to set aside some time to consecrate my life to prayer, meditation and fasting and to cultivate my awareness of God. Because there is no blueprint for what I plan to do, I have simply designed a program that feels right to me.

Last year, I experimented with a sixty-day spiritual program that was outlined in *A Spiritual Philosophy for the New World* by John Randolph Price. The essence of Price's program is surrendering everything in your life, all that you are, to God and to God's will for you and living, essentially, as a spiritual being rather than a human being. My experience from that sixty-day program was wonderful. I gained insight on how to live life more lovingly, peacefully, joyfully, abundantly and freely. I wanted to do a similar program this year, and I wanted to include fasting, which was not part of Price's program.

My aim this time is to distance myself physically from the world, to allow myself time to reflect and renew, to spend quality time in solitude and silence, to simplify and to rediscover my spirituality and my relationship to God, to truth and to the life force in all. I want to find my way back to my own connectedness and learn how to make peace my constant companion.

Oftentimes, in the pursuit of our physical and mental goals, we do not take the time to nurture our spiritual nature, where all joy and peace originate. My spiritual teacher, Paramahansa Yogananda, encourages each of us to become more conscious of the presence of God. He recommends that as we walk or work or perform any of our daily activities, we should try to feel the power of the Infinite behind everything and within our bodies; we should realize that without that divine vitality we couldn't do anything. "It is when you persistently and selflessly perform every action with love-inspired thoughts of God that He will come to you," Yogananda teaches. God alone empowers us.

> Then you realize that you are the Ocean of Life, which has become the tiny wave of each life. This is the way of knowing the Lord through activity. When in every action you think of Him before you act, while you are performing the action, and after you have finished it, He will reveal Himself to you. You must work, but let God work through you; this is the best part of devotion. If you are constantly thinking that He is walking through your feet, working through your hands, accomplishing through your will, you will know Him.

My goal then during my forty-day fast is to devote my life — my thoughts, words, actions, feelings, emotions, beliefs, body, attachments, everything — to God. All that I do during this sequestered time, I will strive to do as a love offering to God.

If you've read *Practicing His Presence* by Brother Lawrence, the seventeenth-century French lay brother of the Carmelites, you know that he spoke of the "inexpressible sweetness" that he tasted when he communed with God. Walt Whitman, in one of the most articulate passages about communing with and living in God's presence, wrote:

> When I undertake to tell the best, I find I cannot.
> My tongue is ineffectual on its pivots,
> My breath will not be obedient to its organs,
> I become a dumb man.

As I undertake to live in God's presence during my forty-day fast, I will be inspired by the words and lives of those spiritual pilgrims who have gone before me. One of the dearest of these to me is Peace Pilgrim, whose life profoundly affected mine when I began to read her works in the early 1980s. Peace Pilgrim was a resplendent woman who began a twenty-eight-year pilgrimage for peace when she was in her mid-fifties. She dropped her given name and all of her possessions, and from January of 1953 to her death in July of 1981, she walked throughout the United States, following this vow: "I shall remain a wanderer until mankind has learned the ways of peace, walking until given shelter and fasting until given food." She lived on faith and on God's guidance and support, calmly trusting that her minimal needs would be provided. She had no money and accepted none. She carried her only worldly possessions — a comb, a toothbrush, pen, paper and correspondence to be answered — in the pockets that encircled the bottom of the short tunic covering her shirt.

In her travels she passed through all fifty states, talking about and demonstrating through her actions her ideas on living peacefully. The people she met always freely gave her food and shelter, paper and postage. Peace Pilgrim walked as a spiritual practice, believing that she needed to take her practice of inner peace out into the world. "I walk prayerfully, and as an opportunity to talk with many people and perhaps inspire them to do something for peace also, in their own way," she said. Peace Pilgrim talked about peace between nations, peace among groups and between individuals, and most importantly, inner peace.

Peace Pilgrim lived her beliefs. Although I never met her, I've read her books (*Peace Pilgrim* and *Steps Toward Inner Peace*) countless times, have watched her videos and listened to her audiocassettes, all of which are available through Friends of Peace Pilgrim. Hearing recordings of her speak, which she did regularly at schools, colleges, churches, in homes or wherever people would listen, I am always struck by her radiance, vibrancy and simple, clear message. (For a free 216-page book, *Peace Pilgrim*, contact friends of Peace Pilgrim in the Resource Directory.)

> When we have found inner peace we feel unity with the Divine within all human beings and unity with God, so all fear is gone from our lives. As long as we feel separate we are afraid to be and act alone — as soon as we feel oneness that feeling is gone. . . . Many people are suffering from spiritual starvation — even though what they need is within them and all around them.

Jesus Christ, perhaps the world's greatest teacher of living peacefully, lovingly and anchored in the presence of God, demonstrated by the way He lived His life that the peace of God is more important than anything the world has to offer and that we can all choose to live a peaceful life. Everything Jesus said and every action He took had its foundation in God, in peace. He didn't care about differences between people; He saw all as innocent children of God. He offered no dogma, just tenderheartedness and compassion. He did not punish people or pass judgment but prescribed love and forgiveness. He was a master of love and peace.

All the words of Jesus are clear and simple. *The Essene Jesus* by Edmond Bordeaux Szekely says that Jesus's teaching can be summed up in two words — creative love — which creates new values everywhere and at all times and changes the kingdom of man into the Kingdom of God.

> If this peace appears in ourselves and among ourselves, if the kingdom of God is in us and among us, then this peace will be universal and there will be no more problems and the teachings of the Son of Man will be fulfilled and there will be peace in and around us. So this higher peace, peace with ourselves, peace with all the forces of nature and peace with all the higher cosmic forces and laws, will be a universal harmony. So Jesus and his disciples always greeted one another: **"Peace be unto you."** This peace is ours in a universal sense, and this peace can be acquired by all of us. He showed to us the way, the truth, the life and the peace.

Jesus advocated fasting for both therapeutic and spiritual benefits. In numerous biblical references, Jesus recommends that we "pray and fast" to purify and renew the body and mind and to make the body the temple of God that it is meant to be.

For the past twenty years, as you will discover as you read further, I have done extensive research on fasting and have fasted several hundred times myself. But until now I have never fasted for forty days to achieve spiritual rejuvenation. In his eye-opening, insightful book, *Spiritual Nutrition and the Rainbow Diet*, physician and author Gabriel Cousens* writes in great detail about fasting and how, if done properly and with the right intention, it

---

* also the author of *Sevenfold Peace* and *Conscious Eating*

enhances the transformation of the spirit. He cites the history of fasting as an essential discipline for the attainment of true knowledge in the spiritual practices of almost all religions. Cousens also notes that fasting for spiritual purposes usually involves some degree of removing of oneself from worldly responsibilities. In addition, he cautions that fasting, to enhance divine communion, should be considered only after a clear signal from the inner self suggests it. I found his discussion on how to prepare for a fast, how to fast and why some people should not fast and his accounts of his own forty-day fast and numerous shorter fasts most enlightening.

Approximately a year ago I received inner direction to embark on a forty-day fast. I was to consume nothing but water and commit myself to living in the presence of God. As I take you through the fast with me, I'll write in more detail about my preparations. For now, I want to give you just the outline of the program I've designed for myself.

First, I will take two months away from my normal worldly activities — teaching, writing magazine articles, traveling, lecturing, counseling and consulting. During these two months, I will live in God-communion, as much as possible as a spiritual being rather than a human being. In the first ten days of this time away from the world, I will taper my food intake and will gradually reduce my diet to fresh raw juices. Then I will begin my forty-day fast, taking in only pure water. At the end of those forty days, I will reverse the process, starting with juices and gradually adding foods until I've returned to my normal diet.

You may wonder why I picked this amount of time, forty days, to fast. In the Bible the number forty, indicates a cycle of completed spiritual growth. Each period of Moses's life was forty years. Jesus went into the wilderness for forty days and forty nights. And my inner guidance said I was to fast for forty days.

During my forty-day fast, I want to accomplish several things. Each day I will spend at least three hours praying and meditating; I will devote some time to simplifying how I live (which probably means giving away a lot of "stuff"); I will read spiritual, inspirational books; I will strive to be conscious of God's presence in my life each waking minute. I want every action, thought and feeling to be imbued with the Infinite. These are my goals. I also plan to write a chapter of this book each day, exploring a different facet of peace in each chapter. At the end of the book, I'll share with you my feelings about the experience.

Please don't think I'm suggesting that you should fast forty days or leave all your worldly responsibilities to turn inward. Not at all. I am delighted simply to have this opportunity to share with you this great adventure in my life. I intend the contents of this book as gentle guidelines and tools, rather than rules and imperatives. As I write each chapter, I will pray that all of you who read it discover and connect with the peace of your being and, in turn, live more peacefully. Only when we all realize that we are divine, peaceful children of God, and act from that awareness, will the presence of peace in the world increase.

The saying, "The ancients have stolen all our best ideas," remains true. What I'm writing about isn't new; it's fresh only in that it's written from my perspective, my way of looking at peace, living fully and celebrating life. In a way, I'm writing this book for myself, as something I can turn to for inspiration and motivation. Clearly, I'll be writing about myself, my thoughts, research, experiences and life. I hope my account evokes in you a desire to live your life more from your inner fountain of peace than from the demands of the world. You may not agree with my chosen path or what I write; all I ask is that you keep your heart tender and your mind open. As you read, continually ask yourself, "Am I practicing the absence of God instead of practicing the presence?" Open yourself to your inner guidance while reading this book; listen to your heart. Keep in the forefront of your thinking the idea of peace and the knowledge that there is a peace beyond all fear, beyond everything — that is God's radiance within each of us all just waiting to become manifest.

I suggest that you read this book through once in its entirety. Then read it again, slowly and deliberately, reading no more than one chapter a day. Think about the topic for the day. Absorb it. Practice living it, if you feel called to do so, and make sure you participate in the "Taking Inventory and Action" and "Today's Affirmation" sections at the end of each chapter. In so doing, you will learn more about yourself and will see more easily what changes you may want to make. Living peacefully usually means making changes. The first step in changing is becoming aware of things you do that are not peacemaking. You may want to consider setting aside forty days to go on your own peace program. You don't need to include fasting, but you might want to read one chapter each day and then see how you can make that particular aspect of peace part of your life.

Books are more than words on a page. You, the reader, bring the words to life. Apply what you read and look for ways you can experience more peace in your life than you've ever felt before. I'm the first to acknowledge that my forty-day fast is out of the ordinary, which seems to be the way I've lived most of my life. As you read this book, you'll get a sense of how I've followed my inner guidance rather than the crowd. I love what Henry David Thoreau said about the books he preferred to read.

> Books, not which afford us a cowering enjoyment, but in which each thought is of unusual daring; such as an idle person cannot read, and a timid one would not be entertained by, which even make us dangerous to existing institutions — such I call good books.

Now is the time to choose to live fully, celebrate life and to live more from inner guidance. Make your life the magnificent adventure it was created to be. I salute your great adventure, and I wish you peace.

> God's answer is some form of peace. All pain
> Is healed; all misery replaced with joy.
> All prison doors are opened. And all sin
> Is understood as merely a mistake.
>
> Peace be to me, the holy son of God.
> Peace to my brother, who is one with me.
> Let all the world be blessed with peace through us.
>
> *A Course in Miracles*
> Lessons 359 and 360

> Two roads diverged in a wood, and I —
> I took the one less traveled by,
> And that has made all the difference.
>
> Robert Frost
> "The Road Not Taken"

CHAPTER 1

Celebrate Yourself and Life

What a piece of work is a man! How noble in reason!
How infinite in faculty! In form, and moving, how
express and admirable! In action how like an angel!
In apprehension how like a god! The beauty of the
world! The paragon of animals!

Shakespeare, *Hamlet*

Have you ever stopped to think about how unique, special and marvelous you are? No one else in the world, now or in the past or in the future, is exactly like you. Never, from amongst all the seventy-five billion humans who have walked this planet since the beginning of time, has there been anyone exactly like you. As I thought about this concept this morning, I thought about the approximately five billion people living on our planet. Then I figured out how long it would take to count all these people if they passed by me single file, one every second.

Imagine this. A clock ticks out the seconds while you sit in a rocking chair on your front porch; without taking time out to stretch your legs, eat your meals or rest your eyes, count each person passing by. How many weeks or months do you think it would take to count the world's population, one per second? You would have to sit there continuously for 150 years. One hundred fifty years! *And by that time you would probably be off your rocker!*

This calculation was another amazing lesson for me in the miraculousness of life. Try to grasp the idea that for 150 years you would never find two people exactly alike. You would never find two whose experiences had been the same or whose fingerprints were alike or who thought, believed, felt or talked alike.

And then to that, add the fact that you are the one special being created from one egg and one out of more than 500 million sperm that traveled an immense distance, overcame tremendous obstacles and won the competition — probably the fiercest and most challenging of your life — at the moment of your conception. You are already a winner. What's more, you are composed of a body, mind and spirit, and you already have everything you need to live up to your highest potential, to become master of your life. I think that calls for a celebration. "You are the temple of the living God." (2 Cor. 6:16) "The place where you stand is holy ground." (Exod. 3:5) You are amazing in who you are and what you can do with your life.

We must honor who we are. Paramahansa Yogananda used to tell his students, "A little gram of your flesh contains enough latent energy to keep the city of Chicago supplied with electricity for a week. And yet," he continued, "you complain of feeling tired! It is because you live too much attached to the body, rather than seeing yourselves as waves of God's infinite energy!"

Of course we must take care of our bodies, and we must also see our bodies for what they are — temples of God. Too often we identify too much with the way our bodies look. Just last week, I saw a television program that horrified me. The subject was plastic surgery. Interviewees were teenagers who were unhappy with their looks. They were getting all types of plastic surgery — breast implants, ribs removed to make their waists smaller, cheek and chin implants, fat sucked out and lips puffed up. To me what was even worse was the encouragement that their parents were giving these teenagers to create the bodies of their dreams. I could see that the parents didn't feel good about their own bodies and were passing that dislike on to their children.

Look at magazine ads or television commercials; either by innuendo or by outright declaration, they are almost all aimed at changing who we are, making us somehow better — smarter, more attractive, slimmer, richer, more secure. You can spend millions of dollars changing your physical features, but that will do little good until you change your attitude about yourself and cultivate a relationship with yourself that incorporates your very own divinity. When you do that, chances are you'll be happy with the physical body that God provided for you, and you will establish a salutary health and fitness program to keep your body temple in peak functioning order.

We must *choose* to be kind and loving toward ourselves — all the time. Self-image is crucial here. Being radiantly healthy, living fully and celebrating life starts with celebrating ourselves. Whether we succeed or fail, enjoy our lives or struggle, depends largely on our self-image. In fact, numerous studies have concluded that the view we have of ourselves is the key to taking control of our lives.

Develop a loving relationship, a warm friendship with yourself. Be your own best friend. Out of that friendship all your other relationships form. Stop being so critical, judgmental and unforgiving of yourself. When you are not feeling good about you, you feel separated from others and God. When you see yourself as a failure, you create a self-fulfilling prophecy. You attract to yourself that which you believe you deserve. Your negative thoughts and attitudes about yourself, whether they originated within yourself or others, convince you of your inability to succeed. If you feel you don't deserve success, don't deserve prosperity, don't deserve to enjoy life, don't deserve happy relationships, joy and peace, you settle for less than that to which you are entitled. When you feel unworthy, you cut yourself off from the fullness of life.

Unconditional self-love and self-acceptance can disconnect this vicious cycle. Whitman wrote, "I celebrate myself . . . and love myself." Through inner work, we can develop genuine self-esteem, self-confidence, self-respect and self-appreciation. The next step is to go beyond our limiting beliefs and realize our importance to ourselves and to the world. Each one of us is unique and has something very special to offer. God doesn't make any mistakes. Understand that you have always done your best at any given time; you don't have to be so hard on yourself. And now, you have the opportunity to choose again. Choose to take wonderful, loving care of yourself, your body temple and your magnificent world. Look within for guidance and for the answers to your questions. If you are willing and open, you will find what you have been seeking.

I was listening to Ken and Barclay on KABC, a Los Angeles radio talk show, this morning and was astounded by something one of the hosts read. He said that the blood vessels in your body, if they were all removed and laid end to end, would circle the earth twice. Then he said that the chemicals in your body are worth just two dollars. But the whole body with all the organs is worth $200,000. Wow! That got me thinking about what price I would put on life. For me, no amount of money in the world could equal the experience of life. When we connect with God and remember how powerful and capable we really are, we live life to the hilt. Life is here to be enjoyed.

Ernest Holmes, who developed a philosophy that he called the Science of Mind, wrote, "You are the only person you can ever know intimately. You are the one with whom you must live eternally." So begin discovering yourself and all the beauty, splendor and wonder housed within you. Who you truly are deep in your heart is so much greater than anything you'll ever achieve in life. Indeed, as Anwar Sadat, former president of Egypt, said, "I have realized that my real self is a greater entity than any possible post or title." Your real self — divine self — is a deep river that connects with God and with all life. At this moment, your real self may be hidden or unexpressed, but it is always available to you, with all its profundity, joy and wisdom. When attuned to this inner self, we are, in the words of mythologist Joseph Campbell, "following our bliss."

Follow the path to your own divinity. When you go home to that special place of peace and light within your being, the whole world opens up to you; you will truly understand what it means to celebrate yourself and to live fully.

There is an irresistible Universal and Divine urge within us to be happy, to be whole, and to express the fullness of Life. The latent Divinity within us stirs our imagination and, because of Its insistent demand, impels and compels our growth. It is back of every invention; it proclaims itself through every creative endeavor; it has produced sages, saints, and saviors, and will, when permitted, create a new world in which war, poverty, sickness, and famine will have disappeared.

Ernest Holmes

Living fully is so much more than just surviving. Surviving means fighting your way through life, rarely being joyful, at ease, fulfilled or peaceful. When you are living fully, each day brings reason to celebrate and work and play become one. Living fully is trusting in God and knowing that you are exactly where you need to be. In *The Warrior Athlete*, Dan Millman writes, "Whatever cycles you pass through — no matter what your pace — it's best to trust in natural order, and enjoy yourself each day, come what may, with all the energy and humor at your command." When you live fully, peak experiences become an integral part of your life because you are open and receptive to God's guidance.

When you celebrate yourself and life, you find yourself doing what you love to do. Strength, confidence, joy and peace are the basis of all your experience. Of course, you will encounter some pain and challenges along the way; these are an inevitable part of being human. But when you are living fully, hardships, when they occur, are short-lived, and you can learn from them and grow and change. Whitman describes splendidly this state of celebrating yourself and life:

> A man realizes the venerable myth — he is a god walking the earth, he sees new eligibilities, powers and beauties everywhere; he himself has a new eyesight and hearing. The play of the body in motion takes a previously unknown grace. Merely to move is then a happiness, a pleasure — to breathe, to see, is also. All the beforehand gratifications, drink, spirits, coffee, grease, stimulants, mixtures, late hours, luxuries, deeds of the night, seem as vexatious dreams, and now the awakening.

Awaken to the splendor within your heart. Your radiant body responds to the blessings of love, praise and gratitude. Take time each day to bless your body temple and acknowledge your oneness with spirit. Place all your cares, worries and problems into the light and ask that only those things necessary for your highest good be returned for your attention. Affirm the presence of God within. When you do that, your body will express health, strength and vitality, and your life will be filled with joy, happiness, fulfillment and peace. Celebrate your magnificence.

Choose to live peacefully and celebrate yourself and life.

Whatever your age, if you learn to listen, your inner voice will speak to you about your path.

Bernie S. Siegel, *Peace, Love and Healing*

Taking Inventory and Action

1. How do you feel about your body? Do you express gratitude each day for your body temple?

2. When you look in the mirror, do you praise and appreciate what you see or do you usually offer disparaging remarks?

3. In what ways could your self-esteem and self-confidence be increased?

4. If your life isn't a celebration now, what changes can you make in your attitude, lifestyle and focus to make your life worth celebrating?

5. You are a divine expression of God. Isn't that worth celebrating?

6. You have everything in you right now to assist you in being master of your life. Turn within for guidance.

7. Change your inner voice from one that might speak negatively about you and your abilities to one that always speaks positively.

8. Compliment yourself. Be gentle with yourself. Give yourself pep talks. Smile often. Love God and walk in His light.

9. Every day acknowledge that you are the temple for God and celebrate that oneness.

10. Live in the presence of God.

Today's Affirmation

The holy presence of God within me heals my mind and body. I am vitally alive, enthusiastic about my life and living life to the hilt. Every day is a new adventure of wonder, joy, magnificence, happiness and peace. I celebrate myself, life and God.

CHAPTER 2

Mastery: Vision, Commitment and Choice

I have lived in the pursuit of a vision, both personal
and social. Personal: to care for what is noble, for
what is beautiful, for what is gentle; to allow
moments of insight to give wisdom at more mundane
times. Social: to see in imagination the society that is
to be created, where individuals grow freely, and
where hate and greed and envy die because there is
nothing to nourish them. These things I believe, and
the world, for all its horrors, has left me unshaken.

Bertrand Russell

Do you have a vision of how you would like your life and world to be? Do you look beyond what you can see and realize that you have the power to live your highest vision? Or, like a beach ball thrown into the ocean's waves, is your life a series of ups and downs, lacking direction, responsibility and choice? Proverbs 29:18 says, "Where there is no vision, the people perish."

I see vision as an essential ingredient to living peacefully and becoming master of your life. Vision is looking deep within and aligning with your spiritual self so that you can then look outward beyond appearances. Oftentimes, instead of choosing our highest vision — the ability to see beauty, possibility and good — we give our power away and believe we must settle for what life hands us, that we must ride the waves and hope that perhaps one day we'll make it to the shore where we may have some say or choice in the direction our lives take.

Mastery begins by taking back our power and choosing to be committed to our vision. For years I've been working on taking back the power that I had given away to self-limiting beliefs. Several years ago, I made a conscious choice to stop allowing myself to go where life pushed and pulled me and instead to acknowledge that I can choose my responses and master life. After making this commitment to take responsibility for my life, I found that just about every area of my life got worse before it got better. I had my vision, but everything outside the scope of that vision kept coming at me so that I could claim it, take responsibility for it and then release it. I saw this in my relationships, my career, my level of prosperity and my creativity. Let me give you an example.

My dad died when I was seventeen. Almost ten years before his death, he had abandoned his responsibilities as a father. For several years after he died, I blamed him for my inability to create lasting loving relationships. I gave away my power to him. Not until I chose to confront my fears, pain and lack of forgiveness toward him did my vision for my life and world start coming to fruition. When I made the commitment to deal with this unresolved chapter in my life, I went through a period of more pain and heartache than I thought I could handle, although I've since realized you're never given more than you can handle. All my repressed emotions needed to surface and to be experienced before I could let them go. I kept my vision of mastery anchored in the divine and was guided through the necessary steps to achieve freedom.

To become master of your outer life, you must first become master of your inner world — master of your mind. Although this book is not about Paramahansa Yogananda and his teachings, I will mention him a great deal. The reason is simple. Next to Jesus, no one has affected my life so profoundly. His teachings have been an important part of my life for almost twenty years. If we want to live our highest potential, Yogananda would say, all we have to do is teach the mind how to think differently: how to be gentle, calm, loving and centered on God. He has taught me that if I want to become master of my life, I must take responsibility, be committed and always choose to put God first.

In the 1960s, Abraham Maslow published *Toward a Psychology of Being* which, I believe, helped turn around psychology. Psychology was my undergraduate major at the University of California at Los Angeles (UCLA), and I was drawn to Maslow's work. He chose to study high-functioning people — those living their highest potential (not people with problems, as was usually the case in psychology). Maslow developed a psychology of being, not of striving but arriving, not of trying to get someplace but living fully. He found a common denominator among all his subjects. You know what it was? *They all had vision, were committed to their vision, took responsibility for the choices they made and believed they had the power to master life.* Do you believe you can master your life? Or does your life feel chaotic, out of control?

Chaos in your life can sometimes reawaken and redefine the human heart and create change for a higher way of living and being, for becoming a master. The key to mastery lies in asking what you can do to change an undesirable situation — and then taking action. Complaining, worrying and thinking negatively are time wasters and create a detour in your path to self-mastery. I have a friend who's having financial problems; she's always feeling frustrated. She complains about her inability to overcome years of accumulating debt and gets depressed about it, but she does nothing to change the situation. And she is unwilling to see the valuable lessons she could learn about herself and her self-imposed limitations.

In my life and the lives of most people I know, the most growth, the greatest lessons and the most rewarding transformations occur from the greatest adversities and challenges. Life has a way of making certain that past misfortunes — if you have worked through them — pay extra dividends in the future. Have you noticed the same negative things recurring in your life? Choosing to complain and taking no action will keep you in a rut. You must have the inner vision to see beyond the appearances of your life. You must *choose* to look at your life from a high vantage point. In quiet and solitude, ask this question: *What is it I need to learn to finish this business so I can move on in my life?* You can choose to turn adversity into opportunity. This transformation begins with taking responsibility for everything you've created in your life.

Taking responsibility is accepting the consequences of your choices, both good and bad. When you are responsible, you don't transfer blame to other people or things outside you. You must be willing to own everything that happens to you. When I began taking responsibility for everything I was or wasn't creating in my life, I was scared. If my life wasn't working, I could blame nobody but myself. And yet, at the same time, I realized that taking responsibility can be very empowering and freeing. This is what living is all about — mastering our lives by becoming all that we were created to be. Spinoza said it best: "To be who we truly are and to become all that we are truly capable of becoming is the only end in life." Thoreau, who wrote, "Most men lead lives of quiet desperation," recognized that most people don't choose to live fully.

The other day I received a letter from Robert Muller, chancellor of the University for Peace in Costa Rica. In it Robert was sharing his feelings about living more fully and he wrote something that touched my heart. "We have ecology, but we have no *livology* (the science and art of living)."

For years, I have had the privilege of counseling people about health and human potential. I have learned so much about myself and life from my clients. One thing is for sure: To live your highest vision and follow through on your commitments, you must be willing to risk. You must be willing to move out of your comfort zones, from certainty to uncertainty, and ultimately from the ordinary to the extraordinary. "Not a victory is gained, not a deed of faithfulness or courage done," said psychologist and philosopher William James, "except upon a maybe. And it is only by risking our persons from one hour to another that we live at all." And T.S. Eliot said, "Only those who dare to go too far can possibly find out how far one can go." When you are willing to risk, you have an opportunity to see that you are far greater and more powerful than you thought. Playing it safe is one of the ways we hide out. Taking risks in your life fosters passion, enthusiasm, and trust. When I'm afraid to take a risk, I remind myself that within me is the omnipotent, omnipresent and omniscient light of God; with that type of partnership, everything is possible.

When you commit to a new program, for example a health and fitness program, be aware of your thoughts and beliefs going in.

Harboring doubts about your ability to succeed will affect your results. As James said, "Our belief at the beginning of a doubtful undertaking is the one thing that ensures the successful outcome of the venture." So if you've made a commitment to health, believe with all your body, mind and heart that you can be radiantly healthy. Weed out doubt, worry and concern so you can blossom and create miracles.

Breakthroughs and miracles occur when people are willing to live from their vision and commitment. A commitment is the honoring of a decision. When you're committed, you allow nothing to deter you from reaching your goal. You are disciplined even when you are not feeling motivated. Making a commitment is being willing to put all of your resources on the line and taking responsibility for the outcome.

Commitment — to a project, a relationship, a spiritual practice, a health and fitness program — can lend stability to the chaotic whirl of everyday life. Daily actions that reaffirm commitments bring a feeling of empowerment and increase self-esteem. *It's through our everyday behavior that we know what really counts.* Yogananda stresses that our commitment must be woven through all of life: our thoughts, our emotions, our words and our actions.

I know many people who say they are committed to being healthy, yet they continually let excuses get in the way. They say they'll have to wait until next Monday to exercise because they're just too busy now; or they won't be able to eat nutritious food for the next two weeks because of birthdays, anniversaries and the church's bake sale coming up. Or they're too stressed to make a major change right now. Commitment means that you get past your excuses and follow through on what you said you were going to do. Make your word count. Be responsible and accountable. How do you ever expect someone to make a commitment to you or think you will follow through on a commitment to them unless you first show a commitment to yourself and what you say? Commitment takes organization and follow-through. If you are ready for commitment, you will be committed. In other words, you will arrange your personal circumstances so that your lifestyle, in every way, supports your commitment. You will do the things you need to do to order your life, eliminate the non-essentials, and consciously focus on what is important.

Lack of commitment is near epidemic proportions in our society. Just look around. People say they're committed to creating a healthier, more harmonious planet; yet they continue to litter or drive cars that pollute. They say they're committed to their relationships; yet at the first sign of difficulty or challenge, they're out the door. People say they're really committed to aligning with the spiritual side of their natures, but they make no time to meditate or commune with God. I know that many people wish they felt more committed, wish they had something really big to commit to. These people do not realize that *you can't be committed to anything if you aren't committed to yourself.* By really committing to yourself, by following through on your convictions and decisions and allowing nothing to stand in the way of your becoming master of your life, you will gain tremendous power. Providence will become your partner. Goethe said:

Concerning all acts of initiative and creation there is one elementary truth, the ignorance of which kills countless ideas and splendid plans: *that the moment one definitely commits oneself, then providence moves too* [my emphasis]. All sorts of things occur to help one that would otherwise never have occurred.

Once you have committed to something, write it down. Putting it on paper makes it sacred. Also, make sure all your choices are in alignment with that commitment. Your choices can be made in two main ways — with full awareness or unconsciously. We've all heard people say, "I don't know what made me do that," or "I don't know what came over me." Unconscious choices stem from an untrained mind seeking immediate gratification rather than looking at the long-term goal. They may even be the result of addictions or compulsive behavior. Enlightened choices are mindful of the long term and are made from inner guidance and vision. The mindful method of choosing is described in *The Child of Your Dreams*, a captivating book by Laura Archera Huxley and Piero Ferrucci.

There is an elegant and simple way of choosing. We can handle things at the source, not when they have solidified, not when we feel regrets and resentments, nor when we have to retrace our steps and pay for the consequences of mindless deeds. Being

blurred by the urgency of physical desires, pretending to over-
look future developments, allowing oneself to be enticed by the
lure of false promises — this is not the way of mindful choice.

Choice and responsibility go hand in hand. In consciously
choosing, you exercise your ability to respond. Being a master,
you choose not to let circumstances or other people dictate how
you are going to feel or react. You act from your vision. Spiritual
vision brings conscious commitment, which brings mindful choices,
which assures mastery. To be in alignment with yourself, you must
commit your life to God. Only then can you take ownership of
your life.

More than a year ago I made a commitment to embark on a
forty-day fast. After I made that commitment, I held fast to my
vision. All my decisions and choices were in alignment with my
goal. I strove to become as healthy as possible so that I would be
physically, mentally, emotionally and spiritually ready to give
forty days to living in the presence of God. There were many
opportunities to stray off my path, and occasionally I did stray.
But for the most part, I followed my vision and the guidance of my
heart. And now, I'm on the second day of my forty-day commitment. I am feeling empowered. Sure, I've already had thoughts of
food. I've wondered whether I should have waited another month
to begin. When such thoughts arise, I send them on their way
knowing that my commitment to myself is also my commitment
to God. My commitment to God requires that I live my highest
and best at all times and in all circumstances. I know the loving
presence will give me the strength and courage to follow through
on my commitment.

My commitment to God means that I am giving up any
dependency on people, circumstances and material things. I'm
putting God and peace first in my life, trusting that my life's
higher purpose is being revealed to me through my spiritual vision
— which sees everything in God's sight, from God's peace. The
good news that came first through Jesus, and later through His
follower Paul, is that God's kingdom of goodness and peace is
available to each one of us if we understand that we must nurture
our inner lives. All life's experiences become manifest from the
within to the without.

The greatest work is done in secret, not as an outer display, for God meets with us within the solitude and stillness of our souls, and in aligning with God we know peace. Peace is not dependent on the outer conditions of life; we will not have world peace until all people have peace within themselves. And inner peace begins by making a conscious choice to be peaceful, to be free, to live your highest vision.

Everything we need to know to be free — to be masters of our lives — is within us right now just waiting to be kindled. A spark of divine power, which creates and sustains all life, which is all wise and loving, is within each of us. "It's in Every One of Us" is one of my favorite songs. It says, "It's in every one of us to be wise, find your heart, open up both your eyes."

What are you committed to in your life? What is your vision? Where does God fit in your life? Do you believe you can know and have everything? Without making a commitment to God, you will never have lasting peace in your life. Peace is the breath of God. Through commitment and living your highest vision, you become one with the breath and life itself.

Choose to live peacefully and choose to commit yourself to living God's vision for you.

This is the true joy in life: being used for a purpose recognized by yourself as a mighty one, and being a force of nature instead of a feverish, selfish little clod of ailments and grievances, complaining that the world will not devote itself to making you happy.

George Bernard Shaw

Taking Inventory and Action

1. In what areas of your life have you not followed through on your commitments? Why not? What were your excuses?

2. If you were living your highest vision now, what would your life look like? Write down your vision on a piece of paper and read it out loud. How would you feel if you were living that vision now? Let yourself experience those emotions of joy and thanksgiving.

3. If you're not living your vision, what unresolved conflict from the past or present do you need to take care of so you can move on in your life?

4. Are you lazy? Do you lack self-discipline? Do you follow through on what you say you're going to do?

5. Are you willing to risk all you've got to be all you were created to be?

6 Health is a choice. Happiness is a choice. Peace is a choice. Choose this day to align yourself with God's thoughts about you.

7. Your daily behavior and actions show what really counts to you. Make your behavior and actions reflect your commitment.

8. Make a commitment to yourself to be healthy, happy and peaceful. Write out some of the steps you must take to live this vision.

9. Commit your life to God. Ask for inner guidance to show you how to do this.

10. Live in the presence of God.

Today's Affirmation

I have the power and ability to live my highest vision. Thank you, Father-Mother God, for the clarity of my vision and for showing me how to see beyond appearances. This day I choose to commit to myself and to live from inner guidance. My commitment is reflected in everything I think, feel, say and do.

CHAPTER 3

A Healthy Way of Living

Let food be your medicine and medicine be your food.
Nature heals; the physician is only nature's assistant.

Hippocrates

I want to take this opportunity to share with you a beautiful philosophy of living, which I have embraced for more than fifteen years. It is called Natural Hygiene. Natural Hygiene is a manifestation of a profound passion for life. "It is a philosophy and a set of principles and practices that lead to an extraordinary level of personal health and happiness," according to James Michael Lennon, executive director of the American Natural Hygiene Society. "But it is much more than that. It is an expression of an unconditional love — a love that encompasses ourselves, our families and friends; a love that encompasses all peoples, all living things, including Earth herself."

Those of us who embrace the philosophy of Natural Hygiene recognize the unity of all life and hold that personal health, environmental health and community health are parts of a whole, none of which will ever be fully achieved until all are achieved. Since the early 1830s, the men and women of Natural Hygiene have worked to make health, happiness, peace and prosperity available to everyone, everywhere. We have long held a vision of a beautiful and bountiful planet inhabited by people with open minds and loving hearts. Those of us who practice Natural Hygiene become great optimists and great realists at the same time. We understand that we must take practical steps every day of our lives to achieve our full potential.

Natural Hygienists believe that the natural human condition is good health. Nature has amply provided all that we require for a healthy, happy life — sunshine; pure air, water and food; a clean, nurturing environment; and the freedom to lead wholesome, productive lives. However, because of the choices we have made, we do not always have access to all of nature's bounty. " . . . every instance of sickness and suffering, unless caused by accident, is caused by some wrong doing, either on the part of the sufferer or others," wrote Harriet N. Austin, a physician who practiced Natural Hygiene in the nineteenth century.

To achieve optimal health, we must choose to live right — to eat fresh, whole natural foods; exercise regularly; get plenty of rest and sleep; learn to handle stress; get plenty of fresh air and sunshine; and avoid all negative influences.

The Natural Hygiene diet program is easy to understand: When you are hungry, eat foods that are attractive, delicious and nutritious in their natural state, in quantities that meet your needs and in a manner that ensures proper digestion. We eat simple, uncomplicated meals. Most of our meals are selected from the vast, ever-changing array of fresh fruits and vegetables. We eat the greatest portion of our diet uncooked. We sit down and eat our meals without rushing or discussing problems. It's important to appreciate and give thanks for the beautiful food and nourishment that you are receiving. Being in a hurry or upset or tired interferes with digestion.

I had the good fortune to spend time at a spa called Cal-a-Vie in Vista, California, where a nutritionist and a chef showed me the importance of having fresh food lovingly prepared and presented beautifully on the plate. We ate in a serene environment that allowed us to get the most from our food. When you eat in a healthy, harmonious way, your whole body is uplifted and enriched — physically, mentally and spiritually.

Natural Hygiene recognizes the benefits of fasting. Because fasting is a period of time without sensory stimulation or vigorous physical activity, it is an extraordinary state of rest for the body. While in this state, the body has a tremendous opportunity to rejuvenate itself. The recuperative powers of the body during a fast are often remarkable.

Natural Hygiene is known primarily for the practices of eating whole natural foods, food combining and fasting. But these are only three tenets of unique philosophy of health. Other distinguishing principles of the philosophy include:

1. **Health is normal.** Health is as simple as living in harmony with nature — especially our human nature. Superior health can be achieved and maintained only through healthful living.

2. **Health and disease are a continuum.** The same physiological laws govern the body in sickness and in health. Sick persons use the same practices, modified if necessary, to recover health that healthy persons use to maintain it. Generally speaking, nothing that makes a healthy person sick will make a sick person healthy.

3. **Healing is a biological process.** Except in extraordinary circumstances, healing is the result of actions undertaken by the body on its own behalf. There are times when assistance, including medical treatment and surgery, is necessary. But recovery is ultimately dependent upon biological processes.

4. **The causes of diseases must be removed.** Natural Hygiene points out the distinction between the *causes* of disease and the *symptoms* — the body's response to the causes. To recover health, it maintains that we should remove the causes of disease, take steps that allow the body to respond to the causes and avoid the common mistake of trying to suppress symptoms.

5. **The body functions as a unit.** For the most part, there can never be partial health or partial (meaning "singular") disease. There is a unity of the body. Every organ and tissue has a function. If one part starts to malfunction, it affects the whole person. Natural Hygiene rejects such notions as, "John is perfectly healthy, except for his high blood pressure." If John's heart isn't working well, chances are John has other problems, too, causing or caused by his heart problems.

6. **Physical, mental and emotional health are inseparably linked.** When thinking about Natural Hygiene, one of the first words that comes to mind is "excellence." It is a philosophy

for people who are looking for the good life — not just a pretty good life, but a *very* good life.

While Natural Hygiene is not the final word on health and will continue to be improved upon year after year, it is certainly worth attending to because of the discoveries it has given us so far. Thomas Aquinas wrote, "The slenderest knowledge that may be obtained of the highest things is more desirable than the most certain knowledge obtained of the lesser things."

We Natural Hygienists are happy because we feel so good; optimistic because we see the very real possibility of peace and plenty on earth; confident because we base our lives on a well-reasoned philosophy; and compassionate because we want good things not only for ourselves, but for everyone. "When we are at our best," Lennon says, "our eyes shine with love, our bodies are growing stronger, our hearts point us toward what is right and good, and our minds are figuring out the best way to get there." Natural Hygiene gives us an opportunity to be all we can be.

The American Natural Hygiene Society is a wonderful organization that I encourage you to join. All members receive subscriptions to the society's award-winning *Health Science* magazine, plus other membership benefits including discounts on the best health books and tapes available and on all of the society's conferences and seminars. Membership is only twenty-five dollars per year and supports some very worthwhile efforts. The Society works in Washington, D.C., for organic food and a clean environment and strongly opposes food irradiation. In addition, the society maintains the Herbert Shelton Library, the most important historical collection of Natural Hygiene books in the world and thousands of books and periodicals on fasting, nutrition and natural health practices dating to the 1830s.

Health Science is a showcase for the world's experts on fasting, nutrition and exercise. The stories and articles will open up an exciting new world for you, and the recipes are delicious! Every issue, I cut off the cover and tape it to my kitchen wall so that I can look at some of the most beautiful pictures of food I've ever seen. *Health Science* has been a source of information and inspiration for me for years.

Do something very, very good for yourself today. Join the American Natural Hygiene Society. (See Resource Directory)

Choose to live peacefully and choose a healthy way of living.

Each patient carries his own doctor inside him.

Albert Schweitzer

Taking Inventory and Action

1. Do you look at your body as a whole unit or separate parts?
2. Does your diet consist of too many concentrated, heavy foods in each meal?
3. When you're not feeling well, do you usually keep eating for fear that you'll lose strength?
4. Do you eat simply and avoid overeating?
5. When you're tired, bored, stressed or depressed and it's mealtime, do you still eat even though you don't have much of an appetite?
6. Commit to a week of not overeating. Stop before you're full.
7. If you're not feeling well, skip meals until your appetite returns.
8. Choose organic produce whenever possible; avoid food that's been irradiated; and eat a variety of fresh food in its natural, uncooked state.
9. Be at peace with your body and our living earth. Give thanks for all her bounty.
10. Live in the presence of God.

Today's Affirmation

Health, happiness and peace of mind are everyone's birthright. I claim them now and commit to a lifestyle that is in alignment with my body's needs and supports Mother Earth. I am healthy, full of energy and enthusiastic about life. God has provided me with so many wonderful blessings, and I share what I live with others.

CHAPTER 4

Prayer and Fasting

The popular mistaken concept is that we cannot gain
strength and build resistance unless we eat. So long
as this illusion persists, thousands will
go to premature graves.

Herbert M. Shelton, *Fasting Can Save Your Life*

By maintaining the practices of right diet and fasting
we help to turn the body into a better superconductor
of the cosmic energy. The cosmic energy or prana
comes from God and is the immediate experiential
"face of God" that we can experience in
every moment of our life.

Gabriel Cousens, M.D., *Spiritual Nutrition and the Rainbow Diet*

During the past twenty years, I have done extensive research on fasting, have fasted myself several hundred times and have also observed many fasts of others. I have in front of me now a 136-page bibliography of research published in medical journals on fasting. I have read more than one hundred books on the topic and have visited several fasting institutions. Fasting is a big part of my life. Some people fast for physical reasons, and others for spiritual reasons. I will tell you briefly about both the physical and the spiritual benefits of fasting. My goal is to inspire and motivate you to do some research on your own. Fasting expert Alan Goldhamer, D.C. says the following: "As a doctor who specializes in the supervision of therapeutic fasting, I have witnessed the incredible self-healing potential of the body when the requirements of health are provided. Fasting is perhaps the most powerful tool in the health care arsenal and, when it is used appropriately, fasting is a safe and effective means of helping the body to heal itself. I suggest that individuals seek appropriate guidance before undertaking a fast."

Before describing some of the many advantages of fasting, I'll first define it. Fasting is the complete abstinence from all substances except pure water. Some fasting advocates refer to a juice-only diet as fasting; I prefer to call that juice feasting.

The practice of fasting is as ancient as life itself and has been practiced by nearly every civilization. In their excellent book, *Fasting for the Health of It*, Jean Oswald and Herbert M. Shelton write the ancient Egyptians used fasting to treat syphilis and believed that fasting three days each month preserved youthfulness. The early Greeks — Hippocrates, Galen, Socrates and Plato — recognized the benefits of fasting. Socrates and Plato are said to have fasted for ten days to "attain mental and physical efficiency." Plutarch, the famous biographer, advised, "Instead of using medicine, better fast a day." Much later in history, Paracelsus, the Swiss physician, claimed "fasting is the greatest remedy." In the nineteenth century, therapeutic fasting was first recorded in the United States by Isaac Jennings, a physician and a pioneer in the evolution of Natural Hygiene.

Herbert M. Shelton was one of the world's leading experts on fasting. His work has had a profound effect on my life. He studied fasting for more than sixty years, supervised more than thirty thousand fasts, wrote more than thirty-six books on healing and fasting and made fasting a regular part of his life. His books, *The Science and Fine Art of Fasting*, *Fasting Can Save Your Life* and *Fasting for Renewal of Life*, are classics and, in my estimation, are required reading for anyone interested in fasting. (These books can be ordered through the American Natural Hygiene Society.)

Shelton inspired millions of people, including Helen Keller and Mahatma Gandhi, to fast and adopt a healthier lifestyle. Gandhi invited Shelton to India to lecture and to teach the principles of his "nature cure" at Indian universities.

Fasting is an efficient way to break bad eating habits and addictions. It provides the body a chance to detoxify and heal. Drs. Jennifer Morano and Alan Goldhamer, co-directors of the Center for Chiropractic and Conservative Therapy in Penngrove, California, provide supervised fasting and health/healing programs. They have seen serious health conditions respond to therapeutic fasting. They write, "In addition to the profound effects of therapeutic fasting in the correction of disease processes, it is also effective as a means of rejuvenation and is an important component of a comprehensive health care program."

If you don't know anything about fasting or you grew up believing that skipping a few meals would make you weak or sick or would kill you, let me correct your misconceptions. Fasting is not the same as starving. From *Yours For Health: The Life and Times of Herbert M. Shelton,* by Jean A. Oswald, Shelton writes:

> The fast provides a physiological rest for the entire body. When digestion and assimilation of food are suspended, the elimination of toxins is increased. Aging and sick cells are renewed and regenerated, providing disease has not reached an irreversible state. Blood pressure decreases during this period of rest. The process of healing is facilitated. Excess fat and abnormal deposits are consumed as food during the fast while the cells and tissues of vital organs are preserved.
>
> Starvation is not the same. To starve means to suffer severely from hunger. To starve means to die from lack of food. Before starvation and death occur, the body will attempt to use its vital organs as a food source. . . . Those knowledgeable in supervising fasts know when to break the fast before starvation begins. The body indicates when the fast should be broken. A clean tongue, sweet breath, light-colored urine, and the return of appetite are signs. When one or all of these occur, the fast has been completed.

In *Spiritual Nutrition and the Rainbow Diet*, the physician Gabriel Cousens offers this on fasting:

> By removing toxins from the system, we not only become healthier, but we remove blocks from the body and therefore enhance the movement of all energy in the system. . . . After the first few days of a fast, our appetites usually fade and the attachment to food diminishes. . . . The more we can experience ourselves as free of these bodily desires in the practice of fasting, the easier it is to maintain this freedom in a nonfasting state.

For twenty years, I have incorporated fasting into my wellness lifestyle. I usually fast one day each week, for three consecutive days each month and for a week with each change of season. During these times, I also meditate, pray and often observe solitude and silence. I am the only one in my family who follows this kind of regimen. However, two years ago, I decided to take my mother with me when I visited a fasting/rejuvenation clinic to conduct research. We went to a Certified Hygienic Fasting Center, which is a favorite of professionals, students and celebrities from all over the world. During our sixteen-day stay, we saw some thirty-five other guests, there for all types of health problems, including arthritis, obesity, smoking, bronchitis, spastic colon, asthma, headaches and chronic fatigue. A few who had no specific health problems were there simply for a few days of rest and relaxation.

Based on medical history, health goals or problems, each person is put on an individualized program. My mom, June, wanted to shed a few pounds, rest and relax and alleviate her painful arthritis. I wanted to lose ten pounds, to experience fasting in a supervised environment and to interview the other guests. Because my mother had never fasted and was on medication, she was not allowed to fast. She was, instead, given a strict nutritional program that usually consisted of fresh orange or apple juice for breakfast, fresh fruit or raw vegetable salads for lunch and a salad and sometimes brown rice or vegetable soup for dinner. I was put on a twelve-day fast, which was followed by a nutritional program similar to my mother's for four days. June left ten pounds lighter and practically free from arthritic pain. I lost twelve pounds and felt fantastic.

No one should go on a fast without consulting with a family physician, holistic health professional or other person qualified in supervising fasts. If you have diabetes, heart disease, ulcerative colitis or epilepsy; if you are expecting or lactating, have not reached full physical maturity or are more than ten pounds underweight; if you're on medication like Dilantin, diuretics, tranquilizers or lithium, you need special supervision.

Keep in mind a few essential points when fasting. First, if you have not fasted before, make sure you read and study the subject as much as you can before you begin. Then, ease into fasting; start off with several twenty-four-hour fasts (lunch to lunch or dinner to dinner), spaced one week apart. After a month of weekly twenty-four-hour fasts, move on to a thirty-six-hour fast, followed the next week by a forty-eight-hour fast. Drink only pure water; relax and rest. During a fast, you should refrain from vigorous exercise. Break your fast with small amounts of fresh, raw juices and light meals made up exclusively of either fresh fruits or vegetables.

The first three days of a fast are usually the most difficult in terms of hunger pains and other physical discomfort. The body is beginning to rid itself of toxic poisons that have built up over years of poor eating habits. If you've never fasted, this can be an uncomfortable process, which is why I recommend that first-time fasters go to a fasting clinic where they can be supervised. After the first day, the tongue is usually coated and the breath becomes foul. Do not be disturbed by these symptoms, rather be grateful for the increased health and well-being that will result. You may experience headaches during this time, especially if you are an avid coffee or tea drinker. These are mild withdrawal symptoms and will pass, though they may be very unpleasant for a time.

Around the fourth day the hunger pains begin to subside, though you may feel weak and occasionally dizzy. The dizziness is temporary, caused by sudden movement. Move more slowly and you will have no difficulty. Feelings of weakness can reach the point where the simplest task takes great effort. Rest is the best remedy. Many find the fourth and fifth days the most difficult phase of the fast, although everyone reacts differently.

By the sixth or seventh day, you will begin to feel stronger, and your sense of concentration will be sharper. You may feel as if you could fast indefinitely, but hunger pains will return anywhere between twenty-one and fifty days or longer. This marks the first stage of starvation and signals that the body has used all its reserves and is beginning to draw on living tissue. The fast should be judiciously broken at this time.

Before embarking on an extended fast, some people are tempted to eat a good deal to "stock up." This is not recommended; in fact, it's best to eat lighter than normal meals for a few days before fasting. I also recommend abstaining from coffee or tea for at least three days before beginning. If your last meals are raw fruits and vegetables, you should have no difficulty with constipation. As I mentioned earlier, I am taking a two-month break from my regular activities to conduct this forty-day fast. Ten days before I began, I tapered my food intake and varied the types of foods I ate. For five days, I ate only raw, fresh fruits and vegetables; then three days of raw fruits only, followed by two days of fresh, raw fruit and vegetable juices. I will reverse this ten-day procedure when I break this fast.

Most people find that fasting itself is not difficult. However, breaking a fast the proper way takes discipline. If you do not break your fast properly, you can undermine all the benefits you gained. I have heard of people breaking a fast by immediately going back to their unhealthy eating habits. This can cause serious physical problems and, in a few instances, has been known to cause death — another reason why I advocate going to an institution that provides expert supervision. Those of you who would like a listing of the health professionals who are certified members of the International Association of Professional Natural Hygienists, specially trained to supervise fasts, should become a member of the American Natural Hygiene Society. You may also want to read *Fasting for the Health of It*, which details the twenty-eight-day fast of co-author Jean Oswald as well as highlighting one hundred fasting case histories.

While I have fasted several hundred times (from one to thirty days) for the purpose of physical rejuvenation, I also fast for spiritual rejuvenation or prayer discipline — the purpose of my current forty-day fast. I want to go deeply into the spiritual side of my nature and to enhance and cultivate my communion with God and open myself more to His presence of peace, light and love. All spiritual fasting should be entered into with a clear sense of inner direction. Two years ago, I fasted for thirty days, followed several months later by a forty-day juice-only diet. The focus of these efforts was on physical, mental and emotional rejuvenation; but spiritual benefits occurred as well. For this current fast, my focus is spiritual; my intentions are clearly to surrender and dedicate my life to God and to purify my body temple.

A year ago, when I was on a vision quest in the mountains, I received inner guidance to go on this forty-day spiritual fast. Creating the time and space for this in the middle of a busy writing, teaching, consulting and traveling schedule was one of my first tasks. I saw it would be eleven months until I could clear enough of my calendar. I took those eleven months to prepare for my fast physically, mentally, emotionally and spiritually.

I do not lack for inspiration in my consecration fast. Lee Bueno, in her wonderful book *Fast Your Way to Health*, provides nearly a hundred Biblical references to fasting, health, and self-control. Her emphasis throughout the book is that prayer and fasting can restore health. She calls fasting "the Lord's best kept secret." Many religious figures have fasted, first among them Jesus. After His baptism Jesus's first act was to begin his forty-day fast in the desert. In *Spiritual Nutrition and the Rainbow Diet*, Cousens comments on the significance of that fast:

> The act of baptism grants fullness of the spirit, and spiritual fullness grants, through fasting, victory over bodily desire. This is the direct teaching of Christ's forty-day fast. Liberation from bodily and worldly desires then makes it possible to merge in the contentment, fullness, and Love of God communion. This sequence of baptism, fullness of the spirit, fasting, victory over the bodily desires, and communion with God is the way that Christ taught by his own life practice. The act of fasting, especially in the forty-day fast, is a mystical sacrifice of the body. Combined with meditation, which on one level is a sacrifice of the mind, fasting becomes a mystical sacrifice of the ego of body and of mind.

The Essenes, an esoteric, ascetic, scholarly Jewish monastic brotherhood, said to have been founded by Elijah at Mount Carmel, used fasting to purify their bodies and enhance their communion with God. The Essenes, whose name means "expectant of the one who is to come," were well-known as great healers and prophets. Many of the Essenes lived to be more than 120 years old, according to *The Essenes by Josephus and His Contemporaries*, translated by Edmond Bordeaux Szekely. Jesus reportedly lived in an Essene community in Egypt after escaping Herod the Great. The core group of the Essenes fasted for forty days once each year. In the *Essene Gospel of Peace*, Book One, Jesus taught:

> . . . the word and the power of God will not enter into you, because all manner of abominations have their dwelling in your body and your spirit; for the body is the temple of the spirit, and the spirit is the temple of God. Purify therefore, the temple, that the Lord of the temple may dwell therein and occupy a place that is worthy of him. . . . Renew yourselves and fast.

The *Essene Gospel of Peace*, Book One, is an excellent book about purification, healing, rejuvenation and rebirth through fasting. Throughout its pages, Jesus teaches that we must purify and renew our physical bodies in preparation for a spiritual rebirth. A spiritual renewal, or rebirth, follows the physical purification from fasting.

Through the years, I have read as much as I could find on Jesus and His fasting. I perused the pages of *The Teachings of Jesus on Diet and Fasting* by the Christian Health Research Institute, *Fasting Your Way to Health* by Lee Bueno and *Why Did Jesus Fast?* by the Rev. Herman Arndt. The more I read, the more I felt inspired to do a forty-day fast. But I needed to do further research first. For more Biblical references, I read about Moses's fasts. Exodus 34:28-29 says, "And he was there with the Lord forty days and forty nights; he did neither eat bread, nor drink water."

Many other Biblical figures fasted. Daniel, after a fast of twenty-one days, received the revelation of "what shall befall thy people in the later days" (Dan. 10:2). Esther fasted for three days to obtain wisdom as well as divine favor (Esther 4:16). On the fourth day of a fast, it was revealed to Cornelius where he would find Peter, through whom he would receive the Gospel (Acts 10:30). Paul and Luke, the apostles, fasted. Elijah fasted forty days, so did John the Baptist. Many great Christians, including Martin Luther, John Calvin, John Knox, John Wesley, Jonathan Edwards and Peace Pilgrim, fasted and spoke of the value of this practice. In her book of the same name, Peace Pilgrim speculates that her spiritual fast of forty-five days may have "helped [her] to learn to pray without ceasing."

Not limited to the Christian faith, fasting is also incorporated into Judaism, Hinduism, Islam and Buddhism for a variety of purposes, such as propitiation, penitence, preparation for initiations and marriage, mourning, development of inner powers, purification and spiritual development. In Hebrew, the word for fasting is *tsoum*, meaning the voluntary abstinence from food with a religious end.

In his Self-Realization Fellowship lessons, Paramahansa Yogananda stresses the importance of eating a healthy diet, exercising, meditating and fasting for cleansing and purification. Upton Sinclair startled the world with his story about recovering from chronic indigestion after a ten-day fast, followed by improved eating and living habits. He writes about how his fasting experience also affected him spiritually in *The Fasting Cure*.

Back to my forty-day spiritual fast . . . In preparation, for almost a year, I practiced strict dietary discipline in order to get into shape so that I could prevent any physical problems for this fast. As I said earlier, I eased into the fast with raw foods and juices. I began drinking only water on Day One and will continue this for forty days.

My spiritual fast is known as a consecration fast meaning a surrender of my desires, my goals, and every aspect of my life to God. Through this type of fast you develop a powerful relationship with God and learn how to put total trust and faith in God's will and plans for you. It's a time to set yourself apart from the world, from food and drink, and from most earthly pleasures and sensual comforts of life. A consecration fast is the best and most powerful way I know to prepare ourselves to receive the fullness of God's blessings in our lives. When we consecrate a fast to God, He releases His wonderful spiritual gifts through us. *Fast Your Way to Health* by Lee Bueno goes into great detail about the different types of fasts, including a consecration fast.

When you fast for spiritual purposes, it is best to remove yourself from worldly responsibilities and, if possible, from other people. Most of these forty days I am spending in solitude and silence. The only people who know I am fasting are my family and a few close friends. Jesus's counsel was to refrain from calling attention to what you are doing. The only ones who should know you are fasting are those who have to know.

My days are filled with meditation, prayer, writing, reading and rest. Occasionally, I take walks outside, visit the beach (a couple of minutes from my home), stretch, do yoga and sing. Every day, I will do my deep breathing, take a ten- to fifteen-minute sunbath and dry-brush my skin. But the most important part of my fast is to commune with God — to live in the presence of God.

During these forty days, I am striving to unite with the Christ within, to live as many of each day's hours as possible in awareness of my divinity and connection to God. I will meditate a minimum of three hours each day. I want to make every task a sacred action. I want to cultivate a gentle receptiveness to the divinity all around me and within me.

Probably more than any other single discipline, fasting reveals what controls us. And this isn't just food. Oftentimes we cover up what is inside us with food and other substances, but while fasting, all these things surface. My experience when fasting has been that attachments to people, things, beliefs, preconceived ideas of the way things should be and emotions all come up for me to look at and release. In Psalms 69:10, David said, "I humbled my soul with fasting." When I do a spiritual fast, I think a lot about what it means to surrender to God's will and how miraculous the human body really is. During this fast, I have been opening myself to God's peace and to ways we can each bring more peace into our lives. Even now, only four days into my fast, I feel a deep sense of joy and peace.

According to Jesus, spiritual fasting can bring breakthroughs in the spiritual realm that may otherwise never be realized. Fasting is a means of God's grace and blessing that should no longer be neglected, as John Wesley writes in *Sermons on Several Occasions*.

> . . . it was not merely by the light of reason . . . that the people of God have been, in all ages, directed to use fasting as a means: . . . but they have been . . . taught it of God Himself, by clear and open revelations of His Will . . . Now, whatever reasons there are to quicken those of old, in the zealous and constant discharge of this duty, they are of equal force still to quicken us.

One of the best books I have ever read on spiritual fasting is Cousens's *Spiritual Nutrition and the Rainbow Diet*. Cousens calls on his training as a medical doctor to describe what happens to the body during a spiritual fast. I consider his book essential reading if you are interested in fasting. I also highly recommend *Fasting and Eating for Health* by Joel Fuhrman, M.D. (1995) to anyone who wants to lose weight, create optimum health and alleviate and prevent disease.

At the end of this book, I will write more about my experiences with this fast and what it meant to me. In the meantime, I hope you are inspired to do some research on your own about fasting and how it can enhance and enrich your life — physically, mentally, emotionally and spiritually.

Choose to live peacefully and incorporate fasting into your lifestyle.

Moreover, when you fast, do not be like the hypocrites, with a sad countenance. For they disfigure their faces that they may appear to men to be fasting. Assuredly, I say to you, they have their reward. But you, when you fast, [He didn't say, 'if you fast'] anoint your head and wash your face, so that you do not appear to men to be fasting, but to your Father who is in the secret place; and your Father who sees in secret will reward you openly.

Jesus
Matt. 6:16-18

Taking Inventory and Action

1. When you have a cold or a fever, do you usually lose your appetite?

2. Were you reared to believe that you could not skip any meals without losing your strength and becoming weak?

3. Have you ever considered fasting from negative thoughts?

4. Are you afraid to fast? Have you read any books on fasting? Do you know anyone who has fasted?

5. Peruse passages in the Bible that refer to fasting; not one of them denigrates the practice.

6. Always check with your doctor before incorporating fasting into your lifestyle.

7. Do a twenty-four-hour fast. Go from lunch to lunch or dinner to dinner without eating.

8. Ask God for guidance on fasting and see what direction you are given. The desire to do a spiritual fast usually comes from a clear sense of inner guidance.

9. At least once a month take a day to commune with God — pray, fast and meditate.

10. Live in the presence of God.

Today's Affirmation

I am a divine child of God. My indwelling Christ guides me, informing me how to cleanse, purify and renew my body so that it is a worthy temple for the spirit of God. I fast from all negative thoughts, feelings and emotions.

CHAPTER 5

Full-Spectrum Living

The human body is its own best apothecary. The most
successful prescriptions are those filled
by the body itself.

Norman Cousins

Health is more than the absence
of disease; being radiantly healthy refers to a vibrant quality of
life. An intricate relationship links the brain, the hormone system
and the immune system, which means that feeling good is a
physical, mental and emotional experience. To be healthy in this
increasingly complicated society takes awareness and commitment
and demands a sound body, mind and spirit.

Being radiantly healthy involves recognizing that all aspects of
life are interrelated and must be integrated if we are to realize our
full potential. Our experience of wholeness of life itself corresponds
with the wholeness of self. The body reflects the mind and
emotions, and the mind and emotions reflect the spirit. For example, when the body is in good shape — fit, toned and strong —
the mind is affected positively, resulting in high self-esteem and
self-confidence. The opposite is also true. The out-of-shape, sluggish and weak body has a negative effect on the mind, which
contributes to lowered self-esteem and a negative outlook on life.

The importance of health to satisfaction and success in life has
always been known. As early as 300 B.C., Herophilies wrote,
"When health is absent wisdom cannot reveal itself, art cannot
become manifest, strength cannot be exerted, wealth is useless
and reason is powerless." And in a 1989 Gallup survey, 75

percent of respondents rated an optimistic attitude, clean environment, stress control, good relationships and satisfying work as very important to health. People who enjoy what they do and who feel a sense of control over their lives tend to be healthier.

Taking charge means acting positively — eating right and exercising regularly. These two elements can do more than add a year or two to your life span — they can improve the quality of life, especially in later years. And Americans are living longer than ever before. By the year 2000, the average life expectancy will be eighty-four — eleven more years than today's life expectancy.

One of the most important nutritional steps you can take to foster heart health is to reduce the amount of fat in your diet. A high-fat diet is linked to heart disease and some cancers, especially of the breast, colon, and prostate. Fat makes up approximately thirty-seven percent of the calories in the average American diet. Many health experts suggest that no more than ten percent of calories should be from fats in the diet.

Also linked to heart disease is high blood pressure and stress. In connection with heart disease, Dean Ornish, M.D., of the Preventative Medicine Research Institute in Sausalito, California, supervised a program for persons suffering from atherosclerosis (artery blocking) and found that this condition could often be stopped and even reversed. His program (described in his excellent book *Dr. Dean Ornish's Program for Reversing Heart Disease*) includes a low-fat vegetarian diet, hatha yoga, and other relaxation exercises, breathing exercises, visualization, meditation, stress management routines, the elimination of harmful behaviors, the cultivation of a loving attitude, and moderate exercise.

So you see, there's more to radiant health than a good diet and exercise. Extensive research in the field of health and wellness over the past twenty years indicates that there are at least twenty essential factors that must be integrated and balanced in our lives if radiant health is what we want. These include fresh air, plenty of rest and sleep, avoidance of addictions, exercise, wholesome nutrition, sunshine, fasting, deep breathing, a clean body, a balanced life, systematic undereating, a deep respect for life, high self-esteem, daily respites of solitude and silence, a positive attitude, a sense of belonging and an awareness and trust in God. In this chapter, I will cover a few of these briefly; the remaining will be addressed in following chapters.

For almost twenty years, I have been a devotee of natural living — wholesome diet, organic foods, fresh air and sunshine, exercise, simplicity, fasting, peace of mind — which all help to keep the body healthy and clean. But it's of the utmost importance to detoxify your body for these elements to achieve their full benefits; they will do little good if your body is toxic and clogged. All of the topics that I will discuss in this chapter relate to detoxification of the body. For those of you who wish to read more about detoxification and rejuvenation once you have finished this chapter, I recommend my book, *Choose To Be Healthy*, in which I offer a detailed 21-day detoxification-rejuvenation program, and my *Celebrate Life!* audiocassette program (see Resource Directory).

Your body has a total of approximately five quarts of blood, which your heart pumps through your body about two thousand times every twenty-four hours. Everything you put into your mouth, whether food or liquid, is broken down into its atomic constituents in the small intestine by the processes of digestion. Through a variety of complex interactions, these atomic elements pass through the intestine walls into the bloodstream, going first to the liver then through the heart for distribution throughout the body. Therefore, the blood is the body's lifeline, delivering nourishment, fuel and cleansing materials for the cells and tissues. If you take in unhealthy food, you create an unhealthy body. Garbage in, garbage out.

Your colon, the last portion in the intestine, is one of the best indicators of your habits and whether your body is healthy. The best health insurance is a clean colon. You can't have a clean bloodstream unless you have a clean bowel. Getting rid of toxic materials is an essential step toward a clean colon and better health. But you also need to balance the cleansing aspect of your program with the building aspect by eating the right foods. Only food builds tissue. Live (uncooked) foods build healthy tissue.

If we burden our bodies' tissue with metabolic wastes, uneliminated drug residues, nicotine, unnatural chemical spray residues from foods, chemicals from polluted air and treated drinking water and other substances the body is unable to expel, the tissue eventually becomes underactive to the point where it falls prey to acute and then chronic disease.

Of the body's elimination system — the bowel, the lungs and bronchials, the kidneys and the skin — the bowel is the key channel. And the best way to attain a healthy, clean colon is through fasting, eating raw whole foods, drinking fresh raw juices, systematic undereating and adopting a Natural Hygiene way of life.

Because all aspects of life are related, this type of diet has spiritual benefits as well. The cleaner the body, the higher the cosmic energy vibrations available to the brain. Clearly, it pays to cleanse the body and maintain the colon's clean and healthy condition.

Systematic undereating is essential to health and longevity. Overeating, even of healthy foods, is one of the main causes of disease and premature aging. Jesus, in the *Essene Gospel of Peace*, Book One said, "And when you eat, never eat unto fullness." In *Spiritual Nutrition and the Rainbow Diet*, Cousens recommends undereating not only for health reasons but also for spiritual benefits. He explains that energy used for digestion is unavailable for meditation, "this is especially true if we want to get up early in the morning to meditate and we have eaten too much the night before." Though undereating "takes precedence over all other dietary advice," Cousens emphasizes that our energy will diminish if we make a practice of "undereating junk foods . . . If raw, whole, organic foods are available, they are still the choice for optimizing our diet for spiritual life." Scientific evidence in his book supports the efficacy of a whole, raw food diet, systematically undereating, for physical and spiritual rejuvenation.

Raw foods provide the highest nutritional value and promote a natural cleansing and detoxification of the body. The energy from live foods allows your body, according to physician Edward Taub, to burn excess fat. I know this may seem hard to believe, but you can eat as much as you want and not gain weight if you eat food unaltered by processing — foods not refined, frozen, irradiated, canned or filled with chemical preservatives. It's been my experience, living mostly on raw foods for several years now, that you tend not to overeat live foods. Taub discusses why the body reacts this way to live foods in *Voyage to Wellness*. Just as your life energy is made up of vibrations unique to you, so live foods have their own natural energy patterns. When you eat foods in their natural, original states, their life energy and yours are completely compatible. When you eat raw nuts, your body can use their calcium and other nutrients. When you eat fresh salad greens and sprouts, your body can easily absorb their vitamins and minerals. When you eat fresh fruits, their abundant life energy imparts life energy to you.

Fruit, if eaten alone on an empty stomach, is the body's best friend when it comes to cleansing. If fruit is eaten in this manner, it proceeds directly into the intestines and is the least fattening, most cleansing food nature provides. With the highest water content of any food and natural sugars acting as a detergent, fruit washes away stored excesses and waste matter clogging the system. Marilyn Diamond writes more about this in her wonderful book, *A New Way of Eating*.

In a classic book on nutrition published in 1923, *Rational Diet*, Otto Cargue states, "Fruits, more than any other products of the soil, receive the beneficial influences of light, heat, and air, through which electric and magnetic forces of the sun are transmitted. Fruits have, therefore, the highest rate of atomic cell vibrations of all foods, and while we cannot determine by chemical analysis this subtle power, we can feel, when eating fruits, their enlivening effects through our whole system."

Ancient cultures throughout the world, including the Greek and Roman, appreciated the superior values of fruits. It has been said that the ancient Gymnosophists of India lived exclusively on fruits and vegetables. The Bible is full of references to fruits, orchards, and vineyards. It's also interesting to note that the word "frugal" refers to fruit, and a frugal diet meant, quite literally, to the Romans of the Republicans age, a diet of fruits.

One day each week for years, I have eaten only fresh, raw fruit in season as a way to cleanse, rejuvenate, energize and spiritualize my body.

One of the most difficult areas of human nutrition is changing eating habits. Severe eating disorders, especially in women, are on the rise. In the insightful book, *The Hungry Self*, Kim Chernin's analysis of the roots of eating disorders led her through a series of revealing psychoanalytical forays into the complexities of early infancy and childhood, emotional relations between mother and daughter, the lack of developmental models for girls and women at important life-turning points and the pressures of male culture for women to conform to aesthetic ideals. All these factors result in the obsessive preoccupations with food, dieting, calories, weight control and tacit self-destruction that currently grip many women.

Even when you know your health demands it, changing your eating habits can be close to impossible simply because likes and dislikes about food can be so rigid. Don't give food power over you. Become a master. Train your mind and body to obey you. From time to time I like to let my body know who's boss by looking for opportunities when I can eat some special, rich, delicious food that's unhealthy and that I really want but choose instead something nourishing that I may not desire. When you first try this, it's hard and your body and mind usually resist. But after a while, you feel a great sense of self-mastery, and you become freer.

I believe that the quality of food is not the only important factor in the way we eat. The way the food is prepared and served is also significant, as is the consciousness in which we eat. Food made, served and eaten with love has a positive effect on our bodies. If we are upset, angry, agitated or in a hurry when we eat, this affects our bodies and spirits. When we take time to appreciate our food, we support efficient assimilation and satisfaction. Each food has a certain vibration. We affect the vibration or energy of the food by our own energy vibration. I always meditate and say grace before a meal, even if it's only one piece of fruit. This simple act of benediction and gratitude has a twofold effect, as Sri Chinmoy writes in his book, *Secrets of the Inner World*:

> If we meditate before we eat, then His Compassion descends on us, and His Compassion is nothing short of energizing power. So, along with material food, if we can receive energizing power, then naturally we will get double benefit from the food.

Our awareness that God is in everything, including the food we eat, gives us a different perspective about eating and caring for our bodies. Focusing consciously on the act of eating can be a most powerful experience. Clear your mind before you eat. Take a couple of minutes to meditate. For me this includes thanking God and Mother Earth for these blessings. Breathe slowly and deeply. Make eating a spiritual delight as well as a physical experience.

In the *Essene Gospel of Peace*, Book One, I read:

> The angels of air and of water and of sunlight are brethren. They were given to the Son of Man that they might serve him, and that he might go always from one to the other. Holy, likewise, is their embrace. They are indivisible children of the Earthly Mother, so do not you put asunder those whom earth and heaven have made one. Let these three brother angels enfold you every day and let them abide with you through all your fasting.

Without sunlight, life wouldn't exist. The life force and the least dense form of energy in our universe, sunlight, according to Cousens, carries the full spectrum of rainbow stimulation to our systems. Cousens recommends at least thirty minutes of sunshine a day over the total body for reenergizing. Both Herbert Shelton and Paramahansa Yogananda recommend ten minutes of sunshine a day. We must have a healthy respect for the sun, however, for her life energy force and revitalizing powers. Early morning or late afternoon sun is much better for you; avoid the midday sun during the summer months. Moderation is the key. Too much sun can age the skin prematurely and even cause skin cancer.

Without the sun, most adults couldn't synthesize vitamin D to keep their bones strong; the body needs this vitamin to absorb dietary calcium. Sunlight also inhibits production of melatonin, a hormone linked to hibernation in bears and lethargy and depression in humans. If we never got sun, we might sleep all day and have rickets, which results from a vitamin D deficiency.

In the insightful book *Sunlight*, author Zane R. Kime, M.D., addresses the relationship of sunlight to human health. Studies from the scientific literature describe sunlight's effects on lowering cholesterol, blood pressure, and blood sugar; and on increasing endurance, sex hormones and, resistance to infection. Crucial dietary suggestions are made in his book to insure a healthy skin when exposed to sunlight.

We all need fresh air and pure water. Air and water are sources of nutrition that the body uses to heal and renew all its cells and tissues. Of course, the quality of both varies depending on where you live. If you live in an area, like I do, that does not provide pure water from the tap, find another source, such as distilled or bottled water processed by reverse osmosis, or get a water purifier. Water is a natural healer and body cleanser. Not only do we need to drink adequate amounts, but we also want to use water that has been energized by the sun. When I swim in the ocean or wade in a stream, I always feel reenergized. We want to obtain the same effect from the water we drink, but distilling water, Cousens asserts, can destroy its life-giving energy. Before drinking distilled water, I usually shake it to reoxygenate it and place it where the sunlight can energize and restructure it.

I recommend taking an air bath daily — exposing your body to fresh air and practicing deep breathing. This is especially important for those who live and work in environments that seal out fresh air. Every morning, immediately after I get up, by going out into my yard or simply opening a window, I let the fresh air caress my body while I participate in a variety of deep breathing exercises. I usually do this in the evening as well. Keeping a window open while you sleep, even if it's only an inch or so in the winter, is also important. You need to breathe in fresh air as much as possible. I can't emphasize enough the importance of the daily practice of deep breathing, which cleanses, detoxifies, energizes and spiritually uplifts the body. For an in-depth look at the effect breathing has on our lives physically, mentally, emotionally and spiritually, I highly recommend *Science of Breath* by Swami Rama, Rudolph Ballentine, M.D., and Allan Hymes. The breathing exercises it suggests are excellent, and I practice many of them regularly.

Rest is another important rejuvenator and healer. No magic number of hours per night works for everyone. How much each of us needs to sleep varies from person to person. I read recently in *Reader's Digest* that both Albert Einstein and Thomas Edison slept only four hours or less each night. You may require ten hours a night. The only way to know how much sleep you need is to take an honest look at yourself. In an article titled "Rest and Sunshine," in *Health Science* magazine, Alan M. Immerman, D.C., warns about overtaxing your energy resources.

When you feel exhausted at night, do you force yourself to stay awake to finish that one last report, clean out that one final drawer, or finish that one last chapter? If this is your regular style, watch out. A physical collapse is in the making. If you are not in good health, if you feel tired all the time and "come down" with frequent illnesses, if you feel too exhausted to exercise, then more radical recuperative measures may be necessary. You may need a period of physical rest much longer than a good night's sleep. Two or three or more days in bed may be needed.

Fasting gives the body a physical rest from digestion, absorption and elimination of food and its by-products. This profound type of rest, says Immerman, gives the body a chance to recover the energy it needs to heal itself.

We also need mental rest. If your body is enervated and you go to bed to rest but occupy your mind with all sorts of work-related problems, you're not getting mental rest. Physical and mental exhaustion undermine health and healing. If you want to rejuvenate and detoxify your body, don't forget the importance of rest and sleep.

Another rejuvenation technique is dry brush massage, which beautifies both the skin and overall health. I've been using this technique for almost twenty years. Paavo Airola, in his book *How to Get Well*, explains why dry brush massage is so beneficial.

. . . your largest eliminative organ is the skin. It is estimated that one-third of all body impurities are excreted through the skin. . . . If the skin becomes inactive and its pores choked with millions of dead cells, uric acid and other impurities will remain in the body. The other eliminative organs, mainly the liver and kidneys, will have to increase their labor of detoxification because of the inactive skin, with the result that they will be overworked and eventually weakened or diseased. Toxins and wastes will then be deposited in the tissues.

You can keep your skin in working order by massaging it daily with a dry brush, then taking a shower. Dry brushes are available in health food stores. Select one with natural bristles and a long handle so you can reach all over your body. (Do not use nylon or synthetic fiber brushes — they are too sharp and may damage your skin.) When I first started dry brushing my skin, I used a softer brush and brushed gently until my skin became "seasoned." Then I moved to a coarser brush.

Making rotary motions, start with the soles of your feet and massage every part of your body. Start gently, especially in sensitive areas like your stomach or under your arms. Because of the sensitive skin on my face, I use a special soft brush only twice weekly in that area. Brush until your skin becomes rosy, warm and glowing, which usually takes five to ten minutes. Make sure you don't rub too hard; as your skin becomes accustomed to massage, your brushing can become more vigorous. Remember, everything is best in moderation, including dry brush massage.

Exercise stimulates all the internal organs and muscle systems, tones the digestive system, rejuvenates the nerves, improves circulation and stimulates the body and skin to release toxins. No health or detoxification program is complete without exercise. For those of you interested in weight loss, exercise is imperative. Your metabolic rate, which determines how many calories your body burns in its day-to-day activities, is directly related to the amount of lean muscle mass on your body. A body with lots of metabolically active muscle burns more calories than a body that carries more fat. Exercise increases lean muscle tissue. And weight training, more than any other exercise, is the best way to develop lean muscle tissue. Aerobics is good for your heart and burns fat, but weight lifters use more calories all day long, even in their sleep.

When you change your lifestyle to one of wellness and detoxification, don't be surprised if you feel worse before you begin to feel better. An initial change for the worse is often a sign that your body is housecleaning. Your body can heal itself; you just have to supply what it needs and avoid giving it what is harmful. It boils down to this: *How much do you want to celebrate life and experience radiant health?* It's up to you. A full-spectrum life brings peace of mind, and, "the mind of peace precedes bodily healing," according to Charles Fillmore in *Jesus Christ Heals*.

Choose today to be in alignment with nature's laws of health and healing. Persistence and commitment are the keys. How you care for your body reveals your inner sense of self-worth. Nourishing your body with fresh foods, pure water, clean air, sunshine, rest and exercise will lead you to the level of radiant health you've always dreamed of having. And if you nourish your body temple so that you can be healthy and strong to live a life of service and oneness with God, you can then even more enthusiastically choose a more natural life. It's the greatest adventure imaginable.

Choose to live peacefully, incorporating the full-spectrum life.

> Because God lives in you, you will want to give Him the very best home that you possibly can. When you obey Laws of nutrition, exercise, and rest, God can do His share to keep you in perfect health.

Mary-Alice Jafolla, *The Simple Truth*

Taking Inventory and Action

1. When was the last time, if ever, you went on a cleansing health program?

2. Do you avoid the sun entirely because you are afraid of its damaging effects?

3. When you're not feeling well, do you automatically resort to drugs or medication to treat your symptoms? (This sometimes interferes with the body's natural healing system.)

4. Do you ever rush through your meals or eat without hunger just because the clock says it's mealtime?

5. Do you love yourself enough to want to take care of your body temple?

6. Find a good holistic doctor who can work with you on a detoxifying/cleansing health program.

7. Eat more fresh, raw foods and always stop eating before you are full.

8. Eat fruit by itself when your stomach is empty. Eaten in this way, fruit is nature's best body cleanser.

9. Take care of your body in a way that promotes peace and spiritual rejuvenation.

10. Live in the presence of God.

Today's Affirmation

I am an expression of radiant health. All of life is mine to use with wisdom, joy and delight. My health is a divine gift. I am perfect strength and I live by nature's laws. I am conscious of God as my life, my mind, my body and my appearance.

CHAPTER 6

Vegetarianism and Reverence for Life

Any religion which is not based on a respect for
life is not a true religion.

Until he extends his circle of compassion to all living
things, man will not himself find peace.

Albert Schweitzer

You may wonder what a vegetarian diet has to do with living peacefully. Everything! As a vegetarian for close to two decades, I powerfully state my commitment to my well-being, animal rights and the environment. My convictions contribute to building a more compassionate, sustainable and healthy world. Through the work of individuals such as John Robbins, Herbert Shelton, John McDougall, M.D., Peter Singer, Michael Klaper, M.D., T. Colin Campbell, Gabriel Cousens, M.D., and others, more and more people are becoming aware of how food choices affect more than just health. When you know the facts, the decision to follow a vegetarian diet is easy.

Environmentalism and vegetarianism go hand-in-hand, declares the Physicians Committee for Responsible Medicine (PCRM), a national network of physicians, scientists and other health care professionals concerned with ethical and practical issues in health. This may come as news to many of America's environmentalists. Only 3 percent of all Americans are vegetarians, whereas 76 percent claim to be environmentalists. Animal agriculture was cited as environmentally disastrous by PCRM's president Neal D. Bernard, who offered the following statistics:

- It takes 4,200 gallons of water a day to feed a meat eater. (Only 300 gallons of water per day are required to feed a vegetarian.)

- Over-grazing by livestock and unsustainable methods of growing feed account for a loss of nearly four billion tons of topsoil each year in the United States.

- A pound of hamburger from cattle raised on cleared tropical rain forest land represents 55 square feet of burned-off forest. Thirty-nine times more energy is required to produce beef than soybeans having the same caloric value.

The PCRM is only one organization taking a wider view of the relationship between our food choices and the state of the environment. In an extraordinary book, *Diet for a New America*, John Robbins, with thoroughness, skill and elaborate documentation, reveals the links between our intake of meat and the current epidemics of cancer, heart disease and numerous other health disorders. Robbins shows, as well, the role our eating habits play in the present ecological crisis — in the depletion of our water, topsoil and forests. He discloses how the production of animal foods puts toxins into our environment and how our consumption of these foods, in turn, increases our susceptibility to these toxins. Robbins merely presents us with facts about the meat and dairy industries — their cruel and dangerous methods of food production — and lets us draw our own conclusions about the way we want to live. Here are a few statistics I garnered from his book:

- Number of acres of United States forest land cleared to create cropland to produce a meat-centered diet: *260 million*

- How often an acre of trees disappears in the U.S.: *every eight seconds*

- Trees spared per year by each individual who switches to a pure vegetarian diet: *one acre*

- Number of people who will starve to death this year: *60 million*

- A driving force behind the destruction of the tropical rainforests: *American meat habit*

- Current rate of species extinction due to destruction of tropical rainforests and related habitats: *one thousand per year*
- Number of animals killed for meat per hour in U.S.: *500,000*
- Diseases that are commonly prevented, consistently improved and sometimes cured by a low-fat vegetarian diet: *stroke, cervical cancer, hiatal hernias, heart disease, stomach cancer, diverticulosis, osteoporosis, endometrial cancer, obesity, kidney stones, diabetes, gallstones, breast cancer, hypoglycemia, hypertension, colon cancer, kidney disease, asthma, prostate cancer, peptic ulcer, irritable colon, pancreatic cancer, constipation, salmonellosis, ovarian cancer, hemorrhoids, trichinosis*

Robbins's book leaves no doubt. The food we eat affects our personal health and our planet. His commitment led him to become founder of EarthSave, a nonprofit organization providing education and leadership for transition to more healthful and environmentally sound food choices, nonpolluting energy supplies and a wiser use of natural resources. (See Resource Directory)

Let's get more specific on how your food choices affect your health. Some of the latest exciting news on this front, recently reported in the *New York Times* by Jane E. Brody, was based on information from the most comprehensive study yet undertaken on the relationship between diet and the risk of developing heart problems, cancer, diabetes, osteoporosis and other diseases. These early findings are challenging much of American dietary dogma.

The study was initiated in 1983 by T. Colin Campbell, a nutritional biochemist at Cornell University, and is expected to yield important data for the next half century. The study, being conducted in China, vividly shows that a plant-based diet is unquestionably healthier than a meat-based one. Some of the findings of this study include:

- Eating a lot of protein generally, and animal protein especially, leads to "diseases of affluence," such as heart disease, cancer, and diabetes.
- Obesity is related more to what people eat than to how much: eating excess protein and animal fat is more likely to produce obesity than is eating starches.

- A rich diet that promotes rapid growth early in life, such as cow's milk, meat and eggs, may increase a woman's risk of developing cancer of the reproductive organs and breasts.

- Chinese women do not suffer from osteoporosis, yet their diet generally excludes dairy products, and they get all their calcium from vegetables.

From his work thus far, Campbell concludes, "We're basically a vegetarian species and should be eating a wide variety of plant foods and minimizing our intake of animal foods." Campbell and his associates in China will continue to assess the data. I hope the results will motivate more people to move toward vegetarian diets.

Being a vegetarian is also a way to show respect for animals and their rights, to live in greater harmony with the environment and to balance our bodies. In *Spiritual Nutrition and the Rainbow Diet*, Cousens writes:

With a vegetarian diet, we avoid the disharmony of killing animals. The vegetables we eat are taken from the ground in their seasonal cycles in harmony with when they are going to die naturally, and fruits are simply the sunshine gift of the living plant to us. There is a natural harmony between plants and humans. Plants take in carbon dioxide as a product of our respiration and convert it to oxygen and carbohydrates; thus we share an important biological life cycle. Each colored plant, as food, is a condensed spectrum band of sunlight color for us to take in for the balancing of our chakras and the physical organ, gland, and nervous systems. When we take in a full spectrum throughout the day, we benefit by having our total chakra system balanced energetically by our plant friends. This is the principle of the Rainbow Diet.

Cousens's book is the best I've ever read on how our food choices affect the spiritual side of our nature. He takes us on a journey into the relationship between nutrition and spiritual life and, like Robbins, fully documents his elaborate work.

This chapter has certainly provided some food for thought, and I hope it has inspired you to consider your food choices. What you eat goes way beyond nourishing your body; it goes hand-in-hand with living peacefully and creating a more peaceful world. Given the threat to our species and our planet, we cannot hesitate in our efforts toward change. You can make a difference by what you choose to eat.

Choose to live peacefully with a reverence for life.

Nothing is more powerful than an individual acting out of his conscience, thus helping to bring the collective conscience to life.

Norman Cousins

Taking Inventory and Action

1. In what ways can you improve your diet?
2. Are your food selections influenced by others?
3. Do you select foods more out of habit than for health benefit?
4. What is your commitment to our Mother Earth?
5. Read *Diet for a New America* and learn what foods you might want to eliminate from your diet to enhance your health and save our planet.
6. If you don't want to give up animal foods, at least choose to cut down.
7. Experiment for this week and choose a vegetarian diet. See how you feel. If you are already a vegetarian, see if you can eat healthier.
8. Include a variety of colorful foods in your diet from the fruit and vegetable groups.
9. Pay close attention to how the foods you eat affect your level of peace.
10. Live in the presence of God.

Today's Affirmation

I am aware that the act of eating can be a powerful statement of commitment to my own well-being and to the creation of a healthier planet. And so, with knowledge and inner guidance, I now choose foods that are in alignment with my commitment. I have reverence for all life.

CHAPTER 7

Juicing

Let your body be henceforth a temple
dedicated to God.

Edmond Bordeaux Szekely, *The Essene Gospel of Peace*

Drinking fresh, raw fruit and vegetable juices heals and rejuvenates the body. Raw juices contain an abundance of vitamins, minerals, enzymes and other nutritive elements that are beneficial in normalizing all the bodily processes. Minerals in juices help restore the biochemical and mineral balance in the tissues and cells. Mineral imbalance in the tissues is one of the main causes of diminished oxygenation, which leads to disease and the premature aging of cells. According to Ralph Bircher, a Swiss physician known internationally for his healing expertise, raw juices contain an as – yet – unidentified factor that stimulates the cells' ability to absorb nutrients from the blood stream and effectively excrete metabolic wastes.

You can incorporate juices into your diet, or you can adopt a juice-only diet, sometimes referred to as a juice fast, although I prefer to call it a juice feast. In *How to Keep Slim, Healthy and Young With Juice Fasting*, Paavo Airola writes, "Make your juice fasting one of your most wonderful experiences, which will recharge, renew and rejuvenate your whole personality — body, mind, and spirit."

Why not eat the whole vegetable or fruit instead of extracting the juice and discarding the fibers? Solid food requires many hours of digestion before its nourishment is available to the cells and tissues of the body. While the fibers in solid food have virtually no nourishing value, they do act as an intestinal broom during the peristaltic activity of the intestines; hence the need to eat raw foods in addition to drinking juices. According to N.W. Walker in his book, *Fresh Vegetable and Fruit Juices* (which I recommend highly to anyone interested in juicing for better health):

> The removal of the fibers in the extraction of the juices enables juices to be very quickly digested and assimilated, sometimes in a matter of minutes, with a minimum of effort and exertion on the part of the digestive system. Whole vegetables and fruits are composed of a considerable quantity of fibers. Within the interstices of these fibers are enclosed the atoms and molecules which are the essential nutritional elements we need. It is these atoms and molecules and their respective enzymes in the fresh raw juices which aid the speedy nourishment of the cells and tissues, glands, organs and every part of our body. The juices extracted from fresh raw vegetables and fruits are the means by which we can furnish all the cells and tissues of the body with the elements and the nutritional enzymes they need in the manner they can be most readily digested and assimilated.

Walker's book explains how to use specific kinds of juice to detoxify, heal and rejuvenate the body. He even breaks down the various physical ailments and discusses which juice or combination of juices will assist the healing process.

When you begin a program of regeneration and detoxification of your body by natural means, you must remember that fresh, raw juices may start a regular housecleaning process throughout your system. You may feel pains or aches in the regions of the body where this housecleaning is taking place. Don't think for a moment that the juices are making you sick. Instead realize that the cleansing and healing process is well on its way. Before too long you will be feeling and seeing a positive difference.

It is important to make your own fresh, raw juices, instead of buying canned or bottled juice from the grocery market. Everything in a can or bottle has been heated. At the present time, federal law requires that foods be run through a pasteurizer for at least a half-hour to kill enzymes and prolong shelf life. But that's not all. Processors add sodium benzoate, benzoate acid, sodium nitrate, propionates, carbons, BHA and BHT. Anything in a can or bottle may have been on a shelf in a warehouse for a long time before you bought it. When you make your own fresh juices, you're in total control. You know exactly what you are putting into your body. I would never drink pasteurized juice from a bottle or can.

Whenever possible, buy organic produce to make your juice. When that's not possible, wash the produce thoroughly. Here's a formula for removing toxic surface sprays from your non-organic produce: (1) Fill your kitchen sink with cold water. (2) Add four tablespoons of salt and the juice of half a fresh lemon. This makes a diluted form of hydrochloric acid. (3) Soak fruits and vegetables five to ten minutes. (4) Soak leafy greens two to three minutes. (5) Soak berries one to two minutes. (6) Rinse well after soaking. Note: Never wash or hull strawberries until just before use. They lose their freshness quite rapidly after washing. Leafy greens store better if spun dry after washing. Store greens in zip-lock bags. Celery stores best in the long plastic produce bags with a little water added to the bottom of the bag. For greater freshness, leave the stalks attached until ready to use. Do not juice celery leaves. They add a bitter taste to the drink.

Many different kinds of juicers are available, and I have tried all of them. My favorite is the Juiceman Automatic Juice Extractor. It's very practical, efficient and easy to use and clean. What I particularly like about this juicer is that it's strong enough to juice skins and all — including pineapples, watermelons and cantaloupes. Many of the most important nutrients are in the skins and rinds; it is a waste of nutrients to throw these skins away. In addition, because of my demanding traveling schedule, I like the idea that the Juiceman juicer is light enough to take along. (See Resource Directory)

The Juiceman juicer was developed by Jay Kordich, author of *The Juiceman's Power of Juicing*, who in 1944 was diagnosed as having terminal bladder cancer. Two years later, there was no trace of cancer in his system. His treatment? Juice therapy under a doctor's supervision. Kordich's juice therapy included fresh carrot and apple juice every hour, thirteen times a day. This miraculous cure convinced Kordich to dedicate his life to promoting raw foods and juice as the way to achieve health and well-being. Now, more than forty years later, "Jay the Juiceman," as he is known,

continues to spread the word about the benefits of a raw food diet
— especially fresh-squeezed juices. He has produced an excellent
series of audio cassettes, which include such topics as an introduc-
tion to juicing, raising children with fresh juices, losing weight
and preventing disease with juices, and how juices boost your
immune system.

Make sure you drink your juice right after juicing. Researchers
at Stanford University found that one minute after the juice is
extracted, the therapeutic qualities begin to dissipate. Orange
juice, if not consumed within five minutes, loses half its vitamin C
content; if it sits for an hour, it loses all of its vitamin C. So always
try to drink your juice when it's fresh. If you want to take juice to
work with you, try this: Moisten the inside of a stainless steel
thermos with water and put it in the freezer overnight. Before
going to work, make your juice and put it directly into the cold
thermos, filling the thermos to the brim. Juice will stay fresh for
up to eight hours this way.

Drink your juices slowly; don't gulp them down in large
quantities. When you drink slowly, the saliva will mix with the
juice, providing the same natural digestive enzymes we get when
chewing food. If the juice is taken too quickly and in large
quantities, it can be harmful. This is particularly true of vegetable
juices (such as parsley and beet), which are generally stronger
than fruit juices. Don't combine fruit and vegetable juices; the
exception being apple juice. Apples combine well with carrots,
celery or other vegetables. Never combine melons with other
fruits. You may combine different types of melons with each
other.

Contrary to popular belief, you can get protein from juices.
The strongest creatures on the planet are strictly vegetarian:
horses, gorillas, elephants. The protein that nurtures these creatures
is in green plant life. The most disease-free humans are vegetarians.
In the cellulose matter of greens lies the finest protein in the world.
Humans can have the same protein sources available to them if
they juice greens. You may be surprised to learn that one large
glass of carrot juice has at least five grams of protein, which is
equal to the protein of two eggs.

Juicing has been an important part of my health program for
twenty years. At least once a month, I incorporate a juice-only

diet for a few days. Every day I drink at least one glass of fresh, raw juice. Last year, as a preparation for this forty-day water fast, I went on a juice feast (juices only) for twenty-one days, followed six months later by a forty-day juice feast. I felt fantastic.

Here are some tips that will help you adopt the habit. Set a time when you will juice each day. Be sure to stock up on the produce you want to juice. Have the produce cleaned and ready to juice. If you have unwanted habits that you would like to eliminate, use this one to replace them. Carry this out faithfully for three weeks, for it takes twenty-one consecutive days for your body and mind to accept a new habit. And before that time is up, you will already be reaping the benefits of juicing.

I would now like to share some of my favorite juices and juice combinations. For me, nothing can compare with a glass of fresh grape, carrot or apple juice, but I also like these following combinations:

carrot, apple, celery and parsley
carrot, beet and cucumber
carrot and cabbage
carrot, beet and spinach
carrot and spinach
carrot, cabbage and lettuce
carrot, beet and lettuce
carrot and apple
carrot, apple and parsley
apple and lemon

apple and lime
apple, lemon and ginger
pineapple and strawberry
tangerine and pineapple
grapefruit, orange and lemon
raspberry, orange and pineapple
blueberry and strawberry
orange and strawberry
grape and apple

Juicing has made a world of difference in my health; and I know it will make a difference for you, too. I encourage you to research the subject of juicing through books, audio cassettes and consultation with health professionals. Remember, health is peace of mind.

Choose to live peacefully and incorporate juicing into your health regime.

The power and effectiveness of foods in healing and in keeping people well is sometimes astonishing.

Bernard Jensen, *Vibrant Health From Your Kitchen*

Taking Inventory and Action

1. Is there room for improvement in your level of health?

2. Are there times when you would like a quick "pick-me-up?"

3. When you're in a rush and don't have time to sit down and eat, have you ever considered making fresh juice your meal?

4. Have you ever wondered how you could get more vitamins and minerals into your diet without taking a plethora of supplements?

5. Did you know that a short term juice-only diet is an easy, effective way to lose weight, increase energy, release food addictions and make you feel radiantly healthy? (Always check with your doctor or other health professional before adopting a juice program.)

6. Have your produce washed and stored in zip-lock bags ready for juicing.

7. Whenever possible, buy organic produce.

8. Drink fresh juices between meals. The sweeter juices, like grape, you may want to dilute with some pure water.

9. Juices help to clear your mind and improve concentration. Mental lucidity promotes deeper meditations.

10. Live in the presence of God.

Today's Affirmation

My body is the temple of the living spirit. I treat my body with the love and respect that it deserves and feed it high quality food and juices. As a result, I am radiantly healthy, filled with energy and light.

CHAPTER 8

Exercise For Life

The strongest advice I can give the beginner
is to exercise often.

Covert Bailey, *The Fit or Fat Woman*

Patterns of modern living have channeled the average American into an increasingly sedentary existence. We human beings, however, were designed and built for movement, and our bodies have not adapted well to this reduced level of activity.

For many adults with sedentary occupations, physical activity provides an outlet for job-related tensions or mental fatigue. In addition to reducing tension in the body, exercise can boost spirits and help us feel good about ourselves. Exercise has also been found to aid in weight control or reduction, to improve posture and to increase energy. Further, my experience indicates that many cases, in fact about half, of lower back pain can be traced to poor muscle tone and inflexibility. Proper exercise can often prevent or correct lower back pain. Research also indicates that much of the degeneration of bodily function and structure associated with premature aging seems to be reduced by a program of vigorous, regular exercise.

Regular exercise is necessary then to develop and maintain not only an optimal level of health, but also a youthful appearance, mental clarity and high energy. Regular exercise increases muscle strength and endurance. It enhances the function of the lungs, heart and blood vessels; increases the flexibility of the joints; and improves coordination and efficiency of movement.

But before you can experience any of the benefits of vigorous exercise, you must take responsibility for your own fitness program and for choosing those activities that promote fitness. My aim in this chapter is to cite research that will convince you of the advantages of following a well-rounded fitness program. I will concentrate on how exercise contributes to your self-image, happiness and peace of mind. I have gone into this topic in much greater detail in my book, *Choose To Be Healthy*; I recommend that you read the chapter titled "Be Fit." In that chapter, you'll find much of the material that follows here, plus a wealth of other information.

"A sound mind in a sound body" is a traditional British motto. Researchers are finding, however, that there's much more to the adage than might first appear. It seems that our sense of happiness and well-being depends on how much exercise we get. Malcolm Carruthers, head of a British medical team, believes that "most people could ban the blues with a simple, vigorous ten-minute exercise session three times a week." He came to this conclusion after spending four years studying the effect of norepinephrine on 200 people. Norepinephrine is a depression-destroying hormone, "the chemical key to happiness," according to Carruthers. Ten minutes of exercise doubles the level of norepinephrine in the body.

Enkephalin is another spirit-lifting chemical produced in the brain during vigorous aerobic exercise. In *Positive Addiction*, William Glasser credits enkephalins as the source of the feeling known as runner's high among the long-distance runners that he studied. Enkephalin is a type of endorphin, morphine-like chemicals that serve as natural opiates, increasing pain tolerance and producing euphoric feelings. A study at Massachusetts General Hospital found a rise of more than 145 percent in endorphins during one hour of vigorous exercise.

Exercise can work in conjunction with psychotherapy to alleviate depression, according to work done at the Menninger Clinic in Topeka, Kansas. "It's not a panacea, but it is a useful adjunct for treating depression," says the clinic's Robert Conroy. One of Conroy's hypotheses is that exercise boosts self-image by changing an individual's world view from that of passive bystander to active participant. People who exercise believe they have control over their health and the quality of their lives.

Exercise works better than tranquilizers to eliminate symptoms of tension and anxiety. Herbert de Vries, exercise physiology lab director at the University of Southern California, conducted a classic study of tense and anxious people. As one part of the experiment, he administered 400-milligram doses of meprobamate, the main ingredient in many tranquilizers. In the second part, he had the same group of people take a walk vigorous enough to raise their heart rates over a hundred beats per minute. De Vries measured tension levels by monitoring the amount of electrical activity in the subjects' muscles. "Measuring electrical activity in muscles is the most objective way to measure a person's nervousness," he says. He found that after exercise, electrical activity was 20 percent less than the subjects' normal rate. After being dosed with meprobamate, the subjects showed little change in the electrical activity in their muscles. "Movement is strong medicine," de Vries concluded.

By releasing tension, exercise alleviates those tension-related bodily malfunctions, such as ulcers, migraine headaches, asthma, skin eruptions, high blood pressure and heart disease. Exercise also leads to a good night's sleep, a key to mental well-being.

Aerobic activity is the kind of exercise that produces truly beneficial psychological and biochemical changes. Vigorous, rhythmical activities such as jogging, brisk walking, running, swimming, aerobic dancing, rowing, cross-country skiing, cycling and stair-climbing appear to send messages to the brain as well as the endocrine system to shape up and feel good.

Exercise is a rewarding and enjoyable means of taking control of our psychological and physical well-being. A well-designed physical fitness program can add years of fulfillment, vibrant health and peace of mind. (And that knowledge alone has a potent positive effect on mental well-being.)

Choose to live peacefully and exercise.

Walk your dog every day, whether you have a dog or not.

Paul Dudley White, M.D.

Taking Inventory and Action

1. Are you at your ideal fitness level?

2. What excuses keep coming up that prevent you from exercising?

3. What is the best time of day for you to fit in your exercise? Do you have any home aerobic equipment?

4. Where would you like to be (fitness-wise) a year from now?

5. Do you lack energy, self-confidence or a zest for life?

6. Start today and really commit to your fitness program. Exercise for twenty-one days in a row as that helps establish new habits.

7. Work out with a friend to help you stay motivated.

8. Make a fitness goal for yourself for the next month, three months, six months and a year from now. Plan your fitness program.

9. Realize that when you exercise, you are caring for your body, which is the temple for God.

10. Live in the presence of God.

Today's Affirmations

I love to exercise and I do so regularly. Exercise brings me more energy, mental clarity, self-confidence and peace of mind. Taking care of my body is my way of saying thank you to God for my health and my life.

Slanting

Healing is a matter of time, but it is also a
matter of opportunity.

Hippocrates

Gravity is the master of our environment. Our lives — from the moment we enter this world to the moment we leave it — are dominated by this universal force. We can avoid unhealthy foods, contaminated water and polluted air, but we cannot get away from gravity. Gravity can have a negative effect on posture, skin tone, circulation, concentration and all of the organs of the body as it relentlessly pulls them down. Gravity never lets up.

Recently some medical professionals have made the connection between gravity and health. Robert M. Martin, founder of Gravity Guiding System, cites drooping, sagging stature; bulged out mid-sections; and unsightly posteriors as examples of the "devastating effects of gravity." Martin Jungmann, founder of the Institute for Gravitational Strain Pathology, says, "It is generally accepted that the force of gravity, which is part of man's natural habitat, has a bearing on his health."

We must learn to work with the law of gravity instead of allowing gravity to work against us. In this regard, I have, for more than fifteen years, advocated lying on a slantboard, which puts the legs higher than the heart and the head lower than the heart. In this position, the pull of gravity on your face, neck, back, organs, legs and feet is naturally and effectively reversed. When I was introduced to the slantboard by Bernard Jensen, I never dreamed that such a simple device would not only improve my physical appearance but would also have a tremendous impact on my overall state of health. I have since been recommending the slantboard in all my counseling and workshops on health and healing. I have seen use of the slantboard reduce or eliminate headaches, insomnia, varicose veins, chronic fatigue and neck and shoulder tension. I have also seen it improve posture, complexion and circulation and foster relaxation and peace of mind. (Always check with your doctor before slanting, especially if you have high blood pressure.)

In her book, *Slanting*, Sharlin Leslie writes about the first time she laid on a board.

> . . . the unfamiliar rush of blood to my head made me feel slightly dizzy and my heart sounded as if it was pounding between my ears. The initial reaction lasted only a few moments, though, and quickly gave way to a feeling of pleasant, soothing relaxation.

Leslie began using the slantboard on a regular basis for fifteen minutes, twice a day. After just two weeks, she discovered, in addition to a new-found state of well-being, a more glowing complexion, healthier-looking hair and the loss of several pounds with no effort. At the end of two months her chronic back pain had subsided enough for her to discontinue her weekly visits to the chiropractor, and the dull, aching sensation in her lower legs was greatly reduced.

I have a slanting session daily as part of my health program. It's a great way to practice deep breathing, concentration, visualization and meditation. My visualizations on the slantboard are always very deep and relaxing; my spine stays straight, which is an important aspect of meditating properly. After ten to thirty minutes of slanting, I always feel refreshed, rejuvenated and relaxed.

Many different types of slantboards are available at sporting goods or other fitness stores. My favorite, and the one I've used for more than fifteen years, is called a Bodyslant. Created by Larry Jacobs, it's functional and practical as well as being the best slantboard developed to date. It also functions as a lounge, bed and ottoman. The picture at the beginning of this chapter shows the Bodyslant and another excellent piece of equipment called the Body Lift. Both are important components of my health program. (For more information, refer to the Resources Directory.)

Choose to live peacefully and let gravity work for you and not always against you.

There has been more interest and scientific research regarding gravity on the moon — and its effects on the human body — than there's been about the earth's gravity and its effects on your body.

Larry Jacobs, founder of Gravity Awareness

Taking Inventory and Action

1. Stand in front of a full-length mirror with your clothes off. Can you see some of the effects of gravity on your body?

2. How is your posture? Do you ever get tense in your neck and shoulders?

3. Does your face lack a healthy glow?

4. Do you ever wake up from a full night's sleep and still feel tired and sluggish?

5. Are you one of the millions of people who experience low back pain?

6. Make slanting part of your daily routine. Start with five minutes and gradually work up to thirty. Then adjust according to your schedule.

7. Always check with your doctor before beginning a slantboard routine.

8. Use your Bodyslant to relax, breathe deeply, concentrate, meditate or simply rest your legs and feet.

9. You might want to turn the lights down low, light a candle, play some soft, relaxing music while you Bodyslant. I love doing this as it brings about calmness and peace of mind.

10. Live in the presence of God.

Today's Affirmation

No longer will I let gravity get the best of me. I use my slantboard daily to refresh and rejuvenate my body. My body temple deserves the best, and I lovingly and consistently care for all my body's needs.

CHAPTER 10

Staying Motivated to Exercise

The sovereign invigorator of the body is exercise,
and of all the exercise walking is the best.

Thomas Jefferson

There's no doubt about it — be-
ing fit and feeling vibrantly alive can enrich every area of your life,
including how peaceful you feel. With the plethora of health and
fitness news in all the media, people cannot help but be aware of
the benefits of exercise. And more people do seem to be exercising. Still there are many who start fitness programs and then
suddenly quit.

Has this ever happened to you? You get all fired up about your
exercise program. You start with a winning attitude only to
discover that in a few weeks (in some cases, days or hours), your
attitude has turned from winning to surrender. This lack of
discipline to follow through on your commitment can undermine
even the best of intentions. I see discipline as the ability to carry
out a resolution long after the mood has left you.

How do you stay disciplined and motivated enough to carry
through on your desire to become fit? First, you must have your
goals clearly defined — for both the short and the long term.
Make sure your short-term goals are fairly easy to reach so that
you receive early reinforcement for your intentions. This creates a
positive mental attitude, builds confidence and tends to neutralize
failure patterns imprinted in the subconscious.

Yes, goals provide a direction and let you measure how you are
doing. What are your goals for exercising and being fit? To lose
weight and reshape your body? To increase your energy and boost

your self-esteem? Perhaps you want to be able to run in a 10-kilometer race or increase your strength and definition.

Write down whatever goals are important to you. Really give some thought to what you want to achieve for yourself in your exercise program.

After you've written your list, post it where you can see it every day, perhaps on the refrigerator door or on the bathroom mirror. As you achieve your goals, make new ones.

In addition to having a concise list of goals, make another list of your plan for achieving those goals. Let's say that you've been jogging for six months, and you're now up to four miles four times a week. Among your goals are running a 10-kilometer race in a month and running a marathon by the end of the year. You would, therefore, map out a jogging program that gradually increases your weekly mileage. This is the procedure I followed when training to run 100 miles from Santa Barbara to Los Angeles.

It's a good idea not only to read your goals daily, but also to evaluate your progress weekly to make sure you're staying on course. You might make three lists of goals: one to cover the next month (these can be changed daily or weekly), one for the next six months (these might change monthly), and one to cover the entire year (these might change quarterly).

I have always found it beneficial to share my goals with my friends and family. It's harder to get off course when a caring, supportive friend checks on you to see how you are progressing toward your goals. Make sure you confide in someone you trust and with whom you feel comfortable, not someone who will bring up your "slipbacks" (and you will have some) at the next office party.

Be realistic. Don't set yourself up to fail. If you've just started a jogging program and are now up to one mile non-stop, don't make one of your goals running a marathon at the end of the month. I'm not suggesting that it's impossible. I believe in miracles, but it would definitely take a miracle for a typical person to get in shape for a marathon that quickly.

Next, once you have your goals clearly defined and written out, take some time each day and creatively visualize achieving your goals, exactly as you want to achieve them. Using visualization on a regular basis will hasten your success, increase motivation and keep you on course. The subconscious part of the brain cannot tell the difference between fantasy and reality, between the visualization and the actual event. So as you vividly imagine achieving your goals and you feel the joy that accompanies that achievement, your subconscious is experiencing your visualization as reality. By using visualization techniques regularly, you will discover the behavior necessary for achieving your goal seems to come more easily and readily, without as much resistance.

Always head in the direction of your dreams and act confidently, as though your dreams were your reality right now. You will discover that success begins to chase you. Acting confidently implies being enthusiastic about your commitment. When you love what you do, you carry that winning attitude with you into everything.

In addition to visualizing your goals every day, you'll want to use affirmations to support your intentions and to motivate yourself. (My tape #7 from my *Celebrate Life!* series offers a variety of affirmations to cover every area of your life. It's a wonderful tape to use as you're falling asleep at night and upon awakening each morning.) An affirmation is a purposeful effort to synchronize thought, speech and feeling toward a desired effect. An affirmation acts like a magnet to draw all your powers of concentration to your specific goal. Affirmations are a way to gain conscious control over thought and attitude.

When you are creating your affirmations, select a phrase that embodies your ideal. Always keep the affirmation in the present tense. Keep the affirmation positive. For example, instead of saying, "I will never eat junk food again and am not fat," say, "I always select healthy foods that support my trim, fit body." Practice using your affirmations every day. I recommend using them right before you go to sleep, just as you are awakening in the morning, and during the day whenever you think about them. finally — and this is very important — use your affirmations with feeling. Experience the joy and enthusiasm you would really have if this affirmation were your current reality.

Repetition is the next key to staying motivated and disciplined to achieve your fitness goals. Repetition is the key to mastery in every area of your life. Behavioral scientists have discovered that it takes at least twenty-one days for your mind and body to create a new habit and to stop resisting. Until then, you can expect to hear that incessant voice in the back of your mind that I call Babbler, because it never shuts up. You can count on Babbler to keep up a running dialogue on how nice it would be to sleep in, how sore your calf muscles are or how heavy the weights feel. Babbler will probably tell you that you look just fine the way you are, that people who really love you don't care about a few extra pounds or inches and that huffing and puffing at the top of the stairs is normal for someone your age.

Don't pay any attention. Instead, when the commentary begins, simply acknowledge Babbler's point of view and remind yourself that for twenty-one days you are going to stick to your new exercise program. If at the end of that time you feel you aren't benefitting from it, you can re-evaluate. That should help keep Babbler happy. Chances are that by the end of the twenty-one consecutive days, you'll no longer have any resistance to exercising. In fact, it's likely you'll have become positively addicted to it.

Another way to stay motivated to exercise is to work out with a friend. You won't want to disappoint a friend who is counting on you as a training companion. I enjoy training alone at times, but many times I'm grateful to friends for getting me through workouts I probably would have skipped if I had been on my own. Working out with a friend helps prevent boredom, which can be a great obstacle to staying with a fitness program. Another boredom alleviator is music. Variety in the exercise program also helps. If you are a serious bodybuilder or weight lifter, make changes in your program monthly so you won't get in a rut. Get involved in more than one sport, and if you get bored easily, alternate days with the sport. This is referred to as cross-training. It helps to relieve boredom, keep you motivated and ensure that all your different muscle groups are exercised. Outdoors, I enjoy swimming in the ocean, jogging, walking, hiking and cycling. Indoors, I work out on my PRECOR fitness equipment. I have a climber, treadmill, stationary bicycle and rower. This combination works well for me. Each day I participate in a different aerobic activity. For example, my weekly routine might look like this: Monday - climber; Tuesday - jogging; Wednesday - rower;

Thursday - cycling; Friday - treadmill; Saturday - hiking; Sunday - stationary bicycle.

Don't progress so quickly that you are constantly in pain. It's hard to look forward to working out when you can hardly move and you ache all over. This gets back to setting realistic goals. It took you quite some time to get into the shape you're in now; don't expect to look like your ideal in a few days.

Finally, you've worked hard, you've achieved your goals — or at least you're still heading in that direction — so reward yourself. Treat yourself to something special. And don't be too hard on yourself if you find you're not motivated to work out on your scheduled day of exercise all the time. That's natural and that's okay. Sometimes it's good to give the body a rest. No one is going to be highly motivated to workout 100 percent of the time.

Today commit to your health and exercise program. Accept and expect the best for yourself and advance confidently and enthusiastically in the direction of your dreams and affirmations. If you do, you will meet with unexpected success in every area of your life, and peace will fill your body and mind.

Choose to live peacefully and exercise for life.

Choose what is best; habit will soon render it agreeable and easy.

Pythagorus

Taking Inventory and Action

1. How do you feel about exercise?

2. What are your fitness and exercise goals for the following month, three months, six months and year? Write them out now.

3. What areas of your body need special attention with exercise?

4. What three exercise activities can you incorporate into your fitness program to relieve boredom, keep you motivated and ensure all muscles get a workout?

5. After you work out, do you ever notice that you feel more peaceful and happy?

6. For the next twenty-one days, make a commitment to do some physical activity — even if it's just stretching. You'll feel great at the end knowing you followed through on what you said you were going to do.

7. Decide what your fitness goals are and either share these with a close friend or, better yet, find a friend who is willing to work out with you.

8. Find ways to get in exercise that does not seem so much like exercise. For example, park a few blocks away from your destination and walk the rest. Carry your grocery bags to your car instead of using the cart.

9. When you feel unenthusiastic about life and your peace of mind is foggy, go out and exercise. Realize that you are the temple for the divine.

10. Live in the presence of God.

Today's Affirmation

I look forward to my workouts knowing that I am loving this body temple. From day to day, I vary my workouts keeping them fresh and fun. Exercise is an important part of my health and peace program.

CHAPTER 11

Relationships

Everything in the future will improve
if you are making a spiritual effort now.

Sri Yukteswar, *Where There is Light*

Oone of the great joys in life comes from the relationships we form with others. At the same time, relationships can also present our greatest challenges, offering us countless ways to grow and get to know ourselves better.

To experience harmony in our relationships, we must learn to see and love the divine in others and understand that lasting relationships result from *being* the right person, not *finding* the right person. A basic spiritual principle is that there is only oneness. We are all one with everyone and everything we encounter. Instead of trying to change or fix someone whom we see as the source of our problems or difficulties, we can remind ourselves what that person really is. Instead of focusing on outer appearance and behavior — quirks, idiosyncrasies, clothes, hairstyles — we can look at another with the thought, "That is a soul, a child of God. That human being is an expression of the Infinite." By doing so, we acquire greater understanding and detached perspective: That person has feelings, just as I do. She has thoughts and opinions, aspirations and dreams that are just as important to her as mine are to me. The life force of God in that person is manifesting in her personality and in the services she performs — in the things she does for me, in the way she treats others, in her way of being. Because I know who I am, a divine child of God who already has everything, I can accept and focus on the divinity in others.

As we absorb this higher image of who we are, many wonderful benefits follow. When you come from the awareness that you are a spiritual being, you no longer relate to yourself as a creature whose satisfaction comes solely from physical pleasures. You stop relating to others in terms of their physical appearance. Because you know that your worth derives from the eternal self within you, and because you are aware that this same self lives in the hearts of all, you relate to everyone with respect, kindness and love, no matter what the circumstance.

This change of attitude about relationships is one of the most joyful benefits of spiritual experience, yet it brings enormous responsibilities. In order to see ourselves in all, we must become detached from our own ego, otherwise we will get emotionally entangled in other people's problems and lose sight of our oneness with spirit. You must practice detachment if you want to create loving, harmonious relationships. Being spiritually detached, which to me is being a very loving person, means being able to stand back from and let go of your own needs and preferences. Without this detachment, you cannot help but manipulate other people, which will only create conflict in your relationships.

Peace comes from practicing detachment continuously — at home, at work, with friends and relatives and especially with difficult people. A spiritually detached person will not let a relationship degenerate to stimulus and response. The test is simple: Even if you are upset or angry with me, can I remain calm, loving and kind with you and help you overcome your anger? If you persist in being upset with me, can I still be loving towards you?

A dislike for people is really a reflection on us rather than on those we do not like. For we tend to see others not as they really are but as we are. Our relationships are always mirrors, reflecting some aspect of ourselves. They are spirit's way of saying, "Look at what we can learn about ourselves." Pay close attention when a particular pattern or behavior is mirrored back to you from three or more different people, for then you can be sure here's something you need to look at. To an angry person, everyone seems angry and full of hostility. To a suspicious person, everybody seems suspect. To a loving, tenderhearted person, everybody is worthy of love; every occasion is an opportunity to offer love and forgiveness and to see the best in the other person. I'm not saying that if you are loving and detached, you'll never experience difficulty in relationships. People will still get angry or fail to treat you nicely. And with people who aren't very nice and treat us unkindly and disrespectfully, we must sometimes look harder to see the divine in them. There may be relationships that are unhealthy and abusive. In those instances, you usually need to remove yourself from the environment while both of you get help. Still, you can love that other person (you don't have to love his behavior) and put him in God's hands.

With practice and commitment to your own divinity, you will see, even if it's only in a very small way, that people begin to come around. Being around someone who's loving, gentle, tender and peaceful softens others' hearts. And when we bring to a relationship our awareness of our divinity and keep our heart open, it is amazing how people's attitudes toward us change.

If we want to get along with others, we should not treat people as objects in our environment, but as human beings who are children of God, worthy and deserving of our love and peace. I once heard Buckminster Fuller say, "We are not nouns, we are verbs." People who have rigid images of others think of themselves and their fellow human beings as nouns, as things. Those who keep the awareness of their oneness close at hand and strive to understand and appreciate others more all the time behave more like verbs — enthusiastic, open, active, creative, able to change themselves and to make changes in the world. They keep one goal in mind: *to identify and remove all the blockages to the awareness of God's presence in everything and everyone, including themselves.*

Everyone wants to feel loved, appreciated, nurtured and supported. This is particularly true for children and teenagers. Our role as parents is to love, support, guide and nurture them and to provide an environment in which our children experience high self-esteem and are free to discover and express their God-given talents. Too often we want to manipulate, force or coerce them into doing and being what we think they ought to be doing. We need to get back to spirit and trust that God is revealing to our children their highest vision. We must help our children believe in themselves and their ability to live their vision. Remember, our children are not here to fulfill our unrealized dreams. Nor do they exist to help us resolve all of our unfinished business. They are God's children, and spirit already has a wonderful journey prepared for them. Our role is to love them unconditionally, to support and guide them and to help them realize how lovable and capable they are. To do this, we must feel lovable, capable and worthy ourselves.

> Your children are not your children; they are the sons and daughters of life's longing for itself.
>
> Kahlil Gibran

Children reflect the consciousness of their parents. When your children are causing problems, look at what needs adjusting in your own life. Case in point: Last month, I went to the movies with a friend and her teenaged daughter. When my friend purchased the tickets, although she should have paid the adult price for all of us (her daughter was thirteen), she said, "Two adults and one child." Just a few days prior, she had been talking with her daughter about the importance of always telling the truth. Which message do you think spoke more loudly to her daughter?

In my counseling practice, people often come to me wanting advice on how to discipline their problem children. Before I even address that question, I first look at the parents, how they feel about themselves and what values and attitudes they are giving their children. Until we deal with our own consciousness and take care of unfinished business, all of our attempts to "fix" a problem child are only going to compound the situation. What I always ask myself in every situation, whether with children or adult relationships, is, "*What is this situation telling me about myself? What is this challenge revealing to me? How can I be more loving and offer that love and tenderheartedness to the other person?*" I know that if I can raise my consciousness to the awareness of my oneness with God, especially in the most difficult and trying of times, then I will be able to see more clearly, respond instead of react and resolve differences instead of increasing conflict.

Gerald Jampolsky has written about all this beautifully in *Out of the Darkness, Into the Light.*

> We withhold love from ourselves by denying it. What happens is we begin to feel depressed, and we think that there is something out there in the external world that we need. We begin to get upset when we don't get it. We try to control people. We try to manipulate people and live a life where there is a lot of attack — a lot of saying I'm right, you're wrong. People don't realize that the battle we see out there in the external world is really just an extension of the battle that goes on in our minds.

Problems usually escalate when the spiritual element is not present in a relationship. Says Jampolsky:

> . . . when we feel separate from our spiritual being, what happens is we feel fearful, and fearful that we are going to be attacked. We begin to listen to the voice of the ego, something that we really manufactured, that has a course of fear.

Letting go of negative thoughts and removing fear improves dealings with individuals in every area of life. If a relationship is truly a giving one, says Jampolsky, the couple will decide together to be gentle and kind to everyone they see. "It's not that you have an exclusive love, but have it only to demonstrate that it is the kind of love that we can have with everyone."

Demonstrating peace, kindness, love and gentleness in daily life means having a loving connection not just to another person, but to ourselves as well, which means surrendering ourselves to God and seeing God in all our relationships. One of the greatest gifts you can give is to help others experience themselves as beautiful, lovable, capable and deserving.

Something happened yesterday that reminded me I have a ways to go in my efforts to establish loving relationships with everyone. I was talking to a close friend on the telephone. He is usually very tenderhearted and kind with me, and that shows in his voice and his way of being with me. But yesterday morning was different; he sounded distant, cold and harsh. He was frustrated with work; he was fighting off a cold; and he wanted to clarify some plans we were making for a special celebration.

of responding to him with love and tenderness, I reacted by saying, "Well, there's no need to be so mean and harsh and so maybe we should talk about this another time when you're in a better mood." As you can imagine, that only upset him more and distanced him further. He became more hostile, and I felt ready to give up. Trying to see the divinity in this man was the furthest thing from my mind. We got off the telephone saying we were both okay, even though neither of us meant it.

I thought about that phone conversation all day. I realized that I was too attached to the way I wanted and expected my friend to be. I was unwilling to acknowledge that anyone can have a bad day. I didn't have to take his attitude as a personal attack. I could, instead, choose to offer my love, understanding and patience. After an entire day went by, I finally got brave enough to give him a call and apologize for my behavior. I told him I would work on being more understanding and loving and wouldn't take his infrequent mood changes and distancing personally. At the same time, he acknowledged that he didn't need to take out his frustrations with work on me and that, because he cared for me so much and knows how much I value others' being tenderhearted and loving, he would work on his behavior and attitude. All in all, through communication and a willingness to feel the fear and move forward anyway, we were able to resolve the conflict and come closer together in spirit.

 I like to think that God's harp strings connect all hearts. When we choose to distance ourselves from others, some of those harp strings break, and the music we hear is no longer very harmonious. When we choose to see the divine in everyone and respond lovingly no matter how someone else treats us, then we create beautiful music. God writes the songs; all we have to do is stay together and play the notes. Let God's celestial music resonate in every relationship you have.

I have a list of goals for creating more harmonious relationships:

1. No game playing
2. No pretense
3. No expectations
4. No defenses

5. Respect for myself
6. Respect for others
7. Respect for life itself
8. A constant awareness that I am a child of God, and so is everyone else

There are some wonderful books on how to create more loving, harmonious relationships. *Are You the One for Me?*, *How To Make Love All The Time*, and *Secrets About Men Every Woman Should Know* by Barbara De Angelis are excellent. De Angelis is practical in her approach to human relations and always brings in the spiritual side as well. I also recommend *The Power of Unconditional Love* by Ken Keyes, Jr., *Love is the Answer: Creating Positive Relationships* by Gerald Jampolsky and Diane V. Cirincione, *Homecoming* by John Bradshaw, *Conquest of Mind* by Eknath Easwaran and *Making Peace With Your Parents* by Harold Bloomfield.

In conclusion, I would like to offer from Jampolsky's Center for Attitudinal Healing the basic principles for creating loving, harmonious relationships.

The Principles of Attitudinal Healing

1. The essence of our being is love.
2. Health is inner peace. Healing is letting go of fear.
3. Giving and receiving are the same.
4. We can let go of the past and of the future.
5. Now is the only time there is and each instant is for giving.
6. We can learn to love ourselves and others by forgiving rather than judging.
7. We can become love finders rather than fault finders.
8. We can choose and direct ourselves to be peaceful inside regardless of what is happening outside.
9. We are students and teachers to each other.
10. We can focus on the whole of life rather than the fragments.
11. Since love is eternal, death need not be viewed as fearful.
12. We can always perceive others as either extending love or giving a call for help.

Choose to live peacefully and let God be your primary relationship so you can bring the divine into all your relationships.

Our purpose in relationships is just to see that spirit of love in each other, the light of love in everyone. That is the only reality.

Gerald Jampolsky, *Out of the Darkness, Into the Light*

Taking Inventory and Action

1. When someone criticizes you, do you react emotionally and/ or distance yourself?
2. Do you depend on your relationships to make you feel happy, lovable, worthy or peaceful?
3. Do you hope your child will become a doctor, lawyer, athlete or other professional? Do you blame your children for your problems?
4. Are you trying to change your partner to make him or her more like you?
5. Have you more interest in being right or in being happy?
6. Sometimes we assume that our families or partners or close friends know that we love them. Don't assume anything. Let them know how you feel.
7. Take care of your unfinished business from the past because you carry that with you into all your relationships.
8. Make peace with your parents, whether they are still living or not. Without that peace, you'll never be able to create lasting, loving relationships.
9. If you don't have high self-esteem, either on your own or with help, change it. If you don't love and care for yourself and treat yourself with respect, how do you expect anyone else to do the same?
10. Live in the Presence of God.

Today's Affirmation

I know that the essence of my being is love and I choose to extend this love to everyone in my life. Regardless of outer circumstances, I remain peaceful and tenderhearted. I love myself and others unconditionally and know that we are all children of God. In our oneness, I see divinity in everything and everyone.

CHAPTER 12

Healing and Embracing
Your Inner Child

*I know what I really want for Christmas. I want my
childhood back. Nobody is going to give me that ...
I know it doesn't make sense, but since when is
Christmas about sense, anyway? It is about a child
of long ago and far away, and it is about the child of
now. In you and me. Waiting behind the door of our
hearts for something wonderful to happen.*

Robert Fulghum, *All I Really Need to Know I Learned in Kindergarten*

Do you find that you are often in bad relationships? Do you have a difficult time expressing your feelings or asking for what you want in relationships? Do you have a hard time saying "No"? Is your self-esteem low? Do you look for things outside yourself to validate who you are? Are you depressed or angry? Do you have addictions or a compulsive personality? Did you survive sexual, emotional or physical abuse, or did you come from any type of dysfunctional family? Do you rarely feel peaceful? If you answered "yes" to any of these questions, chances are you have a wounded inner child who needs to be healed and embraced.

You see, if you didn't get your needs met as a baby or child, those needs are recycled throughout your lifetime. My own pain as a child and adult has led me to do extensive exploration into inner child work. My dad was an alcoholic; he left the family and moved to New York when I was seven (I was the third of four children and we lived in Los Angeles), divorced my mom, moved back to Los Angeles when I was seventeen and, shortly thereafter, died. (A child usually feels the death of a parent as abandonment.)

I never really felt loved by my dad. I believed something was wrong with me and that I had to be perfect for him to notice me. Although my mom was wonderful and made me feel loved and wanted, the lack of love from my dad left a deep hole in my soul — this wounded inner child. When I became an adult, this emptiness and abandonment I felt showed itself in a variety of ways: compulsive working and eating, always feeling I needed to accomplish in my career to be a valuable person, and creating relationships where I abandoned others or was abandoned.

The work of two people have had a very positive effect in my life in healing and embracing my inner child. The first person is David White, a workshop leader at the Ken Keyes Center in Coos Bay, Oregon, who also travels throughout the country giving workshops to assist people on contacting and communicating with your inner child. The work of John Bradshaw has also helped me heal my inner child and turn my life around. Family counselor, public speaker and one of the primary figures in the field of recovery and dysfunctional families, Bradshaw appears regularly on public television. He has written several books, including *Bradshaw On: The Family* and *Healing the Shame That Binds You*. But my favorite among his books is *Homecoming: Reclaiming and Championing Your Inner Child*.

In *Homecoming*, Bradshaw writes:

Three things are striking about inner child work. The speed with which people change when they do this work; the depth of that change; and the power and creativity that result when the wounds from the past are healed.

This was certainly apparent in my life and is evident in the lives of those I now counsel.

Bradshaw also says, "I believe that this neglected, wounded inner child of the past is the major source of human misery." For some of you, that statement may sound strange. You may not realize that what you did as a child has so much to do with how you are as an adult. Take a look at some of your current patterns. Maybe you didn't receive the love you needed and wanted as a child; so, as an adult you are needy in relationships. Or maybe your inner child is angry and rebellious; so as an adult you continue to create financial problems, lack and limitation. You could have been physically abused as a child; so, even though you swore you wouldn't abuse your own children, you do (usually feeling guilty and terrible afterwards) or else you attract people who abuse you. Freud called this "the urge to repeat."

In his excellent book, *Advice from a Failure*, Jo Coudert writes, "Of all the people you will ever know, you are the only one you will never lose or leave." I love that! It touches a responsive chord in me. And since you're going to be with yourself forever, don't you want all the parts of that self to be healthy and whole?

You can play the nurturing, protective parent to your inner child and begin the process of healing. Reclaiming your inner child involves going back through all the developmental stages and finishing unfinished business. The only way out is through. No pain, no gain, as they say in recovery.

If you are like I am, you remember very little prior to the age of seven. Bradshaw says that's normal because we were in another state of consciousness; we were magical and totally egocentric. But you don't need to make your recovery dependent on memories. Look at what you're creating in your life now. All you need is the feeling, i.e. lonely, sad, angry.

Many simple, effective corrective exercises for healing your wounded inner child are described in *Homecoming*. I'd like to share two of them with you here because they had a profound effect on my own inner healing work. One is to write a letter to your inner child. According to Bradshaw, the purpose of this letter is to establish a connection with this inner energy. You want to reclaim and champion this vulnerable part of you — to be the protector, to bring this inner child home, to feel once again in touch with your feelings, needs and wants.

Begin by closing your eyes, taking in some long, slow deep breaths, feeling safe and exploring some of your painful childhood memories or emotions. (Remember, don't make your recovery dependent on memories.) Bradshaw suggests that you might want to start with, "I know better than anyone what you've been through." Then give an example, or if you don't have any specific memories, just share the feelings you're experiencing. Then begin to write.

This is the letter I wrote to establish contact with my inner child:

Dear Little Susan,

I know better than anyone what you've been through. I know you were scared of Dad and wondered why he didn't love you. If he did love you, he wouldn't have left you two times and would have made things easier for Mom and your sisters and brother. I know how terrible you felt when you heard Mom and Dad quarrelling late at night when they thought you were asleep. Most of their fights had to do with lack of money and how expensive it was to raise four children. Dad made it pretty clear he wasn't interested in being a Dad. Because he abandoned you, you basically felt like you never really had a Dad. You didn't even grieve at his funeral and felt very little emotion at all. During your childhood, you spent a lot of time in solitude because Mom was so overburdened with trying to make a living to support the family and couldn't give you the attention you wanted. You felt lonely and not understood. You weren't allowed to express your feelings. In a way you felt responsible for their marriage and thought it was your fault that they divorced. You felt like a burden to Mom and Dad.

My precious little Susan, you deserve love and care and attention. I'm so glad you're here. I will always take care of you, protect you, and make you feel safe. I love you just the way you are.

Love, Susan

Write a letter to your inner child and see what comes up for you. Childhood stuff lasts a lifetime because we don't allow children to grieve.

Here is another corrective exercise you can do. Write a letter to your mom or dad and express how you felt as a child. Use your non-dominant hand for this exercise because you will feel like a child when you are writing. The purpose of this letter is to help you finish the unfinished business with your parents so that you can go on with your life.

Here is the letter I wrote to my dad several years ago:

Dear Dad,

I needed to feel you loved me and really never felt that way. When you left for New York, I thought it was because I wasn't good enough and I cost too much money to raise. You made me feel like something was wrong with me. I needed to know you wanted me. And I always felt I needed to be perfect for you to notice me.

Love, Susan

An amazing thing happened to me about a week after I wrote that letter to my dad. I had been invited to give a keynote address to a gathering of dentists and dental hygienists in Glendale, California, only about thirty minutes from my home. After my presentation was over, for some unknown reason, I felt like taking a different route home. I passed by the Glendale Forest Lawn Mortuary, and all of a sudden my car turned into the driveway. It was as though the steering wheel had a mind of its own. The car rolled into a parking spot, and the engine quit. I made several attempts to start it, but the battery seemed to be dead.

I decided to call my mom (she lives a few minutes from the mortuary) to see if she wanted to visit with me while I waited for a tow truck to come to recharge my battery. When I told her where I was, her first comment was, "Did you know that's where your dad's ashes are buried?" (My dad's memorial service had been at a different location from Forest Lawn. I had never bothered to find out where his ashes were kept.)

When my mom told me this, I felt a flood of emotion rush through me. I knew what I had to do. I found out where Dad's ashes were — Freedom Mausoleum, Niche 26760 — and I went to that building, barely able to control the tears. There was no one around except the gardener. He saw me crying, asked if he could help, took my hand and walked me inside the huge, empty building to Niche 26760 — Verne Smith.

My dad's niche was on the bottom of a row, so I sat on the cold, hard floor and for a few minutes just stared at his name. It's difficult to describe how I felt; it was as though a floodgate had opened; emotions swept through me. For almost four hours I sat, stood, walked, laid down, all the time talking to my dad, sometimes out loud, sometimes silently, usually crying. I told him of my pain, sadness, loneliness and anger. I expressed everything that was inside of me. I told him about my life. Once I started, I couldn't stop until it was all out.

And then the strangest thing happened. After about four hours, my tears were gone, and I actually felt peace. I no longer had any negative feelings for my dad. All that was left was tremendous love for him and the knowledge that he had done the best he could. To this day, I only have the deepest love for my dad and am continually feeling his energy around me, guiding my path.

As Bradshaw said would happen, in a matter of hours after this incident, incredible changes began to occur in my life, including better relationships, release of compulsive-addictive behaviors, an increase in self-esteem and a profound peace of mind I had not felt before.

By the way, when I left the mausoleum and went back to my car to get some change to call a towing service, my car started right up.

In *Toxic Parents*, Susan Forward says that we are not responsible for what happened to us as children but we are 100 percent responsible for healing and taking care of unfinished business as adults. Only when you do this will you be able to live fully and celebrate life. It's not easy, but it's necessary. Commit to this inner work. Reclaim your life.

Choose to live peacefully and embrace your inner child.

You will connect with a fresh vision of your child, enriched by your years of adult experience. This is your true homecoming. It is a discovery of your essence, your deepest unique self.

John Bradshaw, *Homecoming*

Taking Inventory and Action

1. Do you have difficulty expressing your feelings or asking for what you want?

2. Do you easily get angry, feel sad or lonely, give in to temper tantrums or pout?

3. Is your self-esteem low? Are you always seeking approval from others?

4. Is there unfinished business you need to take care of with your parents?

5. Are you depressed a lot for no apparent reason?

6. Do you find you're always attracting unhealthy relationships? Do you have addictions and compulsions? Are you self destructive?

7. Read *Homecoming* and do the corrective exercises recommended.

8. For a couple minutes every day, talk to your inner child. For example, say, "(your name), I'm here for you now. I'm glad you're a girl (or boy). You're safe and protected now. I love you just the way you are and you don't have to do anything to earn my love. I'm glad you're here. Welcome beautiful little child."

9. Get into some type of support group. Most people have a lonely inner child — that is they felt lonely during childhood. So get into some group where you feel loved and nurtured.

10. Live in the presence of God.

Today's Affirmation

I embrace my inner child and hold her (him) in the center of my heart. She (He) is safe and protected. I am glad she (he) is in my life. Welcome to my life. You are loved and appreciated.

CHAPTER 13

Sanctuary

He brought me to the banqueting house, and His
banner over me was love.

Song of Solomon 2:4

We all need a sanctuary in life, a
place of refuge and protection, a place filled with love and peace
where we can recharge our batteries and replenish our souls. For
most people, this place is their home.

Do all you can to make your home a comforting place to be.
During this time of spiritual rejuvenation, I have been spending
most of my time at home and have been more sensitive to
enriching my sanctuary. I notice I'm becoming less tolerant of
clutter; every day I am finding things to give away or throw away.
I feel better when my home is clean and organized. Living simply
appeals to me.

I am also aware of how different colors influence my mood.
One of my rooms is yellow; when I'm in that room, I feel more
energetic and creative. Another one of my rooms is lavender; I feel
more relaxed and peaceful in that room. Walk around your house
and see if any of your rooms could use a facelift. Something as
simple as painting a room can make a noticeable difference in
how you feel. "Color has the ability to serve man's physiological
and psychological needs and to keep him on an even keel in times
of stress," writes Farber Birren in *Light, Color and Environment.*

If you have room, create a garden around your home. It
doesn't have to be very elaborate. If you live in an apartment, you
can have some outdoor container plants. We must stay connected
to Mother Earth, and one of the best ways to do is to touch her

soil and nurture her plants. I rarely feel more peaceful and content than when I'm gardening. I love the smell of rich soil. I love sitting on the ground to plant and prune. When I observe nature's beauty and order, I can't help but feel moved and inspired. Watching my garden grow gives me hope, brings me joy and fills me with peace.

Flowers

The flower opens slowly
Each petal following its own path
Questioning not its outcome or destiny.
  Just opening.
Hope in your heart that the petals of
  flowers never develop intellects.

Rebecca Zinn, *On the Wings of Spirit*

All homes are enriched by bringing nature indoors, too. Fill your home with sunlight, fresh air and plants. While most of you have indoor plants because they are attractive and decorative, did you know that houseplants also contribute to your well-being? That's right. They provide your living environment with oxygen. They also can clear the air of toxic chemicals. When National Aeronautics and Space Administration (NASA) scientists placed fourteen different types of houseplants (one at a time) in a sealed Plexiglas chamber with the air pollutant benzene, they found that certain plants absorbed large amounts of this cancer-causing chemical. English ivy destroyed 90 percent of the room's benzene, while Dracaena marginata, Dracaena Janet Craig, peace lily and golden pothos each had a 75 percent removal rate. Chinese evergreen absorbed half of the airborne poison.

The houseplants' ability to neutralize benzene is particularly noteworthy in light of the recent Environmental Protection Agency study showing that most of our exposure to benzene comes from indoor sources, such as cigarette smoke, latex paints and household solvents.

It won't take a jungle to clean the air you breathe indoors: NASA scientists estimate that one 1- to 12-inch plant per 100 square feet of floor space can dramatically reduce benzene levels.

There are so many parts of a home that can be improved for your physical, mental and spiritual benefit. Consider everything — from noise, lighting and decorating to temperature and cleaning products. Architect Carol Benolia has written an excellent book, *Healing Environments*, about the relationship between humans and buildings. If you care about your health and live indoors, this book is must reading. You will learn how the buildings you inhabit can influence your well-being. And you'll gain valuable information on how to change your indoor environment in ways that steadily improve your health.

Music is another way to bring more peace to your sanctuary. Do you ever notice how some music calms you and some agitates you? Our bodies respond with physiological changes to different types of music. In *Sound Health*, Steven Halpern shows the effects of music and sound on the body, mind and spirit and how to develop a proper "diet of sound" to achieve a calmer, more energetic, healthier self.

I know I'm very moved by some types of music. For example, when I listen to Dave Grusin's music from *On Golden Pond*, I always feel immediately calmer and more peaceful. Pachelbel's "Canon" does the same thing for me. When I listen to the music from *The Sound of Music*, I feel uplifted and more joyful. The music of Kenny G or Michael Bolton stirs love and passion in me. Mozart and Bach give me energy. Heavy metal music makes me feel agitated, tense and off-center. Next time you play some music, pay close attention to how it makes you feel. I often play music with nature's sounds — ocean waves, waterfalls, gentle rain or a babbling brook. Nature's sounds make the best music to me.

A special meditation sanctuary inside the home can be an extremely important place. Pick a room or a corner of a room where you'll always go when you meditate. Keep it clean, simple and inviting. When you come to sit and commune with God, leave all else behind. I have a special corner in my bedroom for my inner sanctuary. I have an altar (it's actually a rattan trunk) upon which I have pictures of Jesus and Paramahansa Yogananda, a candle and the Bible. On the floor in front of the altar, I have a wool rug where I sit to meditate. You may prefer to sit in a chair. Because I have used this area of my home for so many years to meditate, it is surrounded with vibrations of love and peace. When I sit to meditate, I immediately feel the calming effects. I use this corner of my room only for meditation.

I also think we need sanctuaries outside our homes, places in nature where we can go and feel safe, uplifted, empowered and relaxed. I have a few places like that. Top of my list is the Self-Realization Fellowship Lake Shrine in Pacific Palisades, just a couple of minutes from my home. This unique sanctuary was dedicated by Paramahansa Yogananda in 1950, and millions of visitors from all over the world have found inspiration in the peace and serenity that pervade these beautiful grounds. Lake Shrine is home to the Gandhi World Peace Memorial — the first monument in the world to be erected in honor of Mahatma Gandhi. Some of Gandhi's ashes are enshrined there in a thousand-year-old stone sarcophagus from China. Every time I visit Lake Shrine, I feel God's presence and leave feeling peaceful, joyful and inspired.

I also have a special bench that sits on a cliff overlooking Santa Monica Bay. When I'm in town, I visit often to watch the sunset or just to think and relax. This is a special sanctuary where I can go and turn within and feel my connection with Life, spirit and God.

You make a place a sanctuary by personalizing it, by bringing your intention and heart to it. Maybe there's a park down the block where you can go and sit or a flower garden or a fountain. Perhaps you can drive to the beach, the mountains or the desert. Find or create a special place you can visit regularly to fill your spirit with the beauty, tranquility and peace of nature.

Choose to live peacefully and let your sanctuary replenish your soul.

Hope never dies in a real gardener's heart.

C.F. Menninger

Taking Inventory and Action

1. Do you feel peaceful, protected and safe in your home?

2. In what ways can you make your home sanctuary more peaceful and relaxing?

3. Where do you sit to meditate? Can you make that area more conducive to your spiritual aspirations and commitment?

4. Where do you go in nature when you need a drink of tranquility?

5. Have your plants and garden been neglected?

6. Look around your home and see where you can bring more of nature indoors.

7. Mist your plants, wash your windows, put on a happy face and your favorite music, take off your shoes. Relax and enjoy.

8. Create a sanctuary close to your home where you can go regularly to relax, be inspired and feel empowered.

9. Know that wherever you go is holy ground and that God's presence is with you all the time. Tend to your garden. Weed out your worries, doubts, fears and self-limitations. Life is a garden; dig it!

10 Live in the presence of God.

Today's Affirmation

My home is my sanctuary and is filled with the vibrations of peace and love. Everyone who visits my home feels the presence of God. I feel safe, protected and one with the spirit of life.

CHAPTER 14

Discipline

Good habits are your best helpers; preserve their force by
stimulating them with good actions. Bad habits are your worst
enemies; against your will they make you do the things that hurt
you most. They are detrimental to your physical, social, mental,
moral and spiritual happiness. Starve bad habits by refusing to
give them any further food of bad actions.

Paramahansa Yogananda, *Scientific Healing Affirmations*

Discipline is a choice. If we are
to live our highest potential, the way God created us to be, we
must practice self-discipline in every aspect of our lives. It's the
only way to live on higher ground. The mountain of soul-
achievement and fulfillment cannot be scaled by anyone who
lacks control of body, mind and emotions.

Discipline, to me, means *the ability to carry out a resolution
long after the mood has left you.* It also means doing what you say
you're going to do.

Discipline brings freedom and peace to your life. A disciplined
person is not at the whim or mercy of external circumstances but
is in control of what he thinks, feels, says and does. An undisciplined
person is lazy, undirected and usually unhappy. Mind discipline
creates body discipline. And from a disciplined body comes an
exhilarated mind.

We cannot very well discipline ourselves in the great things of
life unless, and until, we have learned and accepted that discipline
must begin with the small things. It's been my experience that
through discipline in small things, the greater tasks that once

seemed difficult become easier. For example, it takes discipline to sit at my desk each day with my Macintosh PowerBook 170 to write this book. As the days go by, however, the writing becomes more enjoyable and I see my vision of a book come to fruition. Similarly, it takes discipline to fast for forty days. But if I take on this adventure one day at a time, I will reach the fortieth day more easily.

We can't address the topic of discipline without also bringing in the power of conditioning. The way we have been conditioned to behave affects all areas of our lives. For example, choosing foods that support well-being requires repeated reinforcement of such choices.

When I'm out skiing, I sometimes notice a small ball of snow that begins to roll down from the top of the mountain. At that point, the snow is easy to stop. But if it continues to roll, it may grow steadily bigger and heavier until an immense mass weighing tons descends. At that size, it is impossible to stop. Our desires work the same way. They gain in power and strength through repetition. Repetition is the key to mastery, or failure. Every time we are negatively conditioned, we lose a little of our freedom and our capacity to choose. When a negative desire first surfaces, we must nip it in the bud, we must eradicate it quickly and firmly. When you have a desire to eat junk food, don't give in. Exercise discipline. Choose something healthy to eat or abstain from all food.

Another way to exercise discipline and train your sense of taste is to stop eating mechanically. How often do you eat compulsively rather than from true hunger? Think of your eating behavior at parties and social gatherings, the movies, when you're watching television or attending sports events. Become aware of what you're eating. Discipline yourself to eat slowly and only when you're truly hungry.

When you repeat a negative behavior, it develops into a bad habit. To eradicate your negative conditioning, to break bad habits and to strengthen your self-discipline, make a twenty-one-day agreement with yourself. Let's say that at mealtime you want to stop eating before you feel stuffed. Make an agreement with yourself to do that. Resolve to stick with your agreement every day for twenty-one days. If you skip a day, you must begin the twenty-one-day cycle again. As I wrote earlier, it takes twenty-one days to form a new habit or break an old one. After twenty-one days, your mind and body stop resisting the change you're trying to make. Twenty-one days isn't a very long time. If you find your mind coming up with excuses, as it will, you can maintain discipline by reminding yourself that you have to continue for only twenty-one days.

I have been incorporating this twenty-one-day program into my life for years. The first of each month, I make an agreement with myself to give up some unhealthful habit or to develop a positive pattern. In this way, I make twelve beneficial changes in my life each year.

Keeping your agreements with yourself boosts your self-esteem. I know how I feel when I say I'm going to do something and I don't follow through on it. I feel lousy. When I stay disciplined and do what I say I'm going to do, I feel empowered. I have great respect for people who keep their word. I lose respect for those who don't. I have a few friends who make a habit of saying they are going to do something, like start exercising regularly; when I check with them to see how they're progressing, I hear a litany of excuses. These people aren't living their highest vision for themselves. As so aptly written by Paramahansa Yogananda in *The Law of Success*:

> It is only when you discard your bad habits that you are really a free man. Until you are a true master, able to command yourself to do the things that you should do but may not want to do, you are not a free soul. In that power of self-control lies the seed of eternal freedom.

One of my favorite heros is coach John Wooden. For twenty-seven years, he molded champions on and off the court at UCLA. His leadership generated excitement all over the Westwood campus and touched the lives of millions of people around this country. His unparalleled string of victories and National Collegiate Athletic Association championships remain the benchmark for basketball teams everywhere. One of the main ingredients in what Wooden calls the "pyramid of success" is practicing discipline in every aspect of our lives and keeping our word with ourselves.

One way to begin to master this art of discipline and to see immediate results is to schedule time every morning to meditate. Even if you are not yet a committed disciple on the spiritual path, meditate for the practical health benefits. I have discovered that through discipline in meditation, I have more discipline in other areas of my life. What's more, being disciplined brings me more peace. And it's from a more peaceful mind and heart that I welcome more discipline in my life.

Now is the time to become a disciplined person. Enrich every aspect of your life with self-discipline. You will discover, as I have, that discipline is the road to freedom, mastery and peace.

Choose to live peacefully and practice self discipline.

> Discipline determines that all aspects of your being obey your will. Your life is then an exciting unfoldment. Discipline over your habits, your thoughts, and your actions is essential. When your mind is disciplined, everything else falls into line. You can determine what you are to think. This is the true dominion.
>
> Donald Curtis, *40 Steps to Mastery*

Taking Inventory and Action

1. In what areas of your life do you lack discipline?
2. If you were a disciplined person, how would your life be different?
3. What bad habits would you like to release?
4. What new behaviors or positive habits would you like to adopt?
5. Do you follow through on what you say you're going to do?
6. Make a twenty-one-day agreement with yourself today to give up a bad habit.
7. Make your word count today. Follow through on all your agreements with yourself and others.
8. Get up before sunrise tomorrow and celebrate a brand new day of possibility. It takes great discipline to rise before the sun, and it's a wonderful way to start the day.

9. Turn all your bad habits, laziness, unwillingness and frustrations over to God and ask for guidance, strength and discipline to live God's will.

10. Live in the presence of God.

Today's Affirmation

I make discipline a way of life for me now. My mind is disciplined, which means my body is disciplined. Thank you Father-Mother God that your discipline shines through in everything I think, feel, say and do.

CHAPTER 15

Change and Patience

When the winds of change blow, go deeper.

Roy Eugene Davis

We live in a changing world. Nature is constantly changing. Your body is different from one day to the next; skin cells die off, and you lose hair. Friends come, and friends go. Feelings ebb and flow. The tide comes in and goes out. The only constant in our world is the divine. To live life fully and peacefully, we must anchor ourselves in God.

Sometimes changes come to us as gentle breezes and other times as tornadoes. When changes occur, we can choose how we will respond. We can try to control and manipulate the situation. We can become upset and depressed. We can become angry or tense. We can allow ourselves to be tossed around in the waves of change. Or we can choose to dive below the surface where the power is, where our strength and understanding lie.

The way to remain peaceful in a changing world is to be aligned with our inner changelessness while adapting as needed to the passing world. Welcome change. It promotes growth and restores equilibrium. There is no situation that cannot be changed. With enough love, there is no problem that cannot be solved. There is no heart that cannot be healed. There is no illness that cannot be made better. Know that when you are in harmony with God, anything is possible.

The key here is how you respond to change. My mom helped me to look at change in my life with the proper perspective. Whenever I experience a challenge, I remember her words to me, "This, too, shall pass."

Are you rigid or flexible? Being flexible is essential if you want to remain peaceful. We all have likes and dislikes. You like romantic, funny movies; your spouse likes suspense-filled, action-packed movies. You like vacationing in Hawaii; he would prefer to tour England. You like fruit and muffins for breakfast; he wants a seven-course feast. Can you make it okay that you have different tastes? Or do you get upset when you can't have your way? Be flexible! Don't make your preferences a barometer of how you are going to feel or react. With a flexible attitude, you will float through life rather than trying to swim upstream. It's fine to have certain likes and dislikes, as long as you aren't compulsively attached to them. Keep your options open. Be ready to change your proclivities, if necessary, as easily as you change your shoes.

It's healthy to break habits and acquiesce to another's preference. Next time he wants to see a television program that doesn't interest you, watch it with him and don't complain. If he wants to have Chinese food and you don't, have it anyway. Train your mind to be happy and flexible and to make the best of all situations.

Accepting change and staying open to it takes patience, which is the ability to be calm and undisturbed no matter what happens. This does not imply being unconcerned or uninterested. When we're patient, we cultivate our inner peace and do not disturb the creative flow in the deep waters below. A person who is patient knows she is on God's time and that everything is unfolding just as it should.

Look at nature. It took thousands of years for the Grand Canyon to be created. It takes a few hundred years for some redwoods to reach their full height.

Relationships take time; self-improvement takes time; learning a new language takes time. Cultivate patience.

Let's look for a moment at your health and fitness program. Maybe at this point you are out of shape yet really motivated to begin exercising regularly and eating more nutritious foods. If you're like most people, you don't think about all the years you've taken to get into the shape are now. You want to see results NOW. It doesn't work that way. But with patience, determination and perseverance, you will begin to see progress. Slowly, you will feel much better and be stronger. All things come to those who are patient.

How do you feel around people who lack patience? The other day, I was driving with a friend to the beach. We were going to take a walk and enjoy the sunshine. Our drive took us through heavy traffic. Often, we were unable to move forward when the light changed to green. My friend got uptight, started honking the horn and lost all his patience. I knew this wasn't exactly the best time to tell him he could choose differently, he could sit back, relax, enjoy my company and simply watch how all the other drivers reacted. By the time we got to the beach, his pulse was high and he couldn't relax.

Oftentimes we will be patient with others but forget to extend the same courtesy to ourselves. We make a mistake and are quick to judge and berate ourselves. When we hurt or are angry, we are seldom willing to give the situation an opportunity to reveal its lesson. We want to feel better now. We want to move through a painful situation quickly.

When we look back on our difficult or challenging situations, we find that eventually they led to greater awareness and faith. Anything worth having in life requires patience. Change and patience are part of the process of living fully and peacefully. Everything that happens to us brings us closer to God. With patience, we keep the door open to God's blessings, knowing that all is coming together for our highest good.

The closing poem is one of my favorites. It says to me that with patience, flexibility and the right attitude about change and life, the world can be ours.

Choose to live peacefully, patiently and welcome change as your friend.

If

If you can keep your head when all about you
Are losing theirs and blaming it on you;
If you can trust yourself when all men doubt you,
But make allowance for their doubting too;
If you can wait and not be tired by waiting,
Or, being lied about, don't deal in lies,
Or, being hated, don't give way to hating,
And yet don't look too good, nor talk too wise;

If you can dream — and not make dreams your master;
If you can think — and not make thoughts your aim;
If you can meet with triumph and disaster
And treat those two impostors just the same;
If you can bear to hear the truth you've spoken
Twisted by knaves to make a trap for fools,
Or watch the things you gave your life to broken,
And stoop and build 'em up with wornout tools;

If you can make one heap of all your winnings
And risk it on one turn of pitch-and-toss,
And lose, and start again at your beginnings
And never breathe a word about your loss;
If you can force your heart and nerve and sinew
To serve your turn long after they are gone,
And so hold on when there is nothing in you
Except the Will that says to them: "Hold on";

If you can talk with crowds and keep your virtue
Or walk with kings — nor lose the common touch;
If neither foes nor loving friends can hurt you;
If all men count with you, but none too much;
If you can fill the unforgiving minute
With sixty seconds' worth of distance run —
Yours is the Earth and everything that's in it,
And — which is more — you'll be a Man, my son!

Rudyard Kipling

Taking Inventory and Action

1. Do you get uptight when things move more slowly than you would like them to?
2. How do you respond to changes in your life?
3. Do you believe that everything has its perfect time?
4. Is your disposition affected when you can't have your way?
5. Do you live by your time or God's time?
6. Write down some of the likes and dislikes to which you are compulsively attached.

7. To let go of rigidity and inflexibility, do something today that is different for you or acquiesce to another's preference.

8. Listen patiently today to others and give them your full attention.

9. In quiet meditation, listen patiently for guidance and know that you are exactly where you need to be. Everything is unfolding perfectly.

10 Live in the presence of God.

Today's Affirmation

I am patient and peaceful today and I welcome change in my life. Everything is working harmoniously for me for I am a child of God. I listen patiently for the inner voice as it gives me guidance now.

CHAPTER 16

Simplify

The simplification of life is one of the steps to
inner peace. A persistent simplification will
create an inner and outer well-being that
places harmony in one's life.

Peace Pilgrim.

Simplify! What a wonderful word
and a powerful process. As part of my forty-day spiritual rejuvenation program, I am simplifying my life — not just my home
environment but every aspect of my life. It is such a freeing
experience. Every day I do something to unclutter my life — clean
a drawer or closet, give away some possessions or spend time just
sitting and watching the birds outside my window.

The death of a dear friend a couple days ago made me sit down
this morning and think about life and about how I could choose
to live more fully. The following words by Alfred D'Souze came to
mind:

> For a long time it had seemed to me that life was about to begin
> — real life. But there was always some obstacle in the way,
> something to be got through first, some unfinished business, time
> still to be served, a debt to be paid. Then life would begin. At last
> it dawned on me that these obstacles were my life.

This reminded me that sometimes our lives are so cluttered it's
difficult to see clearly. In the movie *Dances with Wolves*, I was
deeply touched by the simplicity with which the Sioux Indians
lived — able to gather all their belongings at a moment's notice

and move on to another homeland. We are all trying to orchestrate the complexities and responsibilities of modern life. But
much of the complexity we experience is, in fact, self-imposed. As
we grow in self-awareness and live more internally, life gets
simpler. Instead of getting our cues from the outside world, we
listen for cues from our heart.

Simplifying doesn't necessarily mean we have to restrict our
activities, but it does mean uncluttering our lives so that we can
put all our energy into activities we really care about. Activities,
material things and relationships are all time and energy consumers.
Maybe it's time to take inventory of your life and weed out the
superfluous. Being simple with life — not naive, but clear —
allows us to experience the present fully and deeply.

Plato wrote, "In order to seek one's own direction, one must
simplify the mechanics of ordinary, everyday life." I like that. To
begin uncluttering your life, start with your home. Weed out
everything you don't need, want and use. Spend fifteen minutes a
day working on one area of your home, like a drawer or a closet.
After your home is simplified, look at how you live, what you do
and how you spend your time. For example, look at all the foods
you eat in one meal. It's hard to appreciate any one of them fully
when there are so many mixed together. Similarly, you could have
a fantastic collection of art objects in your home, but if there are
too many then it is difficult to appreciate each piece fully. By the
same token, if you have too many obligations, details and responsibilities, life loses its luster. "Our life is frittered away by
detail. . . . Simplify, simplify," recommends Henry David Thoreau,
in *Walden*.

This theme of simplicity runs repeatedly through the great
spiritual teachings. St. Francis of Assisi is known for embracing a
life of simplicity. (One of my favorite movies, now available on
video, is *Brother Sun, Sister Moon* about simplicity and the life of
St. Francis.) Throughout the Gospels, Jesus teaches about simplicity.
He tells us that in order to enter the kingdom of God, we must
become as little children. In His simplicity, His thoughts are
profound. "As you have believed, so let it be done unto you."
(Matt. 8:13) All the words of Jesus are simple and clear. I believe
He is the clearest teacher of humankind.

Another one of my favorites is Brother Lawrence, who discovered and wrote about the power of living a life of simplicity; he saw God within the most mundane expressions of life. In *Practicing the Presence*, he wrote, "I began to live as if there was none but He and I in the world.

Peace Pilgrim was another personification of simplicity. To the world she may have seemed poor, walking penniless and wearing or carrying in her pockets her only material possessions. But she was indeed rich in blessings that no amount of money could buy — health, happiness and inner peace. Peace Pilgrim knew that material things come and go, that we can all survive quite comfortably with very little. The quality of our lives isn't created outside ourselves. It comes from a healthy self-image, serenity, and our relationship with God. She wrote:

> The simplified life is a sanctified life,
> Much more calm, much less strife.
> Oh, what wondrous truths are unveiled —
> Projects succeed which had previously failed.
> Oh, how beautiful life can be.
> Beautiful simplicity.

One of the greatest lessons Peace Pilgrim taught me was to simplify outer things so that my inner life can take the driver's seat. Living an uncluttered life gives me time for the things I really care about, like time to think, to read, to walk in nature, to meditate and watch the sunset. Through simplification, I am more clear-minded, and, I believe, a kinder, more sensitive person. When there is time to meditate, walk, read, reflect, think, pray and be in the simplicity and beauty of nature, then life has a more natural flow, which is very much like a meditation. Life becomes meditation. The divine becomes perfect simplicity.

You can live very well and still live simply. There seems to be a trend toward simplicity. Stanford Research Institute social scientist Duane Elgin points out in *Voluntary Simplicity*:

> To live with simplicity is to unburden our lives — to live a more direct, unpretentious, and unencumbered relationship with all aspects of our lives: consuming, working, learning, relating, and

so on. Simplicity of living means meeting life face to face. It means confronting life clearly, without unnecessary distractions, without trying to soften the awesomeness of our existence or masking the deeper manifestations of life with pretensions, distractions and unnecessary accumulations. It means being direct and honest in relationships of all kinds. It means taking life as it is . . .

That passage really rings true for me. Letting go of the clutter, living honestly, simply and freely, without pretensions, encumbrances and superfluity is what living fully is all about. Perhaps we can head in that direction by having fewer desires and being more selfless. The venerable Lao-Tzu said:

Manifest plainness
Embrace simplicity
Reduce selfishness
Have few desires.

Having fewer desires starts with being happy with and grateful for what you have. After Gandhi had met with the King of England, a reporter commented on how scantily dressed he had been in the presence of the king. Gandhi replied, "It's okay. The king has on enough for both of us."

Living a simple life brings more peace, serenity and security. As so wisely stated by Paramahansa Yogananda in his book, *Where There Is Light*:

The pleasure of modern man is in getting more and more, and what happens to anyone else doesn't matter. But isn't it better to live simply — without so many luxuries and with fewer worries? There is no pleasure in driving yourself until you cannot enjoy what you have. . . . The time will come when mankind will begin to get away from the consciousness of needing so many material things. More security and peace will be found in the simple life.

There was a time in my life when I found great pleasure in collecting material things. I would delight in buying lots of clothes, appliances, electronics, gadgets and cars until I got to the point where I was seeking fulfillment from what I collected rather than from within. In the pursuit of material possessions, I began to lose sight of the spiritual side of my nature through which all fulfillment, joy, peace and happiness come. I was looking outward to my collection of stuff for my value and worthiness as a human being rather than looking within.

Fortunately, I discovered that it's not what the world holds for you that's important, but what you bring to the world. When I realized that, it became clear to me that I wanted to live more simply. Sure, I still buy clothes and other items, but more often I'm giving away things and finding ways to make my life less complicated.

When we have chaos in our lives, including in our homes, we feel chaotic in our minds. Here is something I've done for years that might interest you. I invite a guest over to my house, at least weekly; it helps motivate me to clean my home and consistently get rid of clutter and the non-essentials.

I want to close by sharing with you a passage I read a few days ago in the wonderful book, *The Simple Life*, by Joan Atwater.

Choose to live peacefully and simply.

> Our lives are over-burdened, and living often seems to us a terribly complicated affair. The problems of the world are so incredibly complex and we see that there are no simple answers. The complexity always leaves us with a feeling of helplessness and powerlessness. And still, amazingly enough, we go on, day by day, always half subconsciously yearning for something simpler, something more meaningful.
>
> So how we look for our lives and living becomes tremendously important. It's up to us to bring this authenticity, this simplicity, this directness, this unburdened clarity into our looking. If such a thing as living life fully interests you, then it's up to you to learn about it and live it.

Taking Inventory and Action

1. Is your home cluttered? How can you begin simplifying it today?

2. What duties can you delegate to free up your time?

3. How do you feel when your life is cluttered and complicated?

4. Are there some relationships that complicate and clutter your life rather than enrich and enhance?

5. Does your self-esteem depend on what you have and how you live rather than who you are in your heart?

6. Take fifteen minutes today to clean out some small area of your home.

7. Look around your home and see what you can give away today.

8. Take a few moments today to simply *be*. Don't do anything. Just pay attention, observe, reflect, enjoy.

9. Let your formula for life be "high thinking and simple living."

10. Live in the presence of God.

Today's Affirmation

I become as a little child today with my arms outstretched to touch the face of God. I dwell in the presence of God's eternal love. I live simply so that I may live in harmony with God.

CHAPTER 17

Enthusiasm and Confidence

Enthusiasm is the mother of effort, and without it
nothing great was ever accomplished. The
successful person has enthusiasm.

Ralph Waldo Emerson

M any years ago, I made a decision about my work that has had great consequences. I decided that I would do only work about which I could be enthusiastic. Instead of accepting writing assignments simply because the payment was generous, I chose to write articles for which I felt great passion. It was a frightening decision for me since I lived alone and at that time was dependent on my writing as a major source of income. But I never regretted the decision; not only did I start making more money than ever before with my chosen assignments, but I also learned a valuable lesson about enthusiasm. Enthusiasm isn't something you find out in the world; it's a God-given quality that you must choose to bring to whatever you do.

From the Greek word, "entheos," enthusiasm means "to be filled with God." Isn't that fantastic? We must identify with and call forth that which is already within us. Charles Fillmore, cofounder of Unity, was in his nineties when he declared, "I fairly sizzle with zeal and enthusiasm." Regardless of our age, our line of work or our purpose in life, we can be enthusiastic. No matter what the challenge may be, we can call forth this God-given faculty of enthusiasm and meet life with faith. Because we know that we are filled with God at all times, we can approach each day with an enthusiastic outlook.

Dale Carnegie gave us this advice: "Act enthusiastic, and you'll be enthusiastic!" In his lectures across the country and in his books, he told people not to wait for circumstances to transform their indifference into enthusiasm. "Even if you feel uninspired, act as though you were overflowing with enthusiasm," he advised. He often gave examples of people who had been failures early in life, but who persevered by having an enthusiastic outlook. Albert Einstein, Charles Darwin and Thomas Edison all did poorly in school. And yet, each possessed a great deal of enthusiasm for his work and, eventually, each one's genius became known. When you act out an attitude — when you become it — it then becomes you. The action itself is a kind of affirmation.

Several months of the year, I travel internationally giving workshops and keynote addresses and doing television, radio and newspaper interviews. One question I seem to be asked more than most others goes something like this: "Your enthusiasm for life shines brightly in all your work. How do you manage to stay so positive and enthusiastic in the face of so many local and global problems?" And I usually respond: "If I chose to be negative and unenthusiastic, that would just add to the problem. I know I can be most effective in making a difference if I remain positive, optimistic and enthusiastic."

The Bible says to be of a happy heart. How we live, how we feel, what we think and what we become all depend on the way we choose. I've discovered that I am the master of my life, co-creator with God. I can choose to celebrate life, live fully and make a difference. Health is a choice! Happiness is a choice! Peace is a choice! And enthusiasm is the elixir that generates change, nourishes the body and feeds the soul. In his refreshing book, *The Power In You*, Wally "Famous" Amos writes: "Age may wrinkle the face, but lack of enthusiasm wrinkles the soul." Living fully and experiencing aliveness and life as a great adventure is always an inside job.

Not long ago, I spent several days in beautiful Coos Bay, Oregon, where I presented a workshop on "Wellness Lifestyling" at the Bay Area Hospital and gave the Sunday service at the Unity Church. While there, I stayed at a bed and breakfast owned and run by a beautiful soul named Johnny. Johnny taught me that enthusiasm, positive thinking and happiness are the main ingredients in being energetic and staying youthful. Eighty-three-years-young, Johnny greeted each day with enthusiasm and lots of energy. After making mouth-watering, healthy breakfasts for me, he would then take me hiking, jogging or tidepool adventuring for a good part of the morning. After that, he would spend most of his day working on remodeling his other home to which he had added a magnificent second story. When I asked him his secret for staying so enthusiastic, he responded, "Never think of your age, always look at the bright side of everything and, if something bothers you, talk it out. Don't ever hold in small grievances with a friend or spouse because they just fester and grow and create much bigger problems." I loved being around Johnny because he brought out my enthusiasm and zest for life.

Enthusiasm resides in your heart, so you must bring your heart to everything you do. Let that heartlight shine with the rays of enthusiasm permeating everything you think, feel, say and do.

Enthusiasm and confidence are intimately connected. How can you not be confident when you're "filled with God?" When you trust in something greater than yourself, enthusiasm and confidence become your natural expression. I have always admired Oprah Winfrey. No matter what her television topic for the day or what appearances she makes, she exudes enthusiasm and confidence. She brings her heart to everything she does. And, as a result, she is successful, loved and supported by millions of people around the world.

My favorite movie of all time is *The Sound of Music*. I've seen it twenty times. As the governess, Julie Andrews personifies enthusiasm. Filled with God's presence, she radiates enthusiasm in everything she does — climbing mountains, playing with the children, singing in the abbey or talking to God. That enthusiasm strengthens her confidence. Do you remember the song she sings called "I Have Confidence"? It says, "I have confidence in sunshine. I have confidence in rain. I have confidence that spring will come again; Besides which, you see, I have confidence in me."

With the right attitude, enthusiasm and confidence are always available. Look at everything you do as service to God, as a way to do God's work and to establish a closer relationship with God. When your life has that purpose, you become filled with enthusiasm and confidence. The smallest tasks take on new meaning. Everything you do becomes special. It's almost as though you're growing new eyes and ears. Acknowledging and living in God's presence brings peace and a whole new dimension to life.

Choose to live peacefully with enthusiasm and confidence.

Plunge into your activities with joy and enthusiasm, because you are doing them for God.

Sri Daya Mata, *Finding the Joy Within You*

Taking Inventory and Action

1. When you wake up in the morning, are you enthusiastic about the day?
2. Do you approach your job with enthusiasm and confidence?
3. In doing household chores, do you lack a positive attitude and dread participation?
4. When you attempt something new, do you believe in yourself?
5. How often do you acknowledge your oneness with God?
6. Notice how young children seem to be filled with enthusiasm no matter how many times they've done something before.
7. Tomorrow morning when you wake up, choose to be enthusiastic and carry that attitude with you throughout the day.
8. Rent the video *The Sound of Music*.
9. If you lack confidence, ask God for guidance.
10. Live in the presence of God.

Today's Affirmation

I greet this day with enthusiasm and confidence. It feels like I'm walking on air. With enthusiasm, I know I can be happy and successful at whatever I choose to do.

CHAPTER 18

Living in the Present

*If you have deep places of emptiness within you,
no partner regardless of how much they love you,
will be about to fill that emptiness.*

Barbara De Angelis, *Are You the One for Me?*

Living in the moment is different from living for the moment. Children seem to be masters of getting totally involved in and focused on whatever they are doing right now. Granted, their attention span is not long, but they are able to focus on whatever is taking place in their lives at the moment. When they eat, they just eat; when they play, they just play; when they talk, they just talk. They throw themselves wholeheartedly into their activities.

I look back on my early childhood and recall I had no sense of time. My family frequently took long trips in the car. Usually within ten minutes of leaving home, I would ask, "Are we there yet?" followed by, "When are we going to be there?" I repeated this set of questions every ten minutes or so. Two hours away didn't mean anything to me. My only sense of time was now.

Carpe diem. That's Latin for "seize the day." Each day offers us an opportunity to look at the world anew and to celebrate being alive. You'll never have an opportunity to live this precious day again. Moment by moment, choose to be aware of everything around you. Pay attention. Participate fully in life.

Have you ever noticed that young children are willing to try anything at a moment's notice? Even though they might have experienced that same thing before, they will express wide-eyed excitement and wonderment. Children don't use a yardstick to measure activities or compare the present with the past. They know they've played the game before, or had someone read the same story just last night, yet the game or the story is still as fresh and as wonderful as it was the first time.

Think about your attitude when doing the dishes, vacuuming or watering the plants. You probably find these activities boring. Have you ever seen a child help with the dishes or vacuum or water the plants? A child can't wait to participate, and acts as though it's just about the most exciting thing he or she has ever done. What a wonderful quality that is! To be excited about life — about every part of life as though it's always fresh and new. Actually, it is. It's only old thoughts and distorted attitudes that get in the way of celebrating each moment.

Often when I'm conducting a workshop in a beautiful natural setting, I ask the participants to go outside for ten to fifteen minutes and stroll the grounds, alone, in silence. I have them practice being totally absorbed in what they see, smell, taste, feel and hear. To be with nature, letting its beauty into your awareness, is a wonderful experience. What I have discovered in taking this kind of walk (and I do this at least once a week) is that I feel a subtle, gentle communion with nature. The flowers, trees, birds, even the insects seem to be in harmony with me. Recently, I spent some time in Big Sur, California, hiking, horseback riding, kayaking, walking and appreciating all the magnificence around me. I was attentive to all the smells, sights and sounds, and experienced living fully in the moment. It was a fantastic experience for me, one I'll never forget. There is a delightful book called *Celebrate the Temporary* by Clyde Reid. It has helped me appreciate and live in the present. *The Precious Present* by Spencer Johnson is another book that will capture your heart.

Do your best each day to simplify your lives, to value and experience the preciousness of nature and every moment. Rather than living with continual five- or ten-year plans, concentrate on living one day at a time, continuing to ask for guidance and direction each day. Don't look back in anger or regret, nor forward in fear or worry, but look around with conscious awareness.

To be fully present each moment, we must free ourselves from the past. To achieve this freedom, we must heal our pasts. If you don't heal the past, the past will repeat itself and keep you trapped in it. When you're trapped in the past, you're not here now; you're not fully present and you can't pay attention to what's happening all around you.

Ralph Waldo Emerson reminded us:

> Be not the slave of your own past — plunge into the sublime seas, dive deep, and swim far, so you shall come back with self-respect, with new power, with an advanced experience, that shall explain and overlook the old.

Most of us have old unresolved residue that needs to be cleansed and released. We must be gentle on ourselves and, with God's help, be courageous and look within. In *Joy Is My Compass*, Alan Cohen says, "The road to healing begins not with a blind leap outward, but a gentle step inward."

The shadow side of our nature is what we've hidden from ourselves out of fear. It is a repository filled with long-forgotten tears, secret anguish and pain, abdicated power and thwarted dreams. It's the locked-away part of your soul. Your shadow is not itself dark; it is hidden in a dark place where you have feared to go. You must take that step. If you feel it's too difficult to do on your own, seek help. There are lots of books that can assist you, including *Homecoming*, which I've mentioned before. *The Power of Unconditional Love*, by Ken Keyes, Jr., is another excellent book. I have an audiocassette available that offers a guided meditation to assist you in getting in touch with your past so you can release it. (Tape #7 from my *Celebrate Life!* series.) Maybe you'll seek out counseling. But whatever you choose, do it soon. Don't put it off any longer. Ask your inner guidance for help. Life will hold you in its hand.

> How should we be able to forget those ancient myths that are at the beginning of all peoples, the myths about dragons that at the last moment turn into princesses; perhaps all the dragons of our lives are princesses who are only waiting to see us once beautiful and brave. Perhaps everything terrible is in its deepest being something helpless that wants help from us. So you must not be frightened if a sadness rises up before you larger than any you have ever seen; if a restiveness, like light and cloud-shadows, passes over your hands and over all you do. You must think that

something is happening with you, that life has not forgotten you, that it holds you in its hand; it will not let you fall . . .

Ranier Maria Rilke, *Letters to a Young Poet*

One of the splendors of being human is our capacity to learn from our past mistakes. Holding on to guilt, shame and pain does not serve any purpose. When we don't heal our past, we tend to sleepwalk through life, never being able to fully experience its glory. Don't let your fear hold you back. Reach out for God's hand, and He will take care of you. "I saw that all things I feared, and which feared me, had nothing good or bad in them save insofar as the mind was affected by them," wrote Spinoza. When you let go of fear, pain will unfold into joy, sadness will unfold to happiness, and hate will turn unto love. A *Course in Miracles* tells us, "The holiest place on earth is where an ancient hatred has become a present love."

When you heal your past, your life will take on a new sense of wonder and celebration. You will become aware of yourself and everything around you. Because of awareness, we are present and able to respond. We become more receptive and, therefore, able to enjoy, to relate and, when necessary, to confront pain. When we live in the present, with awareness, we can live with heart, knowing that the love we are is all that is. We will find ourselves immersed in wisdom and peace and one with the Infinite. Isn't that what living is all about? Don't wait any longer. Now is the time. Trust more in God.

Choose to live peacefully and in the present moment.

The mind of man is capable of anything because everything is in it. All of the past, as well as all of the future.

Joseph Conrad

Taking Inventory and Action

1. What things from your past do you need to heal?

2. Do you believe your future will be a duplication of your past? The future is more important than the past in deciding the present.

3. How often are you fully present in the moment?

4. Do you compare your present with the past?

5. Do you avoid going within because you're afraid?

6. Take a walk in nature today and be fully present. Listen to her sounds and take in all her beauty.

7. Resolve that you will no longer carry extra baggage from past relationships into your current one. Seek help and release the past.

8. Look at and participate in your daily household chores with a new sense of joy and wonder. It helps when you think you are serving God.

9. Live one day at a time. Don't worry about the future. Bless your past and let it go.

10. Live in the presence of God.

Today's Affirmation

I choose to live each moment to the fullest, one day at a time. I let go of the past and know that my future will be bright and happy because I am one with God. Divine order is taking place in my life right now.

CHAPTER 19

Words, Thoughts and Imagination

Always dwell upon the golden age which could
come, to help bring it into materialization. If we
knew how powerful thoughts are we would
never think a negative thought.

Peace Pilgrim

Control of the mind is essential if we are going to live peacefully, joyfully and healthfully. Be firm but loving, for the mind is the rein that controls the horses — the emotions and the body — and guides them to safety along the road of life. Train the mind always to be loving and kind and to see the best in others and in everything. When the road of life is steep, keep your mind even.

What you give your love, time, and attention to, you get more of. We must become aware of our thoughts. Our thoughts determine our experiences. Each of us has the freedom to accept and embrace whatever thoughts we choose. You possess within the silence of your being the ability to think, create and become whatever you want to become. So take your thoughts off the negative and think only about those things you want to be part of your life. The following quote from the inspiring spiritual leader Masaharu Taniguchi comes from Roy Eugene Davis's book, *Miracle Man of Japan*.

Delusive thoughts distort the flow of creative life. When such thoughts are resolved then the creative flow will be smooth and disease will vanish. Infinite power and plenty will be known and all the sufferings of life will disappear naturally and in divine order.

Our lives reflect our thoughts, dreams, expectations, beliefs, hopes, feelings of self-worth and desires. Knowing this, you can consciously modify your inner states to create and live your highest potential and vision. We are not victims of circumstance; we are the architects of our lives. Our conscious thoughts create an image of our lives, ourselves, our feelings; our unconscious reproduces that image perfectly. We create our own heaven or hell. Your thoughts can imprison you or set you free. Complications, conditions or people do not upset you, but the way you think about them causes your upset. Freedom is not possible until we discipline and retrain our minds.

When we take charge of ourselves, of our thoughts, emotions words and actions, all things respond. God has given us free will, but we must accept it. And through the activity of our indwelling Christ, we have the power to retrain our minds and be in control. No matter how long or how often we have misused our minds, we can still mold and use those minds in ways that are positive and uplifting.

You say you're justified in certain thoughts because of what's happening in your life? Negative thoughts bring those negative conditions. You must break the cycle if you are to create a positive peaceful future. As you think, you feel; and as you feel, you radiate; and as you radiate, you attract back the essence of what you express and think. I am always consciously aware of what I'm thinking. Believe me, it took me a few years and lots of discipline to retrain and control my mind. Until that time, I kept repeating negative patterns in my life. Now I strive to focus my thoughts upon what I want for myself and my world. In so doing, I feel empowered and uplifted. In feeling good, I radiate positive energy, which puts me in the magnetic position of attracting that which I consider to be salutary.

Never underestimate the power of your mind as master controller. In Buddha's "Twin Verses" taken from the *Dhammapada*, this affirmation of the powers of the mind is offered:

All that we are is the result of what we have thought: we are formed and molded by our thoughts. Those whose minds are shaped by selfish thoughts cause misery when they speak or act.

Sorrows roll over them as the wheels of a cart follow the hooves of the bullock that draws it.

All that we are is the result of what we have thought: we are formed and molded by our thoughts. Those whose minds are shaped by selfless thoughts give joy when they speak or act. Joy follows them like a shadow that never leaves them.

Jesus, in all His sagacity and simplicity said, "As you think, so shall you be." There's no denying that the quality of your thoughts determines the quality of your life. And one way to get control of your thoughts is to take control of your imagination.

Albert Einstein wrote, "Imagination is more important than knowledge. For knowledge is limited, whereas imagination embraces the entire world, stimulating progress, giving birth to evolution." And Emile Coué observed, "When the imagination and the will are in conflict, the imagination invariably gains the day." That's a wonderful message to me. He's saying that no matter how much we may will something, if we consistently harbor mental pictures undermining that desire, we won't get what we will. Coué built a whole therapeutic practice based on the simple affirmation: "Day by Day, in every way, I'm getting better and better."

In exploring the work of Coué, Philip White, editor of *Unity* magazine, writes, "Coué had hit upon an important idea which the psychological community has generally accepted in our day: the real direction of our lives is contained in our habitual state of mind, despite what we say to the contrary."

Your imagination is what counts. The imagery you use to envision your dreams, goals, desires and hopes is the key to self-mastery.

At least once a day, I incorporate conscious creative visualization into my schedule. Creative visualization is a tool for using your imagination more consciously. You must practice it with feeling, thanksgiving and acceptance. If you want greater health, see yourself, in your mind's eye, as radiantly healthy and energetic. Whatever those mental pictures are for you, make them vivid and real. If you want more peace, visualize yourself as a peaceful person. The same with prosperity, creativity, happiness, relationships and anything else you might want. See your ideal vision and feel the joy and thanksgiving you would have were the vision your current reality. Don't let your ego get in the way. Your ego is where your fears reside. Creative visualization should be no-limit thinking and feeling. Stay open to your possibilities. What's life without your dreams?

Use affirmations in conjunction with creative visualization. Keep your words sweet in case you have to eat them, as the folk wisdom admonishes. Words, especially those with feeling, have power. Speak only words that are loving, true, kind and helpful. Always speak from your highest self and let your words express the truth of your being. You are a divine child of God. As Jesus said, it is "not what enters his mouth that defiles a man, but it is what proceeds out of his mouth."

Using affirmations is one of the great spiritual techniques of our time. Affirmations offer an opportunity to speak the truth about who you are and what you want to create. They encourage us to be true to our words and to our imagination. Soon we are doing more than just saying the right words, thinking the right thoughts and visualizing our goals and dreams. Soon we have adopted a whole new way of being. We have aligned what we think, feel, say and do.

Two good books on visualization and affirmation are *Creative Visualization* by Shakti Gawain and *How You Can Use the Technique of Creative Visualization* by Roy Eugene Davis.

These days most of my visualizations and affirmations have to do with being in perfect harmony with the Christ within and staying open to his guidance. I want to be an open vessel through which God's will is manifest in my life. My human mind is not usually aware of what God's will for me is, but my Divine Mind is. Every day, through prayer and meditation, I consciously surrender all to God, holding nothing back; and I ask for awareness, strength and courage to act on the guidance I receive. In adopting this way of living, I have seen more changes and far greater fulfillment in my life than I could have ever imagined possible. Christ, the spirit of you, makes all things new. This divine power completely regenerates, renews, restores and rebuilds your life and world according to the divine reality. I realize that spirit can do for me only what it can do through me.

In addition to doing your creative visualization and affirmations for your heart's desires, allow yourself time to align with spirit and find out what God's will is for you. Be open. Let peace be your compass on the path to fulfillment.

Choose to live peacefully and think God.

When you unlock the human door you are caught up in the life of the universe where your speech is thunder, your thought is Law, and your words are universally intelligible.

Ralph Waldo Emerson

Taking Inventory and Action

1. When you think about your future, are your thoughts affirmative or negative?

2. Do you expect to get a cold or the flu each winter? Or do you affirm and expect health?

3. Take a close look at all areas of your life. Are you living in Heaven on earth?

4. When you think about your body, family, friends and work, are your thoughts positive, nurturing, healing and uplifting?

5. Do you judge by appearances and feel like a victim of circumstance, or do you know you are the architect of your life?

6. Visualize how your life would be if you were living your highest vision.

7. Write down your visualization in the positive, present tense and accept it with thanksgiving. Turn it over to God.

8. Be true to your highest self. Let everything you think, feel, say and do be in harmony and in alignment with your divinity.

9. Surrender all your hopes, dreams, desires and goals to God and ask for guidance and understanding.

10. Live in the presence of God.

Today's Affirmation

My peaceful, happy thoughts reflect the light and love within me. I do not judge by appearance for I know that new thoughts create new conditions. I now choose to move aside and allow God's thoughts to be my thoughts. I am renewed, regenerated and restored for I am living God's will for me.

CHAPTER 20

Slow Down and Relax

Calmness of mind does not mean you should
stop your activity. Real calmness should be
found in activity itself.

Ram Dass

People are in such a rush these
days, living on the fast track. Talking fast, eating fast, moving
fast. What a difference from thirty years ago. Did you know you'll
probably do more in this year — with appointments, people to
meet, places to go — than your grandparents did their entire lives?
Given our current pace, we barely have time to relax and cultivate
relationships with our spouses and children, friends and nature,
much less with God. Is it any wonder that stress-related diseases
are on the rise? We are under pressure to keep busy even in our
leisure hours. Computers have sped up our lives. We want to do
everything, and we want to do it all at once. We talk on the
telephone while we drive, watch television while we read, conduct
business while we listen to the radio. I see this as a sickness of
epidemic proportions — a "busyness" or "hurry" sickness. If you
understand the speed of life, you slow it down by enjoying it
more.

In *It's All in Your Head: Lifestyle Management Strategies for
Busy People!*, Bruce Baldwin describes some of the signs of "hurry"
sickness. See if you can identify with any of these:

1. Driving Pattern — you routinely drive fast and run yellow
   lights, you jockey for position and constantly change lanes
   and you're impatient with other drivers

2. Eating Habits — you eat in a rush, often while on the go

3. Communication Style — you talk fast, have problems communicating how you feel and rarely find the time to give emotional support to your family and friends

4. Family Involvement — you are not home much and when you are, you're tired and tend to withdraw, or you sit in front of the TV

5. Leisure Activities — your hurried life is so full of undone chores and responsibilities that relaxing has become even more difficult, if not impossible; vacations are rare; when you're not doing something productive, you experience anxiety and guilt

Does this describe your lifestyle?

Everyone knows Aesop's fable of the tortoise and the hare. The tortoise eventually wins the race by taking a slower and steadier pace than the hare. Which track should we choose? We all want to find a way of living that allows us to emerge as winners. The trick is to enjoy the process along the way.

What causes our need to rush? Often the cause is economic — we must make more money to pay for our chosen lifestyles. Sometimes the cause is simply having way too much to do or feeling that something is wrong if we aren't busy. But beyond these reasons is something deeper — a lifestyle that leaves certain basic needs unfulfilled. By crowding our schedules with more — more socializing, more eating, more work, more activity, more appointments — we are trying to fill the emptiness we feel within.

When you direct your attention and energies outward, you lose sense of the wonder, beauty and magnificence within you, from which true happiness, joy and peace originate. By beginning to slow down and to redirect your energies inward, you can train your brain to relax and you can ultimately change your life.

One of the world's leading experts on the brain is Herbert Benson, M.D., author of *The Relaxation Response* and *Your Maximum Mind*. As associate professor of medicine at Harvard Medical School and chief of the Section on Behavioral Medicine of the New England Deaconess Hospital, Benson has developed relaxation techniques that have improved the lives of countless people. What Benson calls the relaxation response is the body's ability to enter into a scientifically definable state characterized by an overall reduction of the metabolic rate, lowered blood pressure, decreased rate of breathing, slower brain waves and a lowered heart rate. According to Benson, this state of relaxation also acts as a door to a renewed mind and changed life, a feeling of wholeness and, often, expanded awareness. Physiological changes occur when you are relaxed; there is harmonizing or increased communication between the two sides of the brain, resulting in feelings variously described as well-being, unboundedness, infinite connection, and peak experience.

To reach this level of calmness, there are several things you can do. One approach is to progressively relax your body, beginning with your toes and ending with your head. For example, you might breathe slowly and deeply as you say to yourself, "My toes are relaxed, my feet are relaxed, my back is relaxed," and on and on until you've gone through your entire body. Then rest for awhile in the quiet and silence. Another way to relax is to visualize yourself feeling relaxed and peaceful. Use your imagination. You can also listen to an audiocassette to assist you in reaching a state of relaxation. (In my seven-tape audio cassette series *Celebrate Life!*, I guide you through different ways to do this.) One of my favorite ways to relax instantly wherever I am is to visit my inner sanctuary. You can create a sanctuary within yourself where you can go any time just by closing your eyes and desiring to be there. Your sanctuary is your ideal place of relaxation, tranquility, beauty, safety and calmness. I visit my inner sanctuary several times a week, for just a few minutes, and I always come back more relaxed and peaceful.

Something else you can do at work or at home to relax your mind and body is to look at a picture of a beautiful landscape. Richard G. Coss, professor of psychology at the University of California, Davis, conducted two studies that measured the effect of certain photographic slides on emotional and physiological response. The first study was designed to find ways of fighting the boredom and homesickness that astronauts experience during extended stays in space stations. Researchers projected a variety of slides on the walls of a room built to simulate the space station's dining commons, then recorded how much the subjects' pupils dilated in response to certain scenes. The second study focused on hospital patients about to undergo surgery. In both groups, pictures of spacious views and glistening water lowered heart rates and produced feelings of calm.

Here in my home, I have a couple of posters I purchased from the Sierra Club. Whenever I look at them, I can sense a difference in how I feel.

Another approach to relaxation and calmness is simply breathing. Take a few minutes and breathe slowly and deeply, really focusing on your breath. You will find that this calms and soothes you and helps you to slow down and get centered.

You might recite your favorite inspirational quote, passage or affirmation a few times, slowly and deliberately while giving it your total attention. One of my favorite affirmations is, "This day I choose to spend in perfect peace." I also use, "I am the ever-renewing, ever-unfolding radiant expression of infinite life, health, wealth, joy and wisdom, unconditional love and universal peace." I also like the *Prayer of St. Francis*.

Prayer of St. Francis

Lord, make me an instrument of thy peace;
Where there is hatred, let me sow love.
Where there is injury, pardon.
Where there is doubt, faith;
Where there is despair, hope;
Where there is darkness, light;
Where there is sadness, joy.

O, Divine Master, grant that I may not
so much seek
To be consoled, as to console,
To be understood as to understand,
To be loved as to love;
For it is in giving that we receive,
It is in pardoning that we are pardoned,
It is in dying that we are
born again to eternal life.

When you make an effort to relax, don't feel that you must live your life in slow motion. Not at all. You can maintain activity. Your goal is to touch your inner fountain of calmness and bring that calmness to everything you do. Being calm brings clarity, richness and divinity to your life. Even in your activity, you are aware of God's presence.

Simply reading these words by Paramahansa Yogananda relaxes me. "Calmness is the living breath of God's immortality in you." I have that quote on a poster depicting a lake and mountain landscape. I often look at it before I meditate.

Speaking of meditation, I know of no more effective way of bringing about relaxation, calmness and a slower pace. All of the physiological changes described in *The Relaxation Response* occur during meditation. The calmness you feel during your daily practice will stay with you in everything you do. Take time to nurture and protect that calmness by meditating regularly. You'll find that your life will become more rewarding, you'll get more accomplished, you'll have more fun and you won't have to miss out on celebrating life.

Choose to live peacefully with calmness lighting your path.

Knowing that you are a child of God, make up your mind to be calm no matter what happens. If your mind is fully identified with your activities, you cannot be conscious of the Lord, but if you are calm and receptive to Him within while being active without, you are rightly active. Each time a swarm of worries invades your mind, refuse to be affected; wait calmly while seeking the remedy. Spray the worries with the powerful chemical of your peace. You cannot buy peace; you must know how to manufacture it within, in the stillness of your daily practices in meditation. When you think that you have reached the utmost depth of silence and calmness, go deeper still. In the silence you will receive from God the answers of your life's problems.

Paramahansa Yogananda

Taking Inventory and Action

1. Do you feel you are suffering from hurry sickness? Is your schedule always filled to the limit?

2. When you have some free time, are you able to relax without feeling anxious or guilty?

3. Do you look for things to keep you busy so you don't have to face being alone?

4. Do you look for things outside yourself to make you feel at ease, at peace or comfortable with yourself? Does your self-esteem come from "doing" instead of "being"?

5. Get up earlier in the mornings so you have time to meditate, relax and start the day off in a calm manner. This sets the tone for the entire day.

6. Simplify your life. Establish priorities. Let go of the superfluous.

7. Create quiet times during the day in which you can breathe deeply, meditate, relax or simply do nothing. Just *be*.

8. Spend time in nature at least once a week. Next to meditating, I know of no better way to slow your pace, bring calmness and peace and help you feel relaxed.

9. Commit to taking time every day to cultivating calmness and offer that calmness to everyone you meet. What a wonderful gift we can give.

10. Live in the presence of God.

Today's Affirmation

I turn within and feel my deep reservoir of calmness. I refuse to get caught up in the frenzy of life. My life is filled with peace and I carry this peace with me wherever I go. I choose to be relaxed and experience the joy and wonder of all God's blessing in my life.

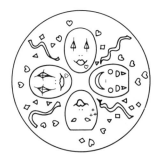

CHAPTER 21

Lighten Up

Make friends with a friendly universe and be grateful
and appreciative for all that is offered to you. In
this way conflicts are avoided and a positive
mental attitude is assured.

Masaharu Taniguchi

When we are anchored in God, no matter what comes our way we can remain positive and look for the good in everything. Easier said than done, right? Attitude makes all the difference. A positive attitude doesn't just happen by itself; we must cultivate it. William James, the noted philosopher, put it beautifully when he said that the greatest discovery of our generation is that a human being can alter his life by altering his attitude.

Indeed, situations will arise in our lives that may seem unpleasant or difficult, but a positive attitude sees problems as opportunities for growth. I believe that nothing happens in life that does not afford us the opportunity to deepen our understanding of and appreciation for life.

With your new positive attitude, you will come to understand that it is not the times, complications of society or other people that cause problems. It is only your inability to cope. Whatever is going on with you at the moment, choose to make it okay. Give up the fear of making mistakes and the need for approval from others. Be yourself. I see so many people living according to how others expect them to be. This just leads to unhappiness. Live more from inner guidance. Understand that there is no absolute way to happiness. Rather, happiness is the way.

A negative attitude acts like an insulator that inhibits the flow of creative energy. Criticism, gossip, anger, fear, envy, suspicion, jealousy, worry, hate, doubt, laziness, anxiety, guilt and shame are all forms of negative thinking. Watch your thoughts. Make them obey you. Train your mind to think constructively and positively at all times. A joyful, thankful attitude will carry you a long way toward the goal of bringing into your life the health, happiness and peace that you desire and deserve.

It's been my experience that if you laugh and smile more, your attitude will tilt toward the positive. And if, by chance, you feel you don't have any reason to smile, let me give you four:

1. Smiling firms your facial muscles.
2. Smiling makes you feel better.
3. Smiling makes people wonder what you've been up to.
4. A smile is the shortest distance between two people.

And here's a fifth reason from Mother Teresa: "A smile is the beginning of peace."

Young children are my greatest teachers on how we can all enjoy and celebrate life. They laugh, tell jokes, play, sing, dance, move and live in their own magical world. I've devoted an entire chapter in my book, *Choose To Be Healthy*, and one of my audiocassettes (#5 from my *Celebrate Life!* series) to being more childlike.

Humor and laughter have both been found to be important components of healing and being radiantly healthy. William Fry of Stanford University has reported that laughter aids digestion, stimulates the heart, strengthens muscles, activates the brain's creative function and keeps you alert. So make up your mind to laugh and be happy. As Abraham Lincoln said, "Most folks are about as happy as they make up their minds to be."

Laughter also helps you to keep your life in better perspective. When you laugh at yourself, you learn to take yourself far less seriously. "Angels fly because they take themselves lightly," says an old Scottish proverb. Isn't that wonderful?

So with the right attitude, with joy in your heart, with a smile on your face and a guard at the door of your mind, you can experience life as a great adventure, a celebration of spirit manifested everywhere and in everyone. You'll come to realize that life was meant to be lived one day at a time with a childlike sense of wonder and expectancy. It's not too late to experience life fully. As long as you're breathing, it's never too late.

A few years ago, I read the following passage in a "Dear Abby" column and, again, just recently, discovered it on a greeting card. It was written by Nadine Stair, when she discovered she was about to die at age eighty-five.

If I Had My Life to Live Over

I'd like to make more mistakes next time. I'd relax. I would limber up. I would be sillier than I have been this trip. I would take fewer things seriously. I would take more chances. I would climb more mountains and swim more rivers. I would eat more ice cream and less beans. I would perhaps have more actual troubles, but I'd have fewer imaginary ones.

You see, I'm one of those people who lives sensibly and sanely hour after hour, day after day. Oh, I've had my moments, and if I had it to do over again, I'd have more of them. In fact, I'd try to have nothing else. Just moments, one after another, instead of living so many years ahead of each day. I've been one of those persons who never goes anywhere without a thermometer, a hot water bottle, a raincoat, and a parachute. If I had to do it again, I would travel lighter than I have.

If I had my life to live over, I would start barefoot earlier in the spring and stay that way later in the fall. I would go to more dances. I would ride more merry-go-rounds. I would pick more daisies.

Choose to make your life a magnificent adventure filled with laughter, love and peace. Choose to live peacefully and lighten up.

While trying to conquer discomfort externally, train the mind to remain neutral to every condition. Mind is just like blotting paper, which readily takes on the color of any dye you apply to it. Most minds take on the color of their environment. But there is no excuse for the mind to be defeated by outer circumstances. If your mental attitude changes constantly under the pressure of tests, you are losing the battle of life.

Paramahansa Yogananda, *The Divine Romance*

Taking Inventory and Action

1. Does your attitude change according to your outer circumstances?

2. When was the last time you really had a good laugh? If you can't remember, it's too long.

3. Do you want to be happy or would you rather be right?

4. Have you ever had a depressing thought in the middle of a good laugh? It's almost impossible.

5. Be aware of your thoughts and stop them from wandering down the negative path.

6. Choose to smile and be happy all day today.

7. Adopt an attitude of playfulness. Be willing to be silly and a little absurd.

8. Let your inner child come out and play and orchestrate your day.

9. Look for the incongruities in life's situations and laugh at yourself. Look for the good in others.

10. Live in the presence of God.

Today's Affirmation

I am laughing my way to enlightenment. My inner child is alive and well and orchestrating my day. I always look for the good in others and in every circumstance. As God smiles at me through nature and other people in my life, I smile back with a joyful heart.

Prosperity and Abundance

Seek first the kingdom of God, and
His righteousness; and all these things
shall be added unto you.

Matt. 6:33

For many people, abundance and prosperity are tied to their level self-esteem. You make a good living, pay your bills and save money, so you feel successful. I define success in a different light. Being successful is not a matter of how much money you have, how many possessions you've collected or what type of lifestyle you live; success can be measured only to the degree to which you have inner peace and, no matter what the circumstance or situation, you can remain peaceful, calm and happy.

I know what some of you may be thinking. Being peaceful doesn't pay my bills or put food on the table. But that's where you may be mistaken. Abundance and prosperity begin inside you. Believe me when I say I speak from experience.

Many years ago, it seemed that no matter what I did or what work I accomplished, I continued to create lack and limitation in my life. When money finally came to me, it disappeared almost instantly. I was frustrated, depressed and confused. One day I decided to do everything possible to change the situation and to live the life God had created for me. I read books, attended prosperity lectures and workshops, prayed and meditated and, after a while, I finally put all the pieces of the puzzle together. This is what I'd like to share with you now.

First, it's important to realize that your thoughts and beliefs affect your level of abundance. Do you feel worthy of abundance? Do you wish for abundance and at the same time worry about how you'll pay your bills? Do you even believe that there's enough money to go around? You will attract to yourself what you believe to be true. Have you closed the doors to prosperity by your beliefs and thoughts? In *The Science of Mind*, Ernest Holmes writes, "Life lies open to me — rich, full, abundant. My thought, which is my key to life, opens all doors for me."

Choosing to open the doors for me also involved being aware of all the abundance around me. Just look at nature — the oceans, the clouds, the sky, the mountains and rivers, the stars; there couldn't be a better lesson in abundance. And then I asked myself, from where does all this come? God is the source and supply of abundance. When I realized this and acted from this awareness, my level of prosperity changed.

You see, up until that point, I had been looking outside myself for the source of my supply. It's not outside you. It's within you. Everything you need to be happy, prosperous and live abundantly is inside you right now. God's kingdom is within you. When you love God with all of your being, you draw His kingdom into your consciousness, and His abundance is made evident in your world. You are an heir to the kingdom of abundance. You must know that and feel it. Recognize a divine sufficiency as constant in all your affairs. If you think in terms of scarcity, you will manifest limitation. Similarly, if you think thoughts of abundance, you will manifest sufficiency, success and happiness.

To open the floodgates of abundance, you must begin by giving away what you have. Some call this tithing; some call it sharing. Paramahansa Yogananda wrote in *Where There Is Light*, "Unselfishness is the governing principle in the law of prosperity." When you give of yourself to another person or group, you always receive more than you give. We are all one; everyone is yourself. So to give to another is to give to yourself. But keep in mind that your giving must always be guided by spirit and not stem from guilt, as John Price mentions in *Mastering Money*. When you come from spirit, you stay in the flow. My financial situation turned around quickly when I started tithing and giving to others. I always receive my gifts back, multiplied.

I realize that it might feel scary to give when you think you can barely pay your bills. I understand. Start off with small donations and gifts, always blessing the money and being grateful that you are able to share what you have. Remember the wise words of Lao Tse: "A journey of a thousand miles must first begin with a single step."

Next, it's important to love what you do. Do you feel passion and enthusiasm for your work? Do you get up every morning eager to accomplish a full day's work? Or do you dread how you spend your day? This can make a big difference in your level of abundance. A recent national poll revealed that 95 percent of the people working in America do not enjoy what they do! This is a staggering statistic. For years, I have done extensive research on people who are successful, and it's clear to me that achievements and financial rewards are directly related to the enjoyment they derive from their work and the service they provide to community and the world.

Right livelihood is predicated upon a conscious choice. Yet, too often, we live our lives according to what others value. When you consciously choose to enter into your work, you can participate fully and know you are making a difference. Sometimes this takes courage and perseverance, but your life will be enriched.

I have a friend who went into dental school right after college because his parents had always wanted him to be a dentist. Although dentistry wasn't his calling, he followed their wishes. After he graduated from dental school, he went into private practice and for almost twenty-five years was quite successful. He married his college sweetheart, had three children, built his dream home and traveled. Still, he never really loved his work; he never felt a great passion for how he spent his days. In one of our counseling sessions, he told me how much he loved to work in his garden. He even said that if he had to do it all over again, he would go to school and learn to be a landscape architect. So I asked him what was stopping him? He said he could never afford to keep up his lifestyle if he gave up his practice. I asked him what was more important — to be happy or to keep up appearances? I also reminded him that prosperity is an inside job. I gave him a copy of *Do What You Love, the Money Will Follow* by Marsha Sinetar, and *You Were Born Rich*, by Bob Proctor. He began taking night classes in gardening and landscaping and after three years, got his degree. With a partner, he opened a landscaping business. At the same time, through another partnership with three other dentists, he cut back his dental office time to just two days a week. He discovered that working twice a week as a dentist made him look forward to his work; he knew he was offering a valuable service to his patients. At the same time, he put in two to three days a week at his landscaping job and thoroughly loved being outdoors, creating and having more time to spend with his family. What's more, he was bringing in more money than he had in his full-time dental practice.

Maybe it's time to take a close look at your line of work. Do you look forward to going to work each day or do you wish you were doing something different? Sometimes it just takes a change of attitude to make your current job more fulfilling. Listen to your heart. Talk to God about this and ask for guidance. Pay close attention to the answers you get and be willing to respond.

Spirit can only do for you what it can do through you. So you must release all obstructions, blockages and interferences that keep you from God's kingdom. Release everything that has caused you fear, anger, frustration, depression, guilt, shame and hurt. Through some inner exploration, you'll probably discover that most of these negative emotions can be traced to your wrong thoughts, wrong words and wrong actions. In *A Spiritual Philosophy for the New World*, John Price writes:

> It is a law of the Universe that whatever you surrender to Spirit is always purified, thus unblocking Spirit's avenues of expression through consciousness. Rather than affirm your way out of a situation, why not simply give it up?

Open your doors and let the light shine through. Become an open receptacle to receive God's gifts of prosperity, abundance and peace. Share what you have. Love what you do. Listen to your heart. Know that you deserve to be prosperous and that everything you need to live your highest potential is within you right now. Claim and accept it.

Choose to live peacefully and prosperously.

Think of Divine Abundance as a mighty refreshing rain; whatever receptacle you have at hand will receive it. If you hold up a tin cup, you will receive only that quantity. If you hold up a bowl, that will be filled. What kind of receptacle are you holding up to Divine Abundance? Perhaps your vessel is defective; if so, it should be repaired by casting out all fear, hate, doubt, and envy, and then cleansed by the purifying waters of peace, tranquility, devotion, and love. Divine Abundance follows the law of service and generosity. Give and then receive. Give to the world the best you have and the best will come back to you.

Paramahansa Yogananda, *Where There Is Light*

Taking Inventory and Action

1. What is success to you?
2. Are you thinking thoughts of lack and limitation?
3. Who is your source of supply?
4. Do you love what you do?
5. Do you feel worthy to live abundantly?
6. Give of your time or money this week.
7. Turn everything over to God, including your financial affairs.
8. Identify and release limiting thoughts, words, emotions and actions.
9. Choose this day to be a prosperous person.
10. Live in the presence of God.

Today's Affirmation

I am consciously aware of the spirit of God within as my source, supply and support. I deserve to prosper. The more I give of myself or my money, the more I prosper. My prosperity is coming to me now and I give thanks.

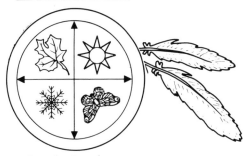

CHAPTER 23

Ritual and Ceremony

Sometimes, when we forget to initiate the sacred
relationship, Mother Earth herself comes forward to
cast the spell. Nature is the great entrancer, water
the master sculptor, wind the supreme musician,
deep veins of volcanoes the great crucibles wherein
are cast the materials of the artist. She prepares a
PLACE which speaks to us and says Listen; watch;
be still, for I am here.

Fredric Lehrman, *The Sacred Landscape*

Our planet, Mother Earth, is
alive, radiant and calling us back home. Too often we forget our
connection to our planet and believe that we are separate and
must do for ourselves. The earth and its atmosphere provide such
constant and reliable support that we take them for granted and
thus unconsciously abuse them.

The American Indians are known for their connection with the
earth, and I believe we have much to learn from them. It's time for
all of us to reawaken to life force that connects us to Mother
Earth. Through ritual and ceremony we can touch the sacredness
in both ourselves and the earth. We are divine beings, thus sacred;
the planet is a divine entity, thus sacred. We are united by a holy
umbilical cord. Wherever we walk is holy ground. The earth
empowers us. We can and must respect and acknowledge her
presence. Together, we can become whole again.

You can go to a place of natural power on this planet and, with
ritual and ceremony, feel transformed and renewed. Or you can
bring the same experience to your daily activities. This is what I

would like to concentrate on in this chapter — bringing sacredness into your life through everyday activities or natural occurrences.

Ritual is the act of taking something ordinary and raising it to the level of the extraordinary. It's taking a daily occurrence and empowering yourself by performing this activity with a high consciousness and awareness. Ritual is a natural part of our lives. Rituals help us gain perspective on changes, offer tradition, support a greater sense of balance, and help us relate to one another. For anyone who wants to consciously recognize life's happenings or bring greater meaning and understanding to the customs they already practice, I highly recommend exploring ritual in your life. One of my favorite books on this subject is *The Art of Ritual* by Renee Beck and Sydney Barbara Metrick.

My dear friend, Kathy Martelli, has been my greatest teacher in the areas of ritual and ceremony. UCLA yoga/fitness instructor, counselor and business owner, Kathy teaches workshops on several topics, including ritual empowerment and connecting with Mother Earth. For years, she has been giving me guidance on how I can live from the highest and most sacred in me. One of the things we love to do together is hike in the Santa Monica Mountains. Sometimes we hike briskly from the beginning to the end just to get an aerobic workout. Other times our hike becomes a ritual, a sacred adventure with Mother Nature. During a ritual hike, we usually talk about what we hope to gain, to learn, to focus on. We hike with attention to all the beauty of nature around us. During one point in our hike, we come to a small waterfall and sprinkle water on our heads, each being empowered in our own personal way. Kathy's ritual might be different from mine or could be the same. During our last hike together, three-and-a-half weeks ago, I saw this water ceremony as a baptism, purifying me and washing away all blockages to the awareness of God's presence in preparation for my forty-day fast.

You see, you can make anything personally sacred for you. Maybe one particular hike is a ritual for claiming your prosperity and abundance as you pay attention to nature's abundance all around you. Another day, the ritual hike might be for opening yourself up to healing and greater health.

I've grown to use every time I'm out in nature as a ritual and ceremony, an opportunity to remember who I am and my connection with Mother Earth. I always use ritual and ceremony with the new moon, the full moon, the four seasonal changes and even sunsets and sunrises. Sometimes I perform these rituals alone, sometimes with a close friend and every so often in a small group. I even take ritual baths and showers and create tea ceremonies.

When I began this forty-day fast, I developed my own special ritual. First I wrote down everything I wanted to surrender to God, which turned out to be everything in my life. It took me about four hours to write everything down. I included my dreams and goals, my friends and family, my health and body, my career, my concerns and worries and all my fears. After reading over the pages, I wrote out a declaration that for forty days I would turn everything in my life over to God, would fast, pray, meditate and live in the presence of God — live as a spiritual being rather than a human being. Not my will but God's will in my life. I then signed it and put it, folded up, on my altar where I meditate everyday.

Then the following morning, Day One of my program, I went down to the beach, which is only a couple of minutes from my home, and walked barefoot by the water, talking to God. I was aware of my connection with Mother Earth and could feel her energy and strength. After the walk, I meditated and then went into the water. With my hands cupped, I poured water over my head and body to purify and cleanse my body and mind. I then went back to the sand and let the healing sun dry me off. Could I have begun the forty-day fast without a ritual? Of course. But I wanted to set a tone and empower myself. Ritual gives my life richness, fullness and sacredness.

The moon lends itself to rituals. Traditionally, all over the planet, people mark the phases of the moon on their calendars each month. The moon has always been connected to female power and energy — its changes paralleling the changes in a woman's body during her menstrual cycle. There are a variety of rituals you can do with the new and full moons.

The new moon occurs once a month every month. Traditionally, this was a time for planting seeds. On a metaphysical level, this time of the month is good for planting the seeds for the changes we want to manifest in our lives. According to the universal law of cause and effect, if we create change in ourselves, changes will manifest around us.

Because the new moon is a time of darkness or no moon, Kathy Martelli recommends you create an environment using darker colors. She wears something that is dark purple, uses dark purple candles and flowers and even writes with a purple pen on purple paper.

In longhand, make a list of the changes that you want to implement in your life on the day of the new moon. You're planting the seeds in your subconscious. I do this ritual, during the new moon time of planting, to acknowledge and honor the ancient tradition and wisdom, to foster clarity and to open myself up to God's goodness and blessing in my life.

You can add a dimension to your life by incorporating ritual and ceremony. You can make sacred any ordinary activity. When you view your body and life as sacred, life becomes richer. And you feel and connect with Mother Earth in a bond of respect, honor and love. Sacredness becomes a way of life. Mother Earth becomes our friend. For further reading on our sacred planet, I recommend the magical book, *The Sacred Landscape*, written and compiled by Fredric Lehrman. It is a literary ceremony, a sequence of words and images that leads the reader on a journey both outward and inward. Through the work of some of the world's finest photographers, the magic that surrounds sacred sites, places of power and natural shrines is evoked and preserved. Writings by contemporary thinkers and by authors of the past open a variety of possibilities for relating to the earth. This book can serve as a doorway into a place of new awareness within yourself and for Mother Earth. It has enriched my life and my connectedness to our planet.

Choose to live peacefully and embrace Mother Earth with open arms and gratitude.

Prayer For The Great Family

Gratitude to Mother Earth, sailing through night and day —
and to her soil: rich, rare, and sweet
in our minds so be it.

Gratitude to Plants, the sun-facing light-changing leaf
and fine root-hairs; standing still through wind

and rain; their dance is in the flowing spiral grain
in our minds so be it.

Gratitude to Air, bearing the soaring Swift and the silent
Owl at dawn. Breath of our son
clear spirit breeze
in our minds so be it.

Gratitude to Wild Beings, our sisters teaching secrets,
freedoms, and way; who share with us their milk;
self-complete, brave, and aware
in our minds so be it.

Gratitude to Water; clouds, lakes, rivers, glaciers;
holding or releasing; streaming through all
our bodies' salty seas
in our minds so be it.

Gratitude to the Sun: blinding pulsing light through
trunks of trees, through mists, warming caves where
bears and snakes sleep — he who wakes us —
in our minds so be it.

Gratitude to the Great Sky
who holds billions of stars — goes yet beyond that —
beyond all powers and thoughts
and yet is within us —
Grandfather Space.
The Mind is his Wife
So be it.

Gary Snyder,
after a Mohawk prayer

Taking Inventory and Action

1. When was the last time you really paid attention to and appreciated your Mother Earth?

2. Have you ever communed with nature — the trees, plants, sunsets, mountains?

3. What activities in your life, through ritual, can you make empowering and sacred?

4. Have you ever jogged or participated in another exercise where you talked with Mother Earth and God and opened yourself up to the energy and power of life and spirit all around you?

5. With each season change, have you ever noticed corresponding changes in your life? Or have you seen changes in your body or emotions with the changes in the moon?

6. Celebrate the next season with a special ritual: Spring Equinox-March 21–23rd, Summer Solstice-June 21–23, Fall Equinox-September 21–23, Winter Solstice-December 21–23. (Refer to Appendix)

7. Make your next bath, shower or cup of tea a sacred time of ceremony and empowerment.

8. Spend some time alone in nature this week and feel her love and energy. Respect. Love. Open yourself up to her lessons and power.

9. Plan to celebrate the next new or full moon. If you don't know the specific date, call your local library and mark your calendar for the year.

10. Live in the presence of God.

Today's Affirmation

I am grateful for all Mother Earth has given me. Her abundance and beauty are everywhere. In stillness, I listen for her guidance and know that every step I take is on holy ground. Divine love, through us both, connects our hearts.

CHAPTER 24

Faith, Trust and Belief

Faith is not a matter of trusting that events
will always occur to our liking, but of trust that,
whatever happens, our inner resources will
be equal to the moment.

John Robbins & Ann Mortifee, *In Search of Balance*

Faith, as usually understood, is an elusive quality. The definition in *Webster's* reads, "unquestioning belief that does not require proof or evidence." So we are told that we'll see it when we believe it. Easier said than done, right? It seems to me that for our faith to take hold and become the wind beneath our wings, we must trust in something greater than ourselves. We must put our trust in God. We must put our faith in our oneness with God.

It is an illusion to believe that any security can be found on earth; the only security is trust in God. Through this trust, all things are possible. Psalms 37:5 says, "Commit your way to the Lord, trust also in Him, and He shall bring it to pass." When you trust, you allow life to be as it is. You remember that you are a child of God and so is everyone else. You come to realize that everything in your life can be a pathway to God.

Trust and faith can work miracles. In the relatively new field of science, psychoneuroimmunology, researchers are discovering that belief and faith play a major role in healing the body. Psychoneuroimmunological studies show an undeniable link between the workings of the mind, the nervous system and the body's ability to fight off disease. Studies also reveal that attitudes are

151

biochemical realities. Medical research has demonstrated, for example, that panic, depression, hate, fear and frustration can have negative effects on human health. In *Head First: The Biology of Hope*, Norman Cousins presents evidence that hope, faith, love, will to live, purpose, laughter and festivity help combat disease.

Faith is intuitive recognition of the truth behind all things. It's not simply passive acceptance, but committed belief, belief put into practice and action. By our own acknowledgement and awareness of the one Presence within us all, we can live up to our highest potential. We can make our dreams come true. In the movie, *Field of Dreams*, there was a line that gave me major goose bumps. Kevin Costner's character said, "Sometimes when you believe the impossible, incredible dreams come true."

Faith, trust and belief will lift all sense of discouragement, defeat and helplessness. They will bring about a change in your consciousness so that the creative flow of life and love and unlimited possibilities can fill your being. So to seek changes in your outer world, you must first make changes in your conscious- ness. We must stop looking outside ourselves for the solutions, answers and changes, and instead put all trust with God.

We live in a friendly universe that is always saying "yes" to us. Our responsibility is to identify and transform those beliefs that have been sabotaging us from accepting and receiving the good that is our birthright. We must learn to trust and love ourselves as much as we are loved by God. When you remove all the blockages to God's presence and align with the love that you are, then abundance, prosperity, peace and success will be yours. Trust God. Believe in yourself. Have faith that nothing is impossible.

The idea that "when you believe, the impossible becomes possible" came alive for me last month. I was having dinner with my dear friend, George, and his teenaged daughter, GiGi. We had just seen a movie starring Tom Cruise. During dinner, GiGi went on and on about how much she adored Tom Cruise and how she would give just about anything in the world to get an autographed picture of him. For most of our meal, this was the only topic of conversation. Tom. Tom. Tom. Well, before we finished, I waxed rhapsodic, as I tend to do from time to time, and told GiGi that if she had enough belief and faith, anything was possible, even getting an autograph from Tom Cruise. I also told her I would try to locate an address or telephone number for his publicist or fan club.

That night, as I was lying in bed, I thought about what I said to her and decided to put my words to the test. With every bit of faith and trust I could muster, I visualized, affirmed and accepted that, somehow, some way, I would make the right contact to get Tom Cruise's autograph for GiGi. I then turned it all over to God and gave thanks that the right path would come to me.

The following week, George and I went to see another movie. During the movie, I leaned over to George and asked if he would like to get an ice cream sundae afterwards. He looked at me in bewilderment. He knows that I rarely indulge in this type of food. I confessed to him that although I didn't feel like having any ice cream, I had an urge to visit an ice cream parlor. George was delighted because he was in the mood for a sundae. After the movie, we walked to the nearest ice cream parlor, only a couple of minutes from the theater. As we approached the entrance, I told George I'd rather go to the one that was closer to my home, about a five-minute drive away. He said fine and off we went.

So there we were standing at the counter. As George ordered, I turned around to see what the person next to me was ordering. I almost fainted on the spot. You guessed it — Tom Cruise was standing about three feet to my left. I quickly turned to George and began to babble that Tom Cruise was right there at the ice cream counter. Not for a second did he believe me. He was used to hearing GiGi claim that most guys she saw looked like Tom Cruise. To humor me, though, George took a look. I thought his eyes were going to pop out. I knew I couldn't let this opportunity pass by, so I tapped Tom's shoulder and asked if he would give me an autograph. Very nicely he said, "No problem, just give me a piece of paper and pen." I grabbed a napkin, borrowed a pen and got his autograph personally inscribed to GiGi. When he left, George and I could hardly speak, not so much because we had just seen and talked with Tom Cruise, but because we had just seen belief and faith in action.

There are many people who would write off the Tom Cruise encounter to coincidence. I don't believe in coincidence. In *Love is Letting Go of Fear*, Gerald Jampolsky writes that coincidence is when God decides to do something but prefers to stay anonymous. And Wayne Dyer says something similar in *You'll See It When You Believe It.*

> We have been taught not to believe something until we see it with our own eyes. Since we cannot see synchronicity or experience it directly with our own senses, we become skeptical of it. Our Western culture teaches that all of the mysterious connections are really only random happenstance, and it is easier to believe in these coincidences than in something which eludes our senses.

I have another story to share with you that I don't think was simply a random happening. See what you think. I ran my first marathon in Culver City (Los Angeles area) the first week of December, 1975. I had devoted a year to training. When race day arrived, my emotions were mixed. On the one hand, I was eager and excited to run, although not quite sure what to expect since I had never done this before. On the other hand, I was feeling sad. The day of the race was the one-year anniversary of my grandmother Fritzie's death. Fritzie had been instrumental in teaching me about my own spirituality, about self-reliance, simplicity and living fully. As I was driving to Culver City the morning of the race, I felt a tremendous longing to visit with her, I missed her so much. In the car, I was actually talking with her out loud as a way to soothe my heart. I even said to her that I was open to her spirit and energy. I asked her to let me know somehow if she could hear me. I asked her to help me through the marathon.

When I arrived at the race site, there were lots of people getting ready. I was wishing I knew someone so I wouldn't have to run alone. The gun went off and so did a few thousand runners. For the first three miles, I was alone and felt great — confident, relaxed and energetic. Around the fourth mile, a man who looked to be in his mid-twenties ran up next to me and we began talking. Before we knew it, we were at mile ten, then fifteen, then twenty. It's amazing the things you'll tell someone you've never met when you're running together. I think it has something to do with the release of certain chemicals in the body and a change in the electrical activity of the brain during aerobic activity. We talked about our lives, families, interests, dreams and goals. I was feeling extremely grateful to him because our conversation made the miles sail by.

Before we knew it, we were at mile twenty-five. At this point in our conversation, we started talking about where we lived. I told him I lived in Brentwood and he told me he lived in Studio City. "That's interesting," I said. "My grandmother used to live in Studio City. What street do you live on?" When he told me the street, I gasped, for it was the same street as Fritzie's. At this point, we were close to the finish line. I had just enough time to inquire about his exact location. We were crossing the finish line when he told me he had moved into an apartment eleven months earlier, that the lady who lived there before him had passed away. I could hardly breathe, not because I was tired but because of what he was telling me. He had moved into Fritzie's apartment.

Coincidence you say? I don't think so. Out of all the thousands of people in the race, how did I end up running with the man who lived in my grandmother's apartment? And how do you explain this happening only a few hours after I had asked Fritzie to give me some sign that she was receiving my communication?

Only believe. Have faith. Trust your inner guidance. Know you are co-creator with God and, with that partnership, anything is possible. Relinquish limited thinking. The world is yours for the asking.

Choose to live peacefully and trust God.

For we walk by faith, not by sight.

2 Cor. 5:7

Taking Inventory and Action

1. Do you look outside yourself for your good and for your answers?

2. Do you give power to effects rather than causes, for to do so will give people, places, things and conditions power over you?

3. What self-limiting beliefs do you have about yourself and your ability to live your vision?

4. Do you feel worthy to receive the unlimited blessings that are your birthright?

5. Do you believe in miracles? Do you expect miracles?

6. Trust in what you cannot see.

7. Don't judge by appearances; look with your heart. Be still. Listen.

8. Give thanks that you have already been given the Kingdom of Heaven.

9. Never underestimate the power of love and faith to heal and harmonize.

10. Live in the presence of God.

Today's Affirmation

The spirit of God within is my source, supply and support. I draw forth the kingdom into my consciousness and the fullness of my blessings is now being made evident in my world. I stand firm in my faith in God. Miracles are a natural part of my life. I trust and I believe.

CHAPTER 25

Tenderheartedness

What do we live for, if not to make
life easier for one another.

T.S. Eliot

Gentleness and kindness usually ride tandem. Gentle means kindly, mild, amiable, not violent or severe. It means compassionate, considerate, tolerant, calm, mild-tempered, courteous and peaceful. But I think that the best synonym for gentle is tenderhearted. I love that word. And I love being around people who are tenderhearted.

To be treated with tenderheartedness, we must first offer that quality to other people. Respond to others exactly as you would want to be treated. No one likes to be rushed or belittled, ignored or unappreciated. Everyone likes kindness, patience and respect. Ephesians 4:32 advises, "Be kind to one another, tenderhearted, forgiving one another, as God in Christ forgave you."

Reaching out with a kind act or word of praise or appreciation can be so simple. Yet sometimes we assume that others "have it together," and do not need our kindness. Wouldn't it be better to move beyond our assumptions and to offer the kind of thoughtfulness we would appreciate receiving — a compliment, a smile, a hug, a pat on the shoulder, a note of thanks or just a question that shows concern. If your kind gesture goes unnoticed or is refused, it doesn't matter, because in giving to another, you give to yourself. You'll feel better. Gandhi said that the pure loving kindness of one gentle soul can nullify the hatred of millions. Now it's time for all of us to live more tenderheartedly.

Take smiling, for example. Everyone can do it. If you're not used to smiling, practice in the mirror by pulling the corners of your mouth up! It's so simple and yet so effective. Learn to smile sincerely, from your heart. No matter what the circumstance, no matter how challenging the situation, put on a happy face. Smile to family and friends, to strangers, to everyone you meet or pass during the day. Do you realize how many lives you can touch simply by smiling? You smile at one person and he catches the good feeling and smiles at another person, and so on until your smile has, indirectly, affected the lives of several thousand people in one day.

Or how about writing a note of thanks or appreciation? You don't need a special occasion to send a card or note to someone. You say you're too busy to offer that kind of kindness? It doesn't take much time. I read an article in a magazine recently about President Bush's penchant for writing thank-you notes. He is able to dash off a dozen small notes with a single flourish and is "probably the most prolific note writer in America," according to his director of correspondence, Shirley M. Green. It's ironic that the busiest among us are the most faithful letter writers. I love to write letters and am very faithful, as most of my friends will attest. Sometimes I'll go to a card store and purchase several dozen cards to have on hand. Isn't it fun to receive a card from a friend for no reason at all?

Another act of kindness and gentleness I always appreciate is a hug or simply the touch of another person. I've been known to give hugs in important business meetings, even when I've just met the person. I've also had my share of awkward looks from people who feel this type of behavior is totally inappropriate. It's how I like to be, and unless someone specifically says to me that he doesn't like to be touched, I will continue following my heart and doing what feels right to me. Touching does so much. At the University of Colorado Medical School, studies have shown that touching increases hemoglobin, increases immune functioning, decreases tension in the body and accelerates healing. Yes, there is great power in our hands.

You can't speak negatively about another without that criticism becoming a part of your own reality. The real you, your Higher Self, which connects with everyone else, has difficulty differentiating between you and another person. It has a tendency to believe that what you're saying about someone else is what you believe about yourself.

In Romans 12:21, Paul admonished, "Do not be overcome by evil, but overcome evil with good." This rang true for me last month when I visited a friend in the hospital. When I walked into her room, she began complaining about the male nurse she had. She said he was forgetful, rude, short with her and not very pleasant. When my friend left the room for her therapy, her nurse came in to change the sheets. I could see the pain and anguish on his face. I offered a few kind words about how much I appreciated his hard work and dedication. That opened the way for him to reveal the incredible hardship in his life. His wife still lived in South Africa and his two children had recently died from medical complications. He was working a double shift, just to make ends meet. When I heard all this, I felt a deep, loving kindness for him. Before he left the room, I gave him a big hug. He started to cry. You know how that can be sometimes? All it takes is a hug or kind word and the emotional floodgates open. During the following couple of weeks, whenever I visited my friend, I took the nurse some of my home-made bread, which he loved and appreciated. Both my friend and I learned a valuable lesson during those two weeks on how important it is to reach out to others with tender-heartedness even though you have no guarantees of what you'll get in return.

Sometimes the kindest gestures can go unnoticed. I love to put coins in parking meters when I walk down the street if I find some that have expired. The drivers of the cars never know but it makes me feel good. Sometimes I send a note anonymously with a kind word or a few dollars when I know the recipient is in need. It takes so little to do so much.

Each of us can make a difference in the world. By our intentions and through our attitudes, we can see Heaven or Hell. Alan Cohen writes in his delightful book, *Joy Is My Compass*:

The difference between a saint and a sourpuss is that the sourpuss sees his daily interactions as a nuisance, while the saint finds a continuous stream of opportunities to celebrate. One finds intruders, the other angels. At any given moment we have the power to choose what we will be and what we will see. Each of us has the capacity to find holiness or attack all about us.

Isn't that wonderful?

It is a strong person who is gentle. We always feel at peace with such a person. When we relax and get centered in the divine flow, we can feel God's gentle arms around us and express this gentle kindness towards ourselves and others.

Richard Bucke was a physician who studied the personality traits of those he felt had "cosmic consciousness." His book *Cosmic Consciousness* is one of the classics of mystical experience. Of Walt Whitman, someone with a supremely well developed mystic sense, Bucke wrote the following which, for me, shows Whitman's tenderheartedness:

> When I first knew Walt Whitman I used to think that he watched himself, and did not allow his tongue to give expression to feelings of fretfulness, antipathy, complaint and remonstrance. . . . After long observation . . . I satisfied myself that such absence or unconsciousness was entirely real. . . . He never spoke deprecatingly of any nationality or class of men, or time in the world's history . . . or against any trades or occupations — not even against any animals, insects, plants or inanimate things, nor any of the laws of nature, nor any of the results of the laws, such as illness, deformity or death. He never complained or grumbled either at the weather, pain, illness or anything else. He never in conversation . . . used language that could be considered indelicate . . . He never spoke in anger . . . never exhibited fear, and I do not believe he ever felt it.

To be gentle and kind to others, we must first be gentle and kind with ourselves. There's no need to be hard on yourself, to beat yourself up when you make a mistake, choose incorrectly or repeat the past. Just as God forgives us, we must forgive ourselves. Through love and forgiveness, we can live from our hearts and live in the heart of God. And when we live in the heart of God, we can let our tenderheartedness shine through in everything we think, feel, say and do.

Choose to live peacefully and tenderheartedly.

Seek to do brave and lovely things which are left undone by the majority of people. Give gifts of love and peace to those whom others pass by.

Paramahansa Yogananda

Taking Inventory and Action

1. Do you reach out in kindness to people you meet, or do you wait to see if you will receive it from them first?
2. Are you too busy to write thank-you notes, and do you feel that a telephone call would be quicker and easier?
3. When you make a mistake, are you hard on yourself?
4. Do you wait for other people to smile at you before you offer a smile?
5. Pay close attention to how you feel next time you are hugged or gently touched.
6. Hug at least three people today and give yourself at least three hugs.
7. Send notes to three friends today and let them know how much you appreciate them.
8. If you encounter anyone today who seems upset, depressed or anxious, go out of your way to bring a little sunshine into their lives.
9. Connect with God's gentleness and bathe in its healing light.
10. Live in the presence of God.

Today's Affirmation

Peacefully and gently I relax in God's light and love. I let go any thoughts of unkindness or unforgiveness towards myself and others. In everything I think, feel, say and do, I let my gentleness and kindness shine.

CHAPTER 26

Solitude and Silence

Always remember that seclusion is the price of
greatness.... Walk in silence; go quietly; develop
spiritually. We should not allow noise and sensory
activities to ruin the antennae of our attention,
because we are listening for the footsteps
of God to come into our temples.

Paramahansa Yogananda

Noise seems to be part of our everyday lives — from the alarm clock in the morning, to the traffic outside, to the never-ending sounds of voices, radio and television. Our bodies and minds appear to acclimate to these outside intrusions. Or do they?

Two decades ago, the Committee on Environmental Quality of the Federal Council for Science and Technology found that "growing numbers of researchers fear the dangerous and hazardous effects of intense noise on human health are seriously underestimated." Similarly, the late Vice President Nelson Rockefeller, when writing about the environmental crisis of our time, noted that when people are fully aware of the damage noise can inflict on man, "peace and quiet will surely rank along with clean skies and pure waters as top priorities for our generation."

More recent studies suggest that we pay a price for adapting to noise: higher blood pressure, heart rate and adrenaline secretion; heightened aggression; impaired resistance to disease; a sense of helplessness. Studies indicate that when we can control noise, its effects are much less damaging.

I haven't been able to find any studies on the effects of quiet in repairing the stress of noise, but I know intuitively that most of us love quiet and need it desperately. We are so used to noise in our lives that silence can sometimes feel awkward and unsettling. On vacation, for instance, when quiet prevails, we may have trouble sleeping. But choosing times of silence can enrich the quality of our lives tremendously. If you find yourself overworked, stressed-out, irritated or tense, rather than heading for a coffee or snack break, maybe all you need is a silence break.

Everyone at some time has experienced the feeling of being overwhelmed by life. Everyone, too, has felt the need to escape, to find a quiet, secluded place to experience the peace of Spirit, to be alone with quiet thoughts. Creating times of silence in your life takes commitment and discipline. Most of the time, periods of silence must be scheduled into your day's activities or you'll never have any.

Maybe you can carve out times of silence while at home where you can be without radio, television, telephones or voices. If you live in a family, maybe the best quiet time for you is early in the morning before others arise. In that silence, you can become more aware, more sensitive to your surroundings, feel more in touch with the wholeness of life.

From quiet time or silence, you recognize the importance of solitude. Silence and solitude go hand in hand. In silence and solitude, you reconnect with your self. Solitude helps to clear your channels, fosters peace and brings spiritual lucidity. When you retreat from the outside world to go within, you can be at the very center of your being and reacquaint yourself with your spiritual nature — the essence of your being and all life.

Outside noise tends to drown out the inner life — the music of the soul. Only in silence and solitude can we go within and nurture our spiritual lives. Within each of us there is a silence waiting to be embraced. It's the harbor of the heart. When you rediscover that harbor, your life will never be the same. In the Bible we read, "There is silence in heaven" (Revelations 8:1). "For God alone my soul waits in silence." (Psalms 62:1).

Mystics, saints and spiritual leaders have all advocated periods of silence and solitude for spiritual growth. St. John of the Cross writes that only in silence can the soul hear the divine. Jesus prayed much by Himself and spent long hours in silent communion with God. Gandhi devoted every Monday to a day of silence. In silence, he was better able to meditate and pray, to seek within himself the solutions to all the problems and responsibilities that he carried. When I read about Gandhi's practice of silence and solitude several years ago, I was so inspired and moved that I decided to adopt a similar discipline in my life. So now one day a week, for two consecutive days once a month and for several days in a row at each change of season, I spend time in solitude, silence, prayer and fasting. Even now, during this forty-day spiritual rejuvenation program, I'm choosing to spend most of my time alone in silence.

How do you feel about being alone? Aloneness is quite different from loneliness. This idea is expressed beautifully by Paul Tillich in *Courage To Be.*

> Our language has wisely sensed the two sides of being alone. It has created the word loneliness to express the pain of being alone. And it has created the word solitude to express the glory of being alone.

Loneliness is something you do to yourself. Have you ever experienced feeling lonely even when you're with other people? We're so used to being with others and so unaccustomed to being by ourselves that we've, in a sense, become a people and not persons. We must reclaim ourselves and reconnect with our wholeness and the peace of solitude. Choose to make solitude your friend.

Even if you're married, you need times of privacy and solitude. In my counseling, I always encourage couples to spend occasional time alone, not only daily, but at regular intervals during the week, month and year. In this way, you regain your identity as individuals. You bring so much more to the marriage when you come from feeling whole, complete and strong. Solitude fosters these qualities.

With a little creativity, a marriage can accommodate solitude and privacy. I have witnessed all types of arrangements, including separate vacations, private rooms in the house, living separately during the week and coming together on weekends, and having special times during the day in which each person is left alone.

I know several people who do everything possible to preclude being alone. Often this is because they have never tried it, they are afraid of loneliness or are simply uncomfortable with themselves. They haven't yet discovered the peace of their own company. It's not scary to be by yourself; it's absolutely wonderful. Loneliness is not a state of being; it's simply a state of mind. You can choose to change your state of mind.

I realize that I live my life differently from most. I go to great lengths to secure my time of solitude and privacy. It's a great comfort to me to be by myself; it's like returning home to an old friend or lover after being away too long. Solitude is not a luxury. It is right and a necessity.

Through the years I have gone on several vision quests. A vision quest is a time of solitude during which an individual can take time for looking into the soul, finding a new direction or path or simply reconnecting with one's Higher Self. On these occasions, I usually go to the mountains or the desert for a time of prayer, meditation, fasting, reflection and aloneness. I spend much of my time outdoors, being open to the beauty and love all around me. In this peaceful, reflective time, the earth, the sky, the wind, the animals, the incredible beauty and divine order of everything takes on a new and personal meaning. I commune with the trees, the moon, the flowers and the animals. My vision quests always show me that the most profound lessons in life come to us through nature, solitude and silence.

It is my contention that all the other good things we endeavor to provide for ourselves, including sound nutrition, daily exercise and material wealth, will be of reduced value unless we learn to live in harmony with ourselves, which means knowing ourselves and finding peace in our own company. This peace is a natural occurrence of spending time alone in silence. In spending time alone we realize that we are never really alone and that we can live more fully by focusing on inner guidance rather than on externalities.

Embrace solitude. Walk in silence among the trees, in the mountains, by the ocean, with the sun and moon as your friends. Be by yourself, and experience a whole new way of celebrating yourself and life. Feel the heartbeat of silence. Bathe in its light and love. Know within yourself that you are a child of God, and in your silence is Heaven.

Choose to live peacefully and choose a time of silence and solitude every day.

> When from our better selves
> we have too long
> Been parted by the hurrying
> world, and droop,
> Sick of its business, of its
> pleasures tired,
> How gracious, how benign is
> Solitude.
>
> William Wordsworth

Taking Inventory and Action

1. What do you do to prevent being alone?
2. How do you feel about aloneness? Lonely? Scared? Uncomfortable? Happy?
3. Do you ever feel lonely being around other people?
4. Do you schedule times of solitude into your life?
5. When was the last time you went to the mountains, the ocean, the desert to listen to the silence of your heart?
6. Today find some time just for yourself and find the peace of your own company.
7. Write down your feelings and thoughts during your time of aloneness.
8. Spend some time with a friend being together and, at the same time, being silent.
9. Look at your calendar and plan a time when you can spend an entire day or two alone. Create your own vision quest.
10. Live in the Presence of God.

Today's Affirmation

In the silence of my heart, I am at peace. In solitude, I feel God's love and guidance in my life. Today I seek out time to be alone, to enjoy the serenity of my own company.

CHAPTER 27

Being Childlike

This ability to see, experience and accept the new is
one of our saving characteristics. To be fearful of
tomorrow, to close ourselves to possibilities, to resist
the inevitable, to advocate standing still when all
else is moving forward, is to lose touch. If we accept
the new with joy and wonder, we can move
gracefully into each tomorrow. More often
than not, the children shall lead us.

Leo Buscaglia, *Bus 9 to Paradise*

So many of us are searching for the "fountain of youth," the secret that will enable us to live long and healthy lives. We have looked to special diets, supplements and exercise. Yet the secret to living a quality life, full of aliveness and celebration, comes from within — from our attitudes, our expressions, our thoughts and how we view ourselves and the world around us. Young children can often provide the keys to celebrating life. They are some of my greatest teachers. They express pure joy.

I marvel at the way young children can be real, sensitive, and open with each other. Living heart-to-heart seems to be so natural for them. There are no masks when they relate to each other. When children meet for the first time, they will often relate as if they were lifetime buddies.

Compare this to your response when meeting someone new. Are you trusting, comfortable and enthusiastic? Or perhaps suspicious, reserved and unwilling to be vulnerable? We reflect our individual attitudes and feelings about ourselves. Every day we have an opportunity to spread some joy in this world by how we relate to other people. It could be something as simple as being a good listener or offering a warm hug. The other person receives your joy and will naturally pass it along to others. It's so simple and yet so profound. What you give comes back multiplied.

Think for a moment about your experiences with very young children. How have you seen them? Were they cheerful, alert, eager, trusting and open? Were they energetic, caring, sensitive, friendly and inquisitive? How about enthusiastic, playful, expressive, spontaneous and natural? And were they both lovable and innocently loving? From my point of view, these natural childlike qualities are the true essences of life. They are the magic we should seek to recapture. (One of my audiocassettes from my *Celebrate Life!* series is all about getting in touch with your inner child and living life more fully.)

As I wrote in my book, *Choose To Be Healthy*, to be childlike is to be innocent of all the strange, authoritarian ideas of what adulthood ought to be; to be trusting and straightforward; to be honest and natural, free from the need to impress others. Being childlike means being more concerned with your experience of life than how you look to others. You do not have to give up being an adult in order to become more childlike. You do not have to become infantile or in the least bit irresponsible or unaccountable. The fully integrated person is capable of the harmonious blending of the adult and the child.

Think about the adults you most like to be with. I'll bet they are genuinely happy, joyful people. From joyfulness flows laughter, a sense of humor and silliness. Too many adults take themselves so seriously that they've forgotten how to look at the bright side of things. You don't always have to be orderly, rigid, serious, and adultlike. Learn to laugh, especially at yourself. Learn to have fun and be a little silly and crazy. In other words, lighten up. When you do this, the whole world will seem brighter and more beautiful.

Within each of us is a child waiting to come forth and express himself or herself more fully. What usually keeps us from getting in touch with the child within is our unwillingness to recognize and accept this child. It seems we often feel that since we're grownups, we have to act our age.

Learning to laugh with children is one way to recover the aliveness and spontaneity that are missing in our lives. Other ways of getting to our inner fountains of joy are simplifying our lives, slowing down, taking time to smell the flowers, talking to the animals, watching the clouds, being with family and friends.

In my life, I have noticed that when my judgmental self rears its ugly head, I tend to be more controlling of people and situations instead of letting go and flowing with life. When I choose to release my desire to be in control and to live more from inner guidance, I notice that struggle dissipates and I feel more joyful and peaceful about myself and life.

The more I pay attention to how children experience and embrace life, and the more I release my fears about being rejected and feeling uncertain, the better life becomes for me and for those people around me, because the gentle, tenderhearted me comes forth. As that happens, the dichotomies in my life soften. My work becomes play; my challenges become wonderful opportunities to learn and grow. My life takes on clarity and purpose as I move closer to becoming a master of the art of living.

According to James Michener:

> The master of the art of living draws no distinction between his work and his play, his labor and his leisure, his mind and his body, his education and his recreation, his love and his religion. He hardly knows which is which. He simply pursues his vision of excellence through whatever he is doing and leaves it to others to decide whether he is working or playing. To himself, he is always doing both.

Make a point of doing something out of the ordinary each day that brings joy to others and to yourself. The results may surprise you. I love teddy bears. Often when I take long trips in my car, my bears accompany me. I also take one when I fly out of town. My bears help keep my inner child alive and happy.

Children accept you totally for your good points and your not-so-good points, too. They don't care about differences in people, about different races, religions or backgrounds. I feel that in a world in which so much conflict exists between people of different religions, races and backgrounds, the best bridge to understanding, peace and joy is built of love and forgiveness. When we reach out to another and offer unconditional love and forgiveness, as children do, joy and peace are the result.

Choose to live peacefully and let your inner child come out and orchestrate your day.

> Let the children come to me and do not forbid them; for to such belongs the kingdom of heaven.
>
> Matt. 19:14

Taking Inventory and Action

1. In what areas of your life are you too serious?
2. Would you describe yourself as a happy, positive person? Are you the type of person you would like to have for a friend?
3. What qualities do you see in children that you'd like to integrate more fully into your life?
4. In what areas of your life are you too rigid and orderly — too adultlike?
5. Do you give yourself permission to act silly and crazy?
6. If you were to regularly let the child in you out to explore, play, be spontaneous and be creative, your life would change in what ways? Describe this on paper.
7. Write down some changes you can make to become a little less serious, to lighten up.
8. You know those things you've wanted to try or do for ages but you keep putting them off. Don't wait any longer. Be spontaneous and live fully. Tomorrow may never come.
9. Do some fun things for those you really care about (for example, write a special note, send flowers, record a song, make a pie, or give someone a teddy bear).
10. Live in the presence of God.

Today's Affirmation

I now choose to let my inner child come out and play and orchestrate my day. I greet each day with joy in my heart and laughter in my eyes. I love my life and know that everything is in divine order.

CHAPTER 28

Self-Reliance and Detachment

Self-reliance, the height and perfection
of man, is reliance on God.

Ralph Waldo Emerson

More than anyone else in my life, my grandmother Fritzie taught me about self-reliance. I wish you could have known her. She was a spirited, happy, shining soul who celebrated life every day. Fritzie loved to travel and did so often, usually alone, all over the world. She took very little with her, just a few basics. She wanted to live simply. She reminds me so much of the Peace Pilgrim. Fritzie was never afraid to visit new places and always made friends wherever she went. Living alone was important to her. Once when I asked her if she ever got lonely, she responded by saying, "Heavens, no! How could I possibly get lonely when God is always with me?" That response led to a long discussion on independence, simplicity, self-reliance and faith in God that profoundly affected my life.

Abraham Maslow characterized his healthiest subjects as independent, detached and self-governing, with a tendency to look within for their guiding values and for the rules by which they lived. He also noted their strong preference, even need, for privacy and their detachment from people in general. My grandmother certainly fits Maslow's description of a healthy person. Maslow discovered that his healthiest subjects were only superficially accepting of social customs, while in private they were quite casual about and even humorously tolerant of them. These people had defied convention when they thought it necessary and judged things by their own criteria. They lived by their own values and not the dictates of society. Maslow called such people *autonomous*.

For more than ten years now I have been living my life autonomously. I spend a great deal of my time alone, and I go to great lengths to protect and nurture my privacy and solitude. Sure I love being with people and, in my work, I come in contact with several thousand people a year. Yet, when I'm not with others, I love to spend time by myself. In fact, on a regular basis, I detach myself from the world and spend time alone. It's a wonderful feeling to be self-reliant and independent. It's true freedom to feel the peace of your own company. I've had friends who didn't understand my desire for solitude and privacy. As a result, these friendships have dissolved, and new and more fulfilling ones have entered my life.

To be self-reliant means you must not judge by appearances. Instead, you become centered in that bedrock of wholeness inside you. Detach from those things that limit you and become one with those things that empower you. Self-reliance, as Emerson suggests, means relying not on our little selves but instead on our Higher Selves. Emerson believed that God could be found in the depths of each person's heart.

Too often in relationships, we rely on the other person to make us feel good or happy or guarantee our self-esteem or self-confidence. John Bradshaw, in one of his television shows said, "The goal of life is to move from environmental support to self-support. So what we look at then is the possibility of going deeper within ourselves."

From my counseling work, I have learned that people emphasize what they do in order to determine how "good" they are. They look outside themselves to establish their self-esteem. Most of us have grown up believing that what others say is more important than what we think or how we feel. We become too attached to "looking right" and valuing others' opinions. With a more detached attitude, we can flow through life without any judgment about how things are supposed to be. We see that what we do doesn't matter; it's the heart we carry with us and the peace we feel that bring us fulfillment. Don't be attached to a specific outcome. With that attitude, you can become centered and allow the divine flow to see you through. Author Carlos Castaneda writes about detachment in *Journey to Ixtlan*:

> Thus a man of knowledge sweats and puffs and if one looks at him he is just like any ordinary man, except that the folly of his life is under control. . . . His controlled folly makes him say that what he does matters and makes him act as if it did, and yet he knows that it doesn't; so when he fulfills his acts he retreats in peace, and whether his acts were good or bad, or worked or didn't, is in no way any part of his concern.

I've seen this same principle in my career. I used to be concerned that my articles or lectures be well-received. When I chose to give up that concern and to speak and write more from my heart, I found that not only did I do much better, but also I began receiving a deluge of offers to write and speak. I allowed myself to work more from the power within me, knowing that the outcome isn't the most essential thing.

Gandhi was once asked by a Western journalist, "Can you give me the secret of your life in three words?" Gandhi replied, "Renounce and enjoy!"

Detachment releases joy and is the secret to health and peace of mind. When I began this forty-day spiritual discipline, part of my surrender was letting go of all the things and people in my life, knowing they were in God's hands. I wanted to detach myself from the outside world for awhile so I could become truly anchored in the divine. Through this process, I've realized that detachment has more to do with what we think and feel and less to do with our actions. I needed to become detached from my judgment and thoughts of the way things should be and more in alignment with how God wants things to be. This realization made me feel free and light. This consciousness of detachment takes away stress and, thus, fosters greater health. You become less occupied with the things of the earth and more focused on God and God's will for you. This is true self-reliance — knowing you already have everything you need to live fully and that peace is only a decision away.

Choose to live peacefully and, in all things, put your reliance in God.

People are so preoccupied with the things of the earth, they have no time for God.

Mother Teresa

Taking Inventory and Action

1. In relationships, do you look to the other person to make you happy or complete?

2. Do you put more value on what others say about you than how you feel in your heart?

3. Do you ever venture out on your own for a day or two to enjoy your own company?

4. Is your level of self-esteem tied to your performance at work or at home?

5. Are you attached to the past, unwilling to give up old hurt or sorrow?

6. Look at every experience with the understanding that a spiritual lesson is inherent.

7. Spend a weekend alone in nature.

8. Your troubles are not caused by your spouse, your boss, your children, your friends or the weather. Turn within. Detach yourself from the situation and allow God's light to shine through so you can see more clearly. Don't be attached to a specific outcome. Put your life in God's hands.

9. What you are emotionally charged about, you are usually attached to. Let go.

10. Live in the presence of God.

Today's Affirmation

I put my reliance in the wisdom and love within me and know that my life is now in divine order. I rely on God for everything, for all that I am is God. We are one.

CHAPTER 29

Courage

Life is either a daring adventure — or nothing.

Helen Keller

It takes daring just to live, but it takes courage to live your vision. Is it possible to be in touch with your true courageousness without being in touch with your divinity? I don't think so. We can soar to the top of the mountain and beyond when we know that the courage we want is part of us; it's our trust in God. Trust in God will destroy the fear that stifles our efforts.

Fear is our misperception of a situation. It's looking through our human eyes and mind rather than the eyes and heart of God. When we face our fears, acting from the awareness that we are one with spirit, we learn and nurture courage. Goethe said, "Whatever you can do, or dream you can, begin it. Boldness has genius, power and magic in it." When we face our fears head on, they begin to evaporate. When we embrace what scares us, we find that we are endowed with a level of courage that we never knew existed. Every day we have so many opportunities to act courageously. Committing to a forty-day fast takes courage. Putting forth new and fresh ideas on paper each day takes courage. Getting up each morning to face the day as a willing and enthusiastic participant takes courage.

I have learned alot about what it means to live with courage and commitment from my friend, Morris Dees, civil rights lawyer and author of the excellent book, *A Season for Justice*. On a quiet Spring night in 1981, two members of the Alabama Ku Klux Klan lynched Michael Donald, a young African American. After the conviction of one of the klansmen, Morris Dees and the Southern Poverty Law Center brought a civil suit against the United Klans of America on behalf of the victims mother. In this landmark civil suit against the Klan itself, he successfully proved a pattern of promoting racial violence and won an historic seven million dollar award, crippling the Klan financially. In addition, in 1990, Dees won a stunning judgement in Oregon against Tom Metzger and the White Aryan Resistance.

In a world plagued by racial and religious hatred, Morris Dees has used the law as "a sword." He believes that the fanatical forces of the Ku Klux Klan, Neo-Nazis and White Supremacists must be fought on his terms, in the courtroom. Since 1971, he has waged a heroic crusade, risking his life to win freedom, equality and justice for every American. He and his colleagues at the Southern Poverty Law Center battle successfully for those with no access to the judicial system.

His courage and commitment to the preservation of justice and the protection of basic liberties is an inspiration to me.

Let your courage be the shield that protects you. Let courage direct your spirit's light to shine on your path and give you strength to live your vision, to dare to risk and go after your dreams. In the end, most people don't regret the things they do. They regret what they failed to do.

With so much negativity in the media and around the world these days, it takes courage to see the good and the positive. When I was in college, I acquired the nickname of "Sunny" because I always had a sunny disposition and, like Pollyanna, chose to look at the bright side of everything. Some felt I was naive and ignorant, but I knew better. I saw the negative but chose to look beyond it, with the eyes of my heart.

Why do you defend your limitations? Why do you let fear paralyze you? You can choose differently. Instead, let spirit be your guide, with courage at the reins. Courage is going after the things you believe in even though they seem impossible. In *Field of Dreams* the character played by Kevin Costner went after his vision. He followed his heart and listened to his inner voice no matter that the world seemed to be against him. That took courage. My mom taught me to be courageous. She gave me the courage to believe I could do things I only dreamed of. She would never allow me to defend my limitations.

What is courage to you? To me, courage is moving through uncertainty. Courage is changing when that's the hardest thing in the world to do. Courage is being responsible for what you've created in your life and relinquishing blame. It's trusting in God when you want to be in charge. It's making difficult choices when, in this fast-paced, over-stimulated world, we're overwhelmed with information. Courage is choosing to live peacefully and simply when everything in life seems to teach the opposite. Some people think that if you have courage, you don't have fear. Not at all! Courage is being fearful but doing it anyway, and courage is admitting you don't know.

My dear friend, the Rev. George Marks, assistant minister at Founder's Church in Los Angeles, has taught me so much about the importance of courage and living my highest potential. In a conversation we had yesterday, he inspired me by saying what courage meant to him. He said, "Courage is trusting again in a relationship, even when you've been hurt or disappointed. Courage is living up to the promises we've made to ourselves and to others. Courage is when we don't complain and we do what we have to do even though we might not want to. With courage, we move beyond ourselves." He also said that one of the most inspiring acts of courage to him was when Jesus, knowing that His arrest, trial and crucifixion were imminent, came out of solitude and entered the city of Jerusalem to face His adversaries, with love and forgiveness in His heart.

Courage Is a Three-Letter Word is a powerful, passionate book, which I just finished reading for the third time. Walter Anderson interviews a variety of celebrities about how they overcame their personal fears and, with courage, achieved their goals. His own personal story showed me that with courage, inner strength, belief and faith, you can overcome any obstacle and make a difference in this world.

The lives of Dave Dravecky and Ryan White are two more inspiring examples of how relentless courage can create miracles. Dave Dravecky, formerly a pitcher for the San Francisco Giants, overcame enormous medical odds in his battle to beat cancer, losing his arm in the process. His courage, determination and faith in God created a miracle. *Comeback* is the account of his battle. It's an empowering story. Dravecky is a hero to me. And so was Ryan White, the hemophiliac youth who was barred from attending school in Indiana after he contracted AIDS. His is a story of true courage. He touched the lives of millions of people by how he chose to live with his challenges.

True courage enables us to live in the present moment and make choices rather than being a victim and settling for what life gives us. It's a God-given quality that can be called upon at any time. I definitely called upon it not long ago when my fear almost paralyzed me.

As I regularly do, I went to the Sierra Nevada Mountains alone for a few days of quiet, meditation, fasting and prayer. On this particular trip, I had a very small cabin next to a placid, beautiful lake. The day before I came home, I decided to take an all-day hike in the mountains. I left at around dawn and hiked uphill for most of the morning. Around two in the afternoon, I decided to sit down, relax and meditate by a tree. It was unusually quiet that day; I passed only five people on the trails. Sitting crossed-legged, with my eyes still open, I could see paradise — several lakes and most of the Sierras. With each breath, I felt more peaceful, relaxed and connected with the spirit of life. I closed my eyes and began to concentrate on my breath, slowly inhaling and slowly exhaling. It felt wonderful. In a few more moments, I was totally absorbed in my inner world, not at all distracted by my surroundings, except for one minor thing. I thought I could hear some leaves moving. Often, when I'm meditating outdoors, I'm extra sensitive to nature's sounds. I figured I was in tune with the leaves and their musical dance. After a few more minutes, however, the sound of the leaves moving got louder. Slightly curious, I opened one eye. What I saw made my heart jump so that I thought it was on the outside of my body. No more than ten feet in front of me was a bear.

My first reaction was unbridled fear. The bear just stood there and stared at me. My second reaction was to ask God what to do. The answer was instant and, as I look back on the situation, somewhat off the wall. Or should I say tree? I was told to breathe slowly and deeply — as best I could. I was also told to smile at the bear and say some kind words from my heart. I gave it my best shot. I told the bear, in three octaves higher than I'm used to speaking, that he was beautiful, his fur was shiny and that I didn't intend on being his lunch. By talking to him, I actually began to feel relaxed. As I acted with courage, the fear slowly began to disappear. For about five minutes, I spoke to the bear. Then something really amazing occurred. I sensed that the bear was talking with me and responding to my comments. He even seemed to smile. Yes, part of me was still a little scared, but not paralyzed or mentally frozen. I paid attention, felt all my emotions fully and actually enjoyed the experience. Then the bear started to move in my direction, and I wasn't quite ready to hold out my hand to pet him. Before he got to me, he turned around and left. As I watched him shuffle away, I reflected on my extraordinary experience, one in which I learned that courage is inside of us all just waiting to rear its beautiful head.

We strengthen and develop our courage by using it. Don't let it go to waste. Trust in who you are and be all you were created to be by living a courageous life. Choose to live peacefully and courageously.

> Courage is that quality of strength which motivates you to move forward to reach your goal and accomplish your purpose even though there may be fear, inferiority, doubt and inadequacy in your mind. Courage is of the soul, and it permeates every aspect of our consciousness. Courage leads us to do that which God has given us to do, regardless of the consequences. Courage puts first things first.
>
> Rev. Donald Curtis, *40 Steps to Self Mastery*

Taking Inventory and Action

1. In what areas or circumstances of your life have you let fear stifle you?

2. Do you have the courage to follow through on what you say you're going to do?

3. In what relationship have you been afraid to risk and ask for what you want?

4. Have you ever gotten a signal from your heart to do something but, out of fear, followed the advice of others?

5. Can you admit a mistake and not give in to self-castigation?

6. Do you have the courage to be who you are and to live your highest vision?

7. What could you do today that you have been postponing because you were scared? Do it!

8. Be courageous today and commit to that health program you've been putting off until you have more time.

9. Look honestly at your life today and see where you must take responsibility, let go of blame, start fresh and make better choices.

10. Live in the presence of God.

Today's Affirmation

Courage is my middle name and is part of my very nature. I am courageous in all my activities today and trust that the spirit within me will show me what to do and what to say. I have the courage to face anything and everything, including myself. I trust in God with all my heart.

CHAPTER 30

Gratitude and Humility

Every day should be a day of thanksgiving for the
gifts of life: sunshine, water, and the luscious fruits
and greens that are indirect gifts of the Great Giver.
The All-Sufficient One does not need our thanks
however heartfelt, but when we are grateful to Him
our attention is concentrated, for our highest benefit,
upon the Great Source of all supply.

Paramahansa Yogananda

An attitude of gratitude opens our consciousness to all the blessings God has showered on us. It's like a magnet that attracts good and multiplies joy and happiness. Just as all good things proceed from a peaceful mind, so all things are nourished from a grateful heart.

In 1789, President George Washington introduced the first national day of thanksgiving and prayer to be devoted "to the services of that great and glorious Being who is the beneficent author of all the good that was, that is, and that will be; that we may then all unite in rendering unto Him our sincere and humble thanks. . . ." During the presidency of Abraham Lincoln, Thanksgiving Day became an official national holiday. Two of our wisest presidents thus acknowledged our need to remember our dependency on the goodness of God.

Sometimes in life we give thanks only when things seem to be going well. When things go badly, we loose sight of all our blessings. The Greek philosopher, Epicurus, warned us, "Do not spoil what you have by desiring what you have not."

Praise everything in your life, even the things that don't look like blessings. In her lovely book, *How to Let God Help You*, Myrtle Fillmore writes:

Thanksgiving and gratitude are qualities of the soul too little understood and exercised. Heaven and earth listen and respond to the soul that is quickened into praise and thanksgiving. Praise is gratitude in action.

A thankful consciousness establishes us in the mainstream of the creative flow. It also recognizes the source from which all things come. Giving thanks multiplies what you have. It increases abundance. Jesus did it. Elisha did it. This same power is in you.

I have a friend whose income barely covers her bills each month. And every month, she complains and gets depressed about her insufficient income. After a couple months of hearing her complaining, I said to her that she could begin to change her financial situation by changing her attitude from lack and limitation to one of thanksgiving. So I told her that for one month, she was to think only grateful thoughts about her work, about her income, about paying bills and about abundance. When the bills came in, I suggested she bless each one, giving thanks for the service and product provided. I encouraged her to write "thank you, with love" on each check. She admitted to me that she found this quite difficult to do the first month. But within two months, not only did her attitude change about paying bills, but she actually had some money left over. Abundance began coming to her from sources expected and unexpected. When she opened up the channels and acknowledged God as her source, her blessings began to multiply.

By appreciating what we have, we increase our ability to harvest the abundance of God's blessings. Paramahansa Yogananda has said:

Everything that is good is God. Whether it manifests in nature or through noble qualities in human beings it is God whom we are beholding. God the Beautiful is manifest in the synchronized scenery of nature. His divinity is smiling at us in the flowers. The qualities of love and peace and joy that grow in the garden of human hearts are reflecting His goodness, His beauty.

Every day think about all you have to be grateful for. It's a perfect way to start each morning, after your time of prayer and meditation. Throughout the day, continue your praise and thanksgiving. For example, I give thanks for things like God's healthy foods, the beautiful clouds, some pure water after a lengthy and vigorous workout, the friends in my life and the comfort of my bed after a long day's work. Even when I'm facing a challenge or am having difficulty with someone, I give thanks for that, knowing God will provide the answer and I will learn from the circumstance.

Gratitude comes from knowing that God is your source. Humility comes from realizing that God makes all things possible. Jesus taught, "I of Myself can do nothing, the Father that dwells within Me, He does the works." (John 14:10). And Paramahansa Yogananda wrote:

> Humility comes from realizing that God is the Doer, not you. When you see that, how can you be proud of any accomplishment? Think constantly that whatever work you are performing is being done by the Lord through you.

When you know that you are one with God, and it's not you but God through you that accomplishes the good, then everything is in better perspective. You're able to see how your ego tries to battle for recognition and esteem. In its fickleness, your ego will puff up with pride and arrogance, always leaving you deflated in its wake. True humility is not a weakness. It is to be ever aware that we live in the heart of God and to affirm, "Lord, not my will, but Thy will be done." If we feel this in our hearts, we can then let go of our personal desires and the frustration of their nonfulfillment, remaining content in the greater desire to do whatever God wants us to do. This is true humility: to put God uppermost in our lives.

So today, choose to live peacefully, with thanksgiving and praise in your heart, knowing that God is your source.

> What a vast world of love and joy is within the soul! We don't have to acquire it; it is already ours. We have only to remove the dark curtain of ego, to tear away the covering of egotistical thoughts and behavior that hides the divine brilliance of the soul.
>
> Sri Daya Mata

Taking Inventory and Action

1. Do you praise everything in your life or only the good things?

2. In matters of income and abundance, who is your source?

3. Do you take your health, your friends, your mate, your family for granted?

4. When you accomplish and succeed, do you take all the credit?

5. Do you limit your thanksgiving to one day each November?

6. Make a list of everything about our body for which you are grateful.

7. Let your family members and friends know how much you appreciate them.

8. Recognize, praise and bless the divine power within you and give thanks for God's blessings in your life.

9. Commit yourself to do God's will today. Be an open vessel for His light and love.

10. Live in the presence of God.

Today's Affirmation

Today I sing a song of praise and gratitude. I see each person in my life as God's gift to me. In each encounter of this day I learn, grow and deepen in my awareness of love's wonder and blessing. I dedicate my life to do God's will.

CHAPTER 31

Forgiveness

When you hold resentment against anyone, you are
bound to that person by a cosmic link, a real tough
mental chain. You are tied by a cosmic tie to the
thing that you hate. The one person, perhaps in the
whole world, whom you most dislike, is the very
one to whom you are attaching yourself,
by a hook that is stronger than steel.

Emmet Fox

Forgiveness changes lives. Choosing to forgive unlocks the gate to healing and health, prosperity and abundance, joy and happiness and inner peace. Jesus said, "Father, forgive them, for they know not what they do." (Luke 23:34) His tremendous love encompassed all. On another occasion, Jesus told His disciples to pray affirmatively: "Whatever you ask in prayer, believe that you have received it, and it will be yours. And whenever you stand praying, forgive, if you have anything against anyone; so that your Father also who is in heaven may forgive you your trespasses." (Mark 11:24-25) The Master always reinforced the need for forgiveness.

Forgiveness is the central teaching of *A Course in Miracles*. The Course shows how forgiveness can heal our minds, dispel our pain and ultimately awaken us from the confines of time and space. The core lesson is that fear is an illusion; only love is real. Forgiveness is the vehicle that helps us to release fear. To forgive is to let go. Forgiveness lightens our hearts and reunites them with God. Through forgiveness miracles occur.

A Course in Miracles teaches that all disease comes from a failure to forgive. Medical researchers are also coming to the conclusion that an unforgiving nature may be one of the major culprits in human disease. One researcher calls arthritis "bottled hurt." If we condemn, criticize or resent, if we feel guilty, shameful or angry toward another, we are only hurting ourselves. And until we practice forgiveness in our lives, the past will continue to repeat itself.

As so aptly stated by Emmet Fox at the beginning of this chapter, you become linked to another person when you don't offer forgiveness. You also give away your power and create a highly charged, emotionally active connection. But when you forgive, you take back your power and can no longer be controlled by the other person. Some may say that forgiveness is a sign of weakness. I don't agree with that. It takes strength and courage and a generous spirit to understand that people do not always hurt us because they choose to, but more because they couldn't help it or because we were in their way.

People do harm to others when they are in pain and are out of alignment with their source. If you give back to another person the same pain that person has given you, you are hurting yourself and making it impossible for a miracle to occur.

You can transform any negative emotion into love. While you can't control another person's feelings, you can choose what you want to experience, how you want to be. Let kindness and tenderheartedness be your goal. Jesus tells us to love our enemies.

I understand how difficult this can be, especially when you believe someone has wronged you. Maybe you ask yourself, "How can I forgive what this person has done to me?" The secret is to get yourself out of the way and let God forgive through you. When you choose to live your life more internally, allowing the Infinite to express itself through you, your heart softens and your life changes. Resentments, anger, guilt and hurt are released. But you can't release these negative emotions yourself. In my prayer time every day, I ask God to show me how to forgive the past, to forgive others and to forgive myself.

Forgiveness has to start with the self. We must be gentle with ourselves. "To err is human, to forgive divine," writes Alexander Pope. When we forgive ourselves, that doesn't mean that we condone or support everything we have done. It means that we claim it and own it. Maybe we accept that we were wrong, that we made some mistakes and now it's time to let go and to move on. Let go of the past. Release all the pain and replace it with God's love. When you forgive yourself, you move back into your heart.

Forgiveness is also an essential ingredient in any healthy, successful relationship. Communication is the key. Be aware of your feelings and allow them to come to the surface for you to recognize and own. Share these feelings with your partner. Never go to sleep feeling angry, resentful or upset. Offer forgiveness, let go and let God purify your emotions and feelings.

What if you can't contact another person or that other person has passed away? It doesn't matter. Forgiveness is a change of heart. It was only a few years ago, long after my dad had passed away, that I forgave him for what I believed he had done to me as a child. I also forgave myself for having unloving thoughts about my dad. God showed me the way to do these things. I wrote my dad a letter. I visited his grave site. And I brought my dad to my mind's eye and talked with him. As a result of practicing forgiveness with my dad, miracles occurred in my life — in my relationships, in my career and in my health. And from this forgiveness, I experienced a profound peace. There's no doubt in my mind that forgiveness is the greatest act of healing; it transforms lives and creates miracles.

Choose to live peacefully and practice forgiveness.

As God is constantly forgiving us, even knowing all our wrong thoughts, so those who are fully in tune with Him naturally have that same love.

Paramahansa Yogananda, *Where There Is Light*

Taking Inventory and Action

1. Do you need to forgive yourself?
2. List the people in your life to whom you need to offer forgiveness.
3. Are you repeating patterns in your life? If so, which ones?
4. Are you giving your power away to others? If so, to whom?

5. Would you like to feel peaceful, be happy and create miracles in your life?

6. Today offer only love and forgiveness to everyone you meet.

7. Bring to mind someone who has hurt you and practice forgiveness.

8. Write down those individuals who continue to negatively charge you and take you out of your heart. Start today and forgive each. Continue until you finish the list. It may take weeks.

9. Write down what it would feel like if you forgave yourself for everything.

10. Live in the presence of God.

Today's Affirmation

Through Christ in me, I offer forgiveness to others and myself. I let go and let God's love purify and cleanse all of my past mistakes and wrong thinking. I have an inward sense of peace and tranquility.

CHAPTER 32

Perseverance and Determination

When faced with a mountain I WILL NOT QUIT! I will
keep on striving until I climb over, find a pass
through, tunnel underneath — or simply stay and
turn the mountain into a gold mine, with God's help!

Robert Schuller

Sometimes the answer to a challenge or the guidance that we seek seems just beyond our reach. This is the time to "keep on keeping on." You can win the race no matter how far behind you are when you start. Perseverance and determination will see you through. Keep your goal clearly in sight, and don't get side-tracked.

Life can be complicated. It's easy to lose sight of our purpose in the midst of our daily lives. We often become wrapped up in living our schedules, paying the bills, rearing children or getting ahead at work. We live our lives from a rabbit's-eye view — our noses pressed up against the blade of grass right in front of us.

Just as grasping the beauty of an entire tapestry is difficult if we view it too closely, we can, similarly, lose clarity if we get too caught up in our day-to-day lives. We must learn to take an eagle's-eye view. Soaring far above the ground, the eagle can see farther and with greater clarity than the earth-bound rabbit. And as the eagle uses the wind to keep it aloft, you can choose to use determination and perseverance to keep you on course.

Yesterday, I finished reading *Women Saints East and West* and was fascinated by Saint Teresa of Avila, also known as Saint Teresa of Jesus. She grew up in the sixteenth-century Spanish town of Avila and was intelligent, beautiful, sagacious and charming. She could have had anything in her life, but while she was still a teen, she began to realize that the things of the world did not have nearly so much appeal for her as the things of the spirit. She prayed for greater awareness, clarity and strength to follow her heart. What was it that made her listen to her heart and follow that guidance? Determination. It's one of the qualities she emphasizes. "Those who have this determination," she reveals, "have nothing to fear."

How determined are you to live joyfully and peacefully? How determined are you to keep on going when the going gets tough? How much do you persevere when nothing seems to go your way? When I began writing, approximately twenty years ago, I received more than a hundred rejection letters from magazines where I submitted my articles. There were times I felt like giving up. Even my close friends and some family members encouraged me to seek another profession. "You can't pay your bills on dreams," they would tell me. "Look for a job that offers security, a regular monthly paycheck and normal hours," was something I regularly heard. Well, I'm glad to say I didn't listen to them. I was determined to be true to my vision and dreams. I chose not to buy into their limited thinking. I believed that with God as my source, anything was possible. Now many years later, I've written four books and over five hundred articles. I often schedule my articles with magazine editors up to a year in advance, and editors approach me to write articles for their magazines. Determination and perseverance always pay off.

I love the following words which appear in Richard Bach's insightful book, *Illusions*: "You are never given a wish without also being given the power to make it true. You may have to work for it, however."

Are you willing to do what it takes to become master of your life? How much do you really want to reach the top of the mountain? Do you have the sheer will to give it your all, and then some, even when the odds of attaining your goal appear to be insurmountable?

I have great respect for world-class athletes who, against all odds, become winners. Take Greg LeMond, for example. In 1985, he finished second in the Tour de France, a twenty-three-day 2,025-mile cycling race through France. Then in 1986, Lemond became the first non-European ever to win the tour at the age of twenty-five. With his prime competitive years still ahead of him, Greg LeMond was on top of the world.

Within a few months, however, his life turned upside down. In April of 1987, LeMond was with his uncle and his brother-in-law on a hunting trip when he was hit by a shotgun blast. His brother-in-law had accidentally shot him. LeMond took approximately sixty No. 2-sized pellets in his back and side. He could barely breathe — his right lung had collapsed. His liver and kidney were hit. So were his diaphragm and intestine. In addition, two pellets lodged in the lining of his heart. LeMond thought he was going to die as he lay in the field waiting for the helicopter that would take him to a hospital. His main concern was whether he would ever see his wife and kids again.

While in the hospital, LeMond learned about real pain. A tube to draw blood out of his collapsed lung had to be inserted into his chest without anesthesia, and it remained there for a week. He had thought he was used to pain because he had pushed himself so hard in competition. But the pain he felt while racing his bike was nothing compared with the pain he felt as he fought for his life.

Miraculously, none of the damage was irreparable. Doctors left thirty shotgun pellets in LeMond, including the two in the lining of his heart. They doubted that LeMond would ever race again. Eight weeks later, however, with sheer determination and perseverance, he started the long road back. Before the accident, LeMond weighed 151 pounds, with a total body fat content of 4 percent. When he was able to start training again, he weighed 137 pounds, with 17 percent body fat. In an effort to survive, his body had consumed vast amounts of its muscle.

He had a rough two years coming back. Months after the accident, just when he was beginning to show signs of real progress, he had an emergency appendectomy. The following year, he had to have surgery to repair an infected tendon in his right shin, forcing him to miss the Tour de France for a second straight year. PDM, the Dutch team, with which LeMond had signed a two-year deal in 1987, wanted to cut his 1989 salary by $200,000. The team had lost all confidence in him. But he had not lost confidence in himself. He believed he could come back, and he didn't give up. Well, you probably know the end of the story.

LeMond did enter the 1989 Tour de France, along with 155 other riders and came out the winner. Determination makes all things possible.

And then there's Pete Sampras, one of my favorite pro tennis players. Did you see him play in and win the 1990 U.S. Open Men's Tournament? At age nineteen, he's the youngest person to achieve that honor. In the tournament, he hit a hundred aces (unreturnable serves), many of which were clocked at 120 miles per hour. I love to watch him play! You can just see the determination and concentration on his face and in his movement. His entire tennis career has been that way — one of willing determination and perseverance. For years, he has been training by playing tennis four to five hours a day, running, cycling, lifting weights and eating healthy foods. He is very goal-oriented. He made it to the top because he went after what he wanted and gave it his all.

Jimmy Connors was also very inspiring to me in the 1991 U.S. Open Tennis Tournament. At age 39, when most professional tennis players have retired, Jimmy had the will and compelling determination to keep on practicing and to come back, even when all the odds were against him. He displayed the will and perseverance to produce his best efforts in the face of fierce competition. His playing is a great metaphor for all of us in life to meet life's challenges with gusto, determination, and enthusiasm, and make it to the mountaintop.

Do you have what it takes to reach the top of the mountain? If you think you don't, dispel that thought immediately. Because you are co-creator with God, you have the power and ability to achieve your heart's desire. Let your perseverance and determination fuel your mind and body into action. Believe in yourself. Know that God is your strength and power. When you feel that connection, peace will be your constant companion.

Choose to live peacefully and never give up. Your success is assured!

The Spirit is Self-Propelling. It is Absolute and All. It is Self-Existent and has all life within Itself.

Ernest Holmes, *The Science of Mind*

Taking Inventory and Action

1. Do you give up easily?

2. When the going gets tough, do you loose perspective and clarity?

3. Is there something you've wanted to achieve but didn't initiate because you believed you didn't have what it takes?

4. How many times have you started a health and fitness program only to fail because you lacked determination and perseverance?

5. Do you allow appearances to run you off your path or turn you in the opposite direction of your vision?

6. Refuse to be discouraged if things don't seem to be going your way. See with God's eyes.

7. Be clear on your goals and never let anyone or anything cause you to doubt your power and ability to achieve your high vision. Be determined.

8. Make a list of some household chores you've been putting off. Begin today with one from your list. Complete the project.

9. When the going gets tough, the tough get going. Don't give up! Talk things over with God.

10. Live in the presence of God.

Today's Affirmation

I keep my sights focused on my goal and refuse to get discouraged. Divine love, through me, gives me the strength and determination to follow my heart and achieve my heart's desires. I will persevere for I know my success is assured. With God as my co-creator, anything is possible.

CHAPTER 33

Intuition

Let us be silent that we may hear
the whispers of God.

Ralph Waldo Emerson

Have you ever been thinking of someone you haven't heard from in a long time when suddenly that person called? Did you ever have the feeling that a friend was in trouble, contact him and find out that he was, indeed? Or have you ever met someone and somehow known that this person was going to be your spouse? Some call it a sixth sense, a hunch, a gut feeling, going on instinct or just knowing deep inside. Psychologists call it intuition — an obscure mental function that provides us with information so that we know without knowing how we know. I refer to it as God's whispering to us and giving us direction. In the heart-warming book, *Words That Heal*, Douglas Bloch writes,

> We live in a world that is undergoing rapid transformation. The old rules and guidelines are no longer valid. There is only one source of information and guidance that you can depend upon — the voice of divinity within you.

How tuned-in are you to this voice within? When you get a message, do you usually write it off as nothing? I have found from countless experiences that the more we pay attention to our intuition, the more we'll find ourselves in the right place at the right time. Case in point. A few years ago, I was driving around Santa Monica doing some errands. I passed by a quaint little cafe and, although I wasn't hungry, I felt I should go in and get something to eat. The cafe wasn't very crowded; only four other tables were occupied. I ordered a salad. Just as it arrived at my table, I noticed the man sitting next to me grabbing his throat. His face was turning red. I knew he was choking. Since I am trained as an emergency medical technician, I quickly went over and asked if he could talk or breathe. He said no and gestured to me that some food was lodged in his throat. I immediately stood him up and performed the Heimlich maneuver. Out popped the food. While all this was happening, the other patrons of the cafe just watched in disbelief. They applauded when it was over. I think I received more hugs that day than I usually do in a week. Most importantly, however, I learned how valuable it is to pay attention to and act on your intuition. I have no doubt that God was making sure I was in the right place at the right time.

The key here is not just getting the message but listening to it and acting on it. According to Nancy Rosanoff, author of *Intuition Workout*, one study asked divorced couples when they first realized the relationship wasn't going to work out, and an astounding 80 percent replied, "before the wedding." Although something told them that the marriage was foolhardy, each couple stood together at the altar, either because they wished too strongly that their intuition was wrong or they didn't identify the message as a kind of knowing they could trust.

I consider myself very intuitive because I have worked on developing that faculty for many years. There are a few people in my life who afford me the opportunity to see my intuitive side in action. My special friend, McGyver, who lives in another state, is always picking up on my energy. We might not have talked for three weeks when I'll sit down to write him a letter. Before the letter is complete, he'll call to say hello. Or I'll get an inner signal to call him just when he's thinking of something he needs to ask me. I am the same way with my mother, who's my best friend. We are always picking up on each other's thoughts and feelings even though we can be thousands of miles apart. I'll get a signal that mom is nonplussed about something and I am supposed to call her. When I do, I usually find out she was hoping I'd call. It can really be quite enjoyable and fun when you let your intuition be your guide.

So how can we develop the intuitive side of our being? The best way is just to sit still and listen. Turn within and pay attention. Too often we run away from ourselves, filling up our lives with constant activity. We don't take time to be still. Often creative geniuses report that their "real world" discoveries are nothing other than self-discoveries from a deep silence within. When someone asked William Blake where he got his ideas, he replied that he stuck his finger through the floor of Heaven and pulled them down. And Michelangelo turned away the congratulations someone proffered him on turning a block of stone into a man, saying the man was in there all the time and just required a little help in getting out. Franz Kafka wrote:

> There is no need to leave the house. Stay at your desk and listen. Don't even listen, just wait. Don't even wait, be perfectly still and alone. The world will unmask itself to you, it can't do otherwise. It will rise before you in raptures.

Intuition can be nurtured in a variety of ways — through prayer, contemplation, walks in nature or time spent alone gazing out a window or thinking. The more you act on your intuitive hunches, the stronger and more readily available they become. As you become more sensitive to your oneness with God and life, you will become more intuitive. Part of receiving those inner messages clearly comes when you learn to give up the analyzing, reasoning, doubting and limiting part of your mind. Practice makes perfect. And intuition is infallible when we anchor ourselves in the consciousness of God. In *The Tao of Pooh*, Benjamin Hoff shares:

> The masters of life know the Way. They listen to the voice within them, the voice of wisdom and simplicity, the voice that reasons beyond cleverness and knows beyond knowledge. That voice is not just the power and property of a few, but has been given to everyone.

Turning into yourself is the basis for being yourself, all that you were created to be — and not just any old self, but your best self. As Dag Hammarskjold, former secretary general of the United Nations, observed, "What you have to attempt [is] to be yourself, to become a mirror in which, according to the degree of purity of heart you have attained, the greatness of life will be reflected."

Choose to live peacefully and intuitively.

> The most beautiful things in the world cannot be seen or even touched. They must be felt with the heart.
>
> Helen Keller

Taking Inventory and Action

1. Do you keep yourself so busy that you don't have time to be still and listen?

2. When you receive an inner "hunch," do you usually write it off as something inconsequential?

3. When you have strong feelings about another person who's not nearby, do you ever contact that person to see if there's any connection with your inner signals?

4. Do your doubts, opinions and limited thinking interfere with your inner guidance?

5. Take time each day to "center" yourself and to simply listen to your inner voice.

6. Go out in nature and listen to her sounds. I have found this to be a wonderful way to nurture my intuition.

7. Be one with God, trust your intuition and be willing to act.

8. Next time you get inner guidance to telephone someone or make contact, do it.

9. Be still, trust and know that you are guided by love.

10. Live in the presence of God.

Today's Affirmation

I am a clear and open channel for the power of love to flow through me. In quietness and confidence, I wait for my guidance. I listen to my intuition and act on what I hear.

CHAPTER 34

Surrender, Let Go and Release

The most exquisite paradox…as soon as you give
it all up, you can have it all…. As long as you want
power, you can't have it. The minute you don't
want power, you'll have more than you
ever dreamed possible.

Ram Dass, *Be Here Now*

When I began this forty-day spiritual discipline of fasting and prayer, I knew it would be successful only to the degree that I surrendered everything to God. So a couple of days before I started, I began looking at everything in my life — all my fears, doubts, worries, and frustrations; all my goals and dreams; all my relationships. The day before I began to fast, I wrote down the totality of my life and surrendered it all to God, knowing that "it is the Father that dwells in me that does the works." (John 14:10). I needed to learn it was enough just to *be*.

If you're like I am, you go through days when you wonder whether you have the wisdom and power just to make it through the day. We need to let go of that concern and trust God to do the necessary work. God gives us dreams, then supplies everything necessary to turn those dreams into reality. We must step aside and allow the divine presence to manifest through us. As *The Course of Miracles* asserts, "It cannot be that it is hard to do the task that Christ appointed you to do, since it is He who does it."

Life is really a process of receiving and releasing; taking in and giving out. Just as you must inhale and exhale to live, you must practice receiving and letting go in all parts of your life. There is no way to know God and true freedom until you know the gift of release, the beauty of letting go. Surrender is traveling lightly through life, ready to release what is no longer helpful or what is creating a blockage to your awareness of God's love and presence. In total surrender, you are given everything. What a deal!

I love what Jessica Tandy said shortly after she won the Academy Award for best actress in *Driving Miss Daisy*. "I never compete. When things are right, they come. When they're not, there's always something else to do." Ah! Sweet surrender.

The well-known and loved Unity minister, Eric Butterworth, also practices letting go and giving way to life. He says that each New Year's Day he goes through his closet and gives away any clothing or items that he has not used during the past year. This releasing of the old and unnecessary, he explains, makes way for the new, the greater and the better.

Surrender means simply allowing things to unfold in divine order instead of trying to force them to happen. I've noticed in my life that most of my difficult moments come from holding on: to unhappy relationships, to past unhealthy behavior patterns, to goals and dreams that no longer serve my highest good or to preconceived notions of how my life ought to look or be. Surrender means being open to new possibilities and, as Butterworth writes in *The Concentric Perspective*, to "give way to life!"

In the marvelous book, *Attaining Personal Greatness*, Melanie Brown writes:

> Everyone has a deeply personal rainbow. What works for another might not work for you, and vice versa. In allowing ourselves to be who we most definitely are, we need to grant others the same privilege. Surrender in relationships — when self-knowledge, integrity, and simplicity are also present — is not a martyr's sacrifice of self, but a sign of maturity. When we refuse to let go in love for fear of losing control, a half-hearted relationship results.

All the people I've met who are truly creative and successful know that surrender is part of the program. They realize that it's the higher power within them who is really doing the work; they are just the vehicles of expression. J.S. Bach said that although he played "the notes in order, as they are written, it is God who makes the music."

When you let go of all blockages — when you clear all your channels — and surrender to God, then you can fully express the best of who you are in every thought, word and action. Jesus was able to accomplish what He did because He kept the channel of His mind open and receptive for this power to flow through it. "Fighting any adverse condition," Ernest Holmes says, "only increases its power over us, because we are making a reality of it. . . . Resistance is the offspring of fear and ignorance; nonresistance is the offspring of love."

When we surrender our lives to God, the veil of ignorance is lifted and all things become new. No qualifications here. Your entire world is changed from ego-directorship to reflect the Heaven that is. In 1926, William James wrote:

> The further limits of our being plunge, it seems to me, into an altogether other dimension of existence from the visible world. Name it the mystical region, or the supernatural region, which-ever you choose . . . . When we commune with it, work is actually done upon our finite personality, for we are turned into new men.

Here is an exercise you might want to do to assist in letting go of the past and clearing your channels for divinity to flow. Using a notebook or paper, write a page or more about one of your deep inner hurts. Maybe it's something you've never shared with any-one. Perhaps you've kept it hidden in the deep recesses of your mind and have been afraid to look at it yourself. Open up. Breathe deeply. Be willing to embrace your fear or pain. Write down how you were hurt and what it felt like. If another person was involved, let that person know in writing how you felt. Allow yourself to feel any emotions of sadness, heartache, anger or pain. When you've done that, go on to another page and describe another incident, and then another and another. After you have filled several pages, read them over a couple of times as you ask God to help you see the past in a different light. Ask for guidance so you can release and let go of the hurt and pain and take with you the wisdom and love you garnered. Let God show you how to forgive and love again. This may take some time — a few days or even weeks, but it is well worth it. When it feels right for you, take these pieces of paper and, creating some type of ritual or ceremony, burn them. See your past hurts and pain becoming ashes before your eyes. You are closing a chapter so you can move on and write a great new adventure, filled with comedy, romance and success.

I understand that letting go and surrender may frighten you at first until you discover its enriching and liberating effects in your life. As Veronica Ray wrote in *A Design for Growth*, "It's like learning to swim. If we thrash about in the water tense and fearful, we'll sink as surely as a stone. But if we completely relax and let go, the water will lift us up and we'll float. We can now relax into the flow of the river of life, trusting our Higher Power to take care of us."

My spiritual teacher, Paramahansa Yogananda, in one of his lectures said:

Surrender yourself to God and you will find that your life will become like a beautiful melody. If you try to do everything in the consciousness of God, you will see with joy that every day He is choosing certain duties for you to perform.

Are you choosing to *Let Go and Let God* or are you trying to force things to happen? Are you holding on to the past or living in sweet surrender to a glorious and peaceful present and future? Do you want to continue repeating the past or would you like to experience Heaven on earth? The choice is yours. In faith, let go of everything you think you were, are and want to be and surrender your life to the light. Live in the consciousness of God. Maybe the following passage will inspire you, as it did me, to embrace sweet surrender:

LET GO

To Let Go does not mean to stop caring, it means I can't do it for someone else.
To Let Go is not to cut myself off, it's the realization I can't control another.
To Let Go is not to enable, but to allow learning from natural consequences.

To Let Go is to admit powerlessness, which means the outcome is not in my hands.

To Let Go is not to try to change or blame another, it's to make the most of myself.

To Let Go is not to care for, but to care about.

To Let Go is not to fix, but to be supportive.

To Let Go is not to judge, but to allow another to be a human being.

To Let Go is not to be in the middle arranging all the outcomes, but to allow others to effect their own destinies.

To Let Go is not to be protective, it's to permit another to face reality.

To Let Go is not to criticize or regulate anyone, but to try to become what I dream I can be.

To Let Go is to Fear less, and to Love more.

Anonymous

I know it might seem scary to let go of the familiar for something uncertain. It takes faith and courage. Just take the first step. God will do the rest.

Choose to live peacefully and surrender all that you are and want to be to God.

God is ready to give great things when we are ready . . . to give up everything.

Meister Eckhart

Taking Inventory and Action

1. Are you the type of person who likes to be in control of everything and everyone?

2. What from your past do you need to release? What no longer serves your highest good?

3. What are you afraid would happen if you surrendered everything to God?

4. What would your life look like if you carried no excess baggage from the past?

5. Do you have faith that God can make all things new?

6. Letting go and letting God requires faith. Take that first step of faith today and ask God to teach you what it means to surrender your life to Him.

7. Let go of unsatisfying relationships, preconceived notions of how life ought to be and goals that are no longer appropriate.

8. Be fully awake and wholehearted in what you could be if you got yourself out of the way and let the divine circuits take over. Stay open to possibility.

9. When your life looks the darkest and you don't know what to do, talk with God and you'll see the way to fly. "What the caterpillar calls the end of the world, the master calls a butterfly." — Richard Bach

10. Live in the presence of God.

Today's Affirmation

I allow my inner wisdom to direct and guide me in everything I do. I know that when I let go and let God, everything works out for my highest good. I go forth today to meet every challenge with faith and courage. Not my will but Thy will be done.

CHAPTER 35

Happiness and Service

I don't know what your destiny will be but the one
thing I do know; the only ones among you who will
be truly happy will be those who have sought
and found how to serve.

Albert Schweitzer

The search for happiness, in itself,
will prove to be disheartening. For happiness will not be found in
people, places and things; it is a quality of the heart, a byproduct
of living a life centered in God. Happiness begins inside us.

Changing one's approach from an outward view to an inward
one was the basic premise of the work of Charles and Myrtle
Fillmore, founders of the Unity Church. Their work now reaches
more than three million people in nearly every country in the
world. The Unity view turns over the cares and concerns of life to
God and sees God everywhere.

Connie Fillmore writes in an issue of *Unity* magazine:

All the time we think we're looking for something outside ourselves,
we're really looking for something that lies easily within our grasp
—as the poet says, "Closer is He than breathing, and nearer than
hands and feet." No matter what the question, God is the answer.
No matter what the need, God is the fulfillment. No matter what
the emptiness, God is the fullness. No matter what the lack, God
is the abundance. No matter what you think you're looking for,
you're really looking for a greater experience of God.

When happiness is lacking in our lives, all we need to do is seek God. It's important to realize that happiness is not the result of fulfilling some desire or achieving a goal or even escaping some difficulty. Happiness comes from our awareness that God is our source and has given us the kingdom already. Happiness is a choice. Thinking that you'll be happy when circumstances change or people change keeps happiness just beyond your reach.

One way to cultivate happiness is by being of service to others. In an issue of his *Truth Journal*, Roy Eugene Davis writes:

> Generous people may be more emotionally and spiritually healthy. This is the opinion of researchers who have examined the lives of persons who demonstrate their concerned interest by helping others in need and by actively participating in useful community projects.

Davis reports that people who are emotionally healthy and spiritually aware are naturally more in tune with their world and naturally want to contribute to the happiness and security of their neighbors and friends in the extended world community. Self-centered people tend to be, if not actually neurotic, at least self-focused and caught up in their real or imagined personal problems.

In *Secrets of Forever Happiness*, Davis explains how any self-responsible person can be as happy as he or she decides to be, and that the basis for true and lasting happiness is not in outer relationships but in the understanding and experience of one's own being. When inner satisfaction is known, outer harmony naturally and spontaneously unfolds. Davis encourages the reader to dedicate his or her life to the service of humanity and to become a servant of God.

We were put here on earth not to see through one another but to see one another through. As you give, so shall you receive. Giving brings joy and puts us in touch with the love that we are. The great Chinese philosopher, Lao Tzu, wrote that "kindness in words creates confidence, kindness in thinking creates profoundness, and kindness in giving creates love."

When you give of yourself, you'll feel better about yourself.

Members of Alcoholics Anonymous learned long ago that reaching out to help someone else give up drinking can make it easier to beat their own addiction. Recovering alcoholics are expected to call or visit their struggling peers, to be there when they're needed, even if that's at three o'clock in the morning. They quickly realize that being in the role of helper increases their inner strength and helps them overcome their own problems.

It's been found that helping others also brings real physical benefits, according to epidemiologist James House and his colleagues at the University of Michigan's Survey Research Center. They studied 2,700 people in Tecumseh, Michigan, for more than a decade to see how their social relationships affected their health. Regular volunteer work, more than any other activity, was shown to dramatically increase life expectancy. Men who did no volunteer work were two-and-a-half times as likely to die during the study as men who volunteered at least once a week. (The health benefits of volunteerism were less clear for women — perhaps because most women already spend a lot of time looking after other people, whether they join a volunteer group or not.)

The study pointed out that one key benefit of volunteering is that it's a way of connecting with people. Some of the data from House's study indicate that those with many social contacts tend to live longer than more isolated individuals. People who spent a lot of time reading, listening to the radio or watching television, as opposed to being more social, had a higher-than-average mortality rate.

Corroborating these findings was one of the largest surveys ever done by epidemiologist Lisa Berkman of Yale and H. Leonard Syme of the University of California, Berkeley. They studied nearly 5,000 residents of Alameda County, California, over a nine-year period. What they found was that those who were unmarried, had few friends or relatives and shunned community organizations were more than twice as likely to die during that time than people who had these social relationships. This was found to be true regardless of race, income, level of activity and other lifestyle factors.

So get out there in the mainstream of life and find ways to participate, to be of service, to give of yourself.

When we think of giving, often what comes to mind is giving our money to worthy causes. In *Bus 9 to Paradise*, Leo Buscaglia sheds some light on how we can expand our view of giving.

We sometimes take a narrow view of what it means to give. We associate giving with money. Of course money is important, but there is no amount that can buy the value of someone who will sit with a dying person who would otherwise be alone. Or someone who will deliver a warm meal to an elderly housebound individual, or volunteer to teach reading, or just listen to a person who is afraid, lonely or rejected.

What it all boils down to for me is being a servant of God. This idea is beautifully emphasized in Robert Muller's book, *The Birth of a Global Civilization*. We best serve God's will by seeing to our spiritual, mental, emotional and physical health and by living a disciplined, wholesome life. As we commit our lives to God and stay aware of our oneness with God, we will be shown in what capacity we can best serve. We must live a committed life. Martin Luther King, Jr., just two months before his death, stated that the only possession he would have to leave behind was a "committed life." Twenty years later, a national holiday commemorates his life of service.

Take a close look at your life. See all the ways you can be of service and spread some happiness. Maybe it's a smile or listening to someone's heartache. Perhaps it's giving your money to an organization or person that's doing some valuable work. Extending your peacefulness to others is a beautiful way to serve humanity. It doesn't matter what form your service takes; if you do it with heart, everyone wins and all lives are enriched.

Choose to live peacefully and as a servant of God.

Consciously or unconsciously, every one of us does render some service or other. If we cultivate the habit of doing this service deliberately, our desire for service will steadily grow stronger, and will make not only for our own happiness, but that of the world at large.

Mahatma Gandhi

Taking Inventory and Action

1. In what ways do you give of your time to others?
2. In what ways in your life can you be of greater service?

3. Do you look to others to bring you happiness?

4. Do you ever think that you'll be happy when you get the perfect job, or you meet the perfect person, or you buy a house or lose twenty pounds?

5. How can you be a more committed servant of God?

6. Make up your mind to be happy today no matter what happens.

7. Smile all day. A smile on your face puts a smile in your heart.

8. Reach out to others in need and let them know you care.

9. One of the best gifts you can give another is your peace of mind. Be peaceful and extend that peace to others.

10. Live in the presence of God.

Today's Affirmation

I know that my happiness is not dependent on any special person, place or thing but results from my recognition and acceptance of the divine love expressing itself through my life. I look for ways to let my light shine in service to others. Everywhere I look, I see opportunities to serve, and I do so joyfully and peacefully.

CHAPTER 36

Wholeness and Oneness

The Spirit of all Life seeks expression through those
individuals who, through Divine Love, open their
hearts to one another and reflect the Light so
all may live together in peace.

Rev. George Marks, Assistant Minister,
Founder's Church, Los Angeles, California

Ａs our changing, complex civilization approaches the twenty-first century, there is a greater need than ever to live life from a different perspective — a higher perspective; we must view the world from the top of the mountain rather than from deep in the valley. The need for a harmonious and unifying approach to living is now emerging as an absolute necessity. "Think Globally, Act Locally" is the slogan I see all around these days on bumper stickers. We can all make a difference on this planet with how we choose to live our lives. As Carl Jung wrote, "It all depends on how we look at things, and not on how they are in themselves." We must dwell on the harmony that underlies the universe. With clarity and inner guidance, we begin to see correlations between events and between circumstances. We see that everything works by the law of cause and effect. To expect otherwise is to have a fractured perspective. A fractured view of life brings mental confusion; an expansive, unified view heightens consciousness and invites wisdom.

This we know: All things are connected
Like the blood which unites one family.
All things are connected.
Whatever befalls the Earth
befalls the sons of the Earth.
Man did not weave the web of life.
He is merely a strand in it.
Whatever he does to the web,
  he does to himself.

Chief Seattle, upon surrendering his tribal lands, 1856

For peace to exist, you must first love yourself and then love each other. As Gandhi said, "Peace between countries must rest on a solid foundation of love between individuals." In simply taking loving care of ourselves, we can enrich the quality of life on this planet. *You* make a difference.

Our bodies are made up of trillions of cells — all of these cells constitute our person. In order to maintain perfect health, each of these cells must operate at peak performance. If we have sick or weak cells, then our healthy cells must work harder so that the body as a whole can be healthy.

Our planet is like a body, and we are all its individual cells. We are not separate from our fellow humans. There is no room for negative thinking, a withholding of forgiveness, bitterness toward others or selfishness. What happens in one area ultimately affects the whole of the world. It is our responsibility to this body that we call our planet to be a healthy, happy, peaceful cell that radiates only goodness, positiveness, oneness and love.

Although the physical body and the body of humanity work along the same principles of harmony and cooperation, there is one difference. The cells of the body don't choose how they function. Theirs is an inherent working and functioning wisdom that seems to take charge most of the time. But people do choose how they live and cooperate with one another. Harmony is not thrust upon us. We have a choice. And when we choose not to work together harmoniously, when we elect to stay separate and uncooperative, we experience collective illness — just as the body experiences disease when its components don't work well together. When we do work well together in cooperation, with compassion and peaceful hearts, we experience collective well-being — life as it is meant to be. This is the key to creating a world of peace and aliveness: harmonious cooperation.

I have long considered Albert Einstein one of the most brilliant minds of this century. Not only was he a scientist, he was a deep-thinking metaphysician who recognized the unity and oneness behind all life. He conveys that thought in this following passage:

> A human being is a part of the whole called by us "Universe," a part limited in time and space. He experiences himself, his thoughts and feelings, as something separated from the rest, a kind of optical delusion of his consciousness. This delusion is a kind of prison for us, restricting us to our personal desires and to affection for a few persons nearest to us. Our task must be to free ourselves from this prison by widening our circle of compassion to embrace all living creatures and the whole of nature in its beauty.

The separation and division that has so long colored our thoughts and beliefs regarding our lives on this planet must now be examined and corrected. To create peace on earth, we must stop dividing the world, the nations, the races, the religions, the sexes, the ages and the resources, and know that it's time to come together and live in harmony and love. Jesus, the greatest teacher who ever lived, said "Love one another."

In his extraordinary book, *The Hundredth Monkey*, Ken Keyes, Jr., tells of a phenomenon that scientists observed when they studied the eating habits of Macaque monkeys. One monkey discovered that by washing sweet potatoes before eating them, they tasted better. She taught her mother and friends until one day there were ninety-nine monkeys who knew how to wash their sweet potatoes. The next day, when the hundredth monkey learned how to wash sweet potatoes, an amazing thing happened. The rest of the colony miraculously knew how to wash sweet potatoes, too. Not only that, but monkeys on other islands all started washing their potatoes. Keyes applies this "hundredth monkey" phenomenon to humanity. When more of us individually choose to make a difference with our lives — when we realize we do make a difference and start *acting* like that, more and more of us will hop on the bandwagon, until we reach the "millionth person" and peace spreads across the globe!

Let's take a closer look at the incredible wholeness and oneness of our bodies. On a television program not long ago, I saw something that dissolved the outer limits of my perception of wholeness and the body. In this study, a woman gave a blood sample from which the white cells were isolated and then attached, with an electrode, to an electroencephalograph (EEG). The woman was then put in a room next door, not in any way connected to her extracted cells. She was asked questions, some of which evoked an emotional response. The response was registered by her cells in the room next door.

Next, she was asked to walk in a high-crime, dangerous area of downtown San Diego at night to see if her extracted cells could pick up her emotions from a distance of several miles. At one point, she was approached and harassed by a pimp. Immediately her cells back in the lab room registered her fear.

Don't ever underestimate the power of thought and the wholeness of your body, mind and spirit. View life as a unity. Recognize that throughout all life, there is oneness. We all share the commonality of spirit. Even scientists and theologians are now coming together to recognize and affirm the one force working behind everything. In *God and the Astronomers*, astrophysicist Robert Jastrow writes:

> For the scientist . . . the story ends like a bad dream. He has scaled the mountains of ignorance; he is about to conquer the highest peak, as he pulls himself over the final rock, he is greeted by a band of theologians who have been sitting there for centuries.

Albert Szent-Gyorgyi, Nobel Prize-winning biochemist, writes about syntropy, a drive toward greater order as a fundamental principle of nature. This is an inherent drive of life to perfect itself and to reach higher and higher levels of organization, order and dynamic harmony, moving toward a synthesis of wholeness and self-perfection.

English physicist David Bohm, who was a colleague of Einstein, believes that the information of the entire universe is contained in each of its parts. Under all the separate things and events is a wholeness that is available to each part.

The way I like to approach oneness and wholeness is from a spiritual point of view. Your life is God's life. Your being and God's being are one. God is not only outside you but within you as well. The Rev. George Marks reminded me of this last month when I heard him give an inspiring sermon on "The Three Os." God is Omnipotent — all powerful; God is Omniscient — knowing all things; God is Omnipresent — present in all places at the same time. Isn't that fantastic? It's cause for celebration.

As I said at the beginning of this chapter, we live in a busy, constantly changing complex world. Yet beyond all the external movement there resides a divine, unchanging, ever-present spirit that is the source of all happiness, prosperity, joy and inner peace. We must open our hearts and receive this spirit of life. We must align ourselves with the purposes of Heaven and act in accord. When we do that we will have all of the natural forces working with us, supporting us, helping us.

> It is in our own heart, our own mind, our own consciousness, our own being, where we live twenty-four hours a day, awake or asleep, that that eternal share of the Infinite comes to us, because every man is some part of the essence of God, not as a fragment, but as a totality.
>
> Ernest Holmes, *Sermon by the Sea*

As a constant reminder that we are one with God and each other, I practice this beautiful Indian salutation, *Namaste*. Translated it means "I honor (or salute) the divinity you are (in you)." In the East many people greet their friends with folded hands and the word *Namaste*. I usually do this silently and without folding my hands. When I meet someone, or simply think of someone, I inwardly acknowledge, "I honor the divinity you are." In this way I bless myself by being reminded of the truth and bless others by seeing their real spiritual essence and the spiritual connection between us. This salutation sounds a note of reverence and spiritual awareness. Practiced with faith and dynamic intent, it helps to build the kind of inner attitude that externalizes itself in harmonious human relations. *Namaste* is also a way to develop and demonstrate the ability to function simultaneously at two levels — that of the personality and that of the soul. Finally, it's a gentle reminder that behind all the changes and complexities of our world, there is that omnipotent, omniscient and omnipresent loving light that also resides at the center of our hearts. When you rest in that knowledge, you float in an ocean of peace.

Choose to live peacefully and see God in everything and in everyone, including within yourself.

> Whenever you choose, you walk away from your maps and models for times of being, times of insight, times of peaceful attunement with All That Is. On these occasions you leave behind your beliefs and ideas, no matter what culture or society or geography you are living in. You leave behind all the forms of your understanding, no matter how accurate you believe those forms to be. You leave them all behind, mere foam on the surface. You relax into a deeper knowing. Your identity expands beyond your individuality. You experience yourself in perfect unity with the external Spirit at the source of your life. You rest in that knowledge, in that oneness, in the infinite ocean of eternity's peace.
>
> Ken Carey, *Return of the Bird Tribes*

Taking Inventory and Action

1. At what times do you feel most connected with other people?

2. When you are not feeling very good with yourself, do you find you feel most separate from other people?

3. When you are consistent with your exercises or wholesome nutrition program, does that result in a more positive attitude about yourself and life?

4. Take a close look at all areas of your life. Do you see a cause-and-effect relationship between what you believe to be true and what you receive or have in your life?

5. Do you know that God is the essence of who you are and is there in your heart just waiting to give you the Kingdom of Heaven? Remember, by our awareness of our oneness with Him, we share His powers and attributes.

6. Take a walk in nature and seek the presence of God in all the beauty around you. God is everywhere.

7. When someone smiles at you, realize that is God smiling at you. When someone is upset or angry at you, still choose to focus on the divinity in that person.

8. In all relationships, understand that we are all basically the same. We all just want to be loved, appreciated and supported.

9. Between all hearts are the connecting harp strings of Heaven playing beautiful celestial music. Listen. Pay attention. Focus on your shared divinity. Feel the magic of what happens when you align with the Spirit of life. Open your hearts. Rejoice and celebrate. The Kingdom has come.

10. Live in the presence of God.

Today's Affirmation

I am lovingly connected to all beings and to all creation. I see God in everyone I meet and feel His presence in my heart and in my life. I rejoice in His oneness knowing that I have the Spirit of life supporting me and loving me as I journey to the top of the mountain. I am one with God.

CHAPTER 37

Environmental Peace

The supreme reality of our time is the
vulnerability of our planet.

John F. Kennedy

The earth is our home, and a home
is something to take care of and protect, not abuse and destroy.
Even though you are just one person, you can make a difference.
It's true. Everything you do contributes to the quality of life on
this planet — from the type of products you buy, to how you heat
your house, to the type of food you eat.

This is not to say that corporations or the government should
be let off the hook. Not at all. We must demand a cleaner, safer
environment and a healthier world. And we must, of course, hold
industry and government accountable for the many actions they
take that affect the health of the earth and the future of the planet.

But we are responsible, too. In *Save Our Planet*, Diane
MacEachern reminds us:

> This is our world, and it's the only one we've got. By making small
> but substantial decisions about the things we do, the goods we
> buy, and the laws we support, we can make a better life for
> ourselves while helping to ensure a world that's fit for the future.
> If we expect others to be accountable, then we must be held
> accountable, too, starting with our own lives.

Environmental peace begins, I believe, with our attitudes about
the earth. I see the planet earth as a living, breathing organism.
Her spirit breathes; she takes care of her children — provides

them an abundance of food and material for clothing and shelter and gives them air to breathe. She is totally balanced, in perfect equilibrium and harmony.

The Native Americans had a close connection with Mother Earth and her spirit. They had a sacred relationship with her, an attitude of reverence for her. What is your relationship with our home?

In *Return of the Bird Tribes*, Ken Carey offers this:

The self to reflect on is the self that you truly are — the Creator, the Eternal One, the spirit of God. You reflect on those aspects of the Great Spirit that manifest before you as the men, the women, the children, the plants, the animals, the crystals, the creatures of the world entrusted to your care. First and foremost you are a steward of your immediate world. You care for the earth, not in some nebulous way, but *directly* as an individual representative of God. You take responsibility for bringing love and understanding into every environment through which you pass.

As the birds welcome the morning sun with their song, when you act totally in life, you welcome the Great Spirit into your world. You become a conscious cell in the awakening earth. The physical atoms of your body sing together, vibrating in perfect harmony. Your integrity and unity of being, your integration of purpose and expression brings resonance to everything you are and to everything you perceive. You become a natural channel for the vast and powerful energies of creations. Through you they flow into the healing and transformative work of these decades.

We know we must take care of our planet, yet some people continue to contribute toward her destruction. Why? Perhaps it's through ignorance and greed. Maybe they say, "I can't make a difference." But we all can. Whatever changes occur in the next ten years are up to us. It's not too late. But we can't wait. The earth needs our help. She needs our love and compassion and cooperation. She needs our discrimination.

Discrimination is pure, detached love in action. Without discrimination, in regard to our planet, the future is in great danger. It seems to me that although we've made tremendous advances, we still lack discrimination. We have difficulty seeing how our choices and values are violating the unity of life. For example, the more unrecycled paper we use and throw away and the more animal products we eat, the more we are adding to the indiscriminate cutting down of forests. I think that this lack of discrimination more than anything else in life is causing our world to become very fragile.

The spirit of life that runs through our bodies is the same spirit that pulsates through our planet and connects us. All of us are one with and part of an indivisible family. Love your Mother Earth. Let your perspective be one of unity and oneness.

Lewis Thomas envisioned the planet as one gigantic cell. In *The Lives of a Cell* he wrote:

> I have been trying to think of the Earth as a kind of organism, but it is no go. I cannot think of it this way. It is too big, too complex, with too many working parts lacking visible connections. The other night, driving through a hilly, wooded part of southern New England, I wondered about this. If not like an organism, what is it most like? Then, satisfactorily for that moment, it came to me: It is most like a single cell . . . . Viewed from the distance of the moon, the astonishing thing about the earth, catching the breath, is that it is alive. The photographs show the dry pounded surface of the moon in the foreground, dead as an old bone. Aloft, floating free beneath the moist, gleaming membrane of bright sky, is the rising earth, the only exuberant thing in this part of the cosmos. If you could look long enough, you would see the swirling of the great drifts of white cloud, covering and uncovering the half-hidden masses of land. If you had been looking for a very long geologic time, you could have seen the continents themselves in motion, drifting apart on their crustal plates, held afloat by the fire beneath. It has the organized, self-contained look of a live creature, full of information, marvelously skilled in handling the sun.

Isn't that fascinating — looking at the entire planet as one big cell? It makes sense to me. Just as each of our body's cells carry the blueprint for the entire body, our planet carries the blueprint for all life.

Atmospheric chemist James Lovelock has postulated a new, holistic way of understanding and appreciating the ecosystem that is earth. He calls his view Gaia. Lovelock posits that *all* living organisms on the planet, from the great whales to the tiny plankton they eat, make an integral contribution to their environment. Unlike Darwin, who believed in "the survival of the fittest" as the biological basis of evolution, Lovelock sees mutual benefit as the engine of biological progress. In the Age of Gaia, it's cooperation, not competition, that makes the world go 'round. In the twenty years since Lovelock first offered the Gaia hypothesis to explain the apparent self-regulation of the earth's atmosphere, the Gaia — named after the earth goddess of ancient Greece — has become synonymous with the concept of a totally integrated, self-organizing, self-regulating living planet of which we are an inextricable part. We are part of the living processes of the planet itself. We all share the sunlight, the air, the oceans, the water and other life forms from this planet-sized living system, the Gaia. Being an integral part of the living system, we are nourished and sustained by its currents of energy and patterns of organization. And as I said earlier, it's not only our bodies that share this life; the human spirit within every one of us depends, for its vitality, on the exuberant health of the natural world.

The more deeply we seek to heal our planet, the more we realize how essential spiritual resources are for solving the ecological crisis, for the threat to our outer world has its deepest roots in the inner environment of our own thoughts. "Only spiritual consciousness — realization of God's presence in oneself and in every other living being — can save the world," said Paramahansa Yogananda. At the dedication of the Prayer Room at the United Nations, Dag Hammarskjold observed:

> Man has reached a critical point in history, where he must turn to God to avoid the consequences of his own faulty thinking. We must pray, not a few of us, but all of us. We must pray simply, fervently, sincerely, and with increasing power as our faith grows. . . . The ability of every individual to seek divine help is a necessary link in the golden chain of harmony and peace. You can help change the world by your prayers and your prayerful action.

As we embrace this last decade before the millennium, I see more and more people realizing that our highest priority should be to find God. In finding Him within ourselves, we begin to see the same God in everyone. We begin to behave as brothers and sisters and friends toward one another and this home we all share — Mother Earth. Awakening to that consciousness will save our planet. As religion and ecology scholar Thomas Berry reminds us:

> If we have a wonderful sense of the divine it is because we live amid such awesome magnificence. If we have such refinement of emotion and sensitivity it is because of the delicacy and fragrance and indescribable beauty . . . in the world about us. If we have strength and grow in vigor of body and soul it is because the earthly community challenges us.

For those of you who would like to do more reading in this area of ecology, ecosystems, saving our planet and understanding our relationship to her, I suggest the following books: *The Ages of Gaia* by James Lovelock; *Diet for a New America* by John Robbins; *The Overview Effect* by Frank White; *The Home Planet* edited by Kevin Kelley; *The Sacred Landscape* written and compiled by Frederic Lehrman; *The Healing of the Planet Earth* by Alan Cohen; and *Save Our Planet* by Diane MacEachern. You might also want to contact the Aspen Institute on Global Change, which operates under the auspices of the Windstar Foundation (co-founded by John Denver). This institute is bringing together some of the world's top scientists and educators to discuss what we know and don't know about our environment.

Let's get down to the practical side and highlight some ways we can all help save our planet. Here are some of the tips I've written down from my research. See which things you can incorporate right away.

1. Don't waste water. Fix leaky faucets. When you take showers, make them five minutes or less. Shower instead of bathe. Install an energy-efficient shower head.
2. Recycle. Find a recycling center in your neighborhood or start one yourself. In my home, I have four bins: one for

glass, one for paper, one for cans and one for leftovers that I put into a compost heap and use on the garden.

3. Don't use aerosol sprays. Most contain chemicals that damage the atmosphere by destroying the thin layer of ozone that protects us from ultraviolet light. Use pump action sprays instead.

4. Shun disposable pens, razors and lighters, which end up in landfills and are not biodegradable.

5. Never dump motor oil, cleaning solvents or other toxic fluids down the drain or into storm drains, lest cancer-causing pollutants wind up in your town's water supply. Use your town's disposal center.

6. Don't use paper or plastic bags at the supermarket. Instead, take your own reusable bags or baskets.

7. Buy recycled goods, especially paper products.

8. Get a home energy checkup from your utility company.

9. Plant shade trees on the west side of your house. In summer, the leaves will block the sun and lower temperature indoors ten to fifteen degrees.

10. Cut back on animal and dairy products in your diet. Cattle require land that could be left as forests.

11. Buy an inexpensive insulation blanket for your water heater; turn water temperature down to 120 degrees to save energy and money.

12. Buy organic produce whenever possible. Or ask your grocer to stock organic produce. I have found in my local markets that if enough people ask, they'll do it. Grow sprouts in your own kitchen.

13. Organize carpools, take the bus or ride the train whenever possible. This will reduce auto emissions and slow the greenhouse effect. Better yet, walk, ride a bike or rollerskate.

14. Use cloth diapers. Disposable, plastic diapers burden landfills.

15. Line-dry clothes or keep your dryer's lint screen clean.

16. Buy rechargeable batteries for appliances. Nonchargeable batteries contain toxic substances that eventually leak into the environment.

17. Use hand-powered mowers and gardening tools instead of electric ones.

18. Use a hand-powered can opener instead of an electric one.

19. If you eat tuna, buy it only from companies that release the dolphins that get caught in their tuna nets.

20. Buy products in bulk instead of in small, wasteful packaging.

21. Buy products that were not inhumanely tested on animals.

22. Check tire pressure. Under-inflated tires make a car use extra fuel.

23. Don't wear real fur — it looks better on the animals.

24. Plant trees. They provide oxygen.

25. Get in touch with your own divinity. When you do that, you will feel your oneness with Mother Earth and want to do everything possible to take care of her.

There is so much we can all do to help make the world a better place to live. The survival of our planet depends on all of us — on you and on me. When you come from that awareness and act on it, transformation occurs. We can create a peaceful, healthy planet. My vision is bright and clear.

Choose to live peacefully and love and take care of your Mother Earth.

We don't inherit the earth from our parents, we borrow it from our children.

Anonymous

Taking Inventory and Action

1. Have you ever looked at a picture of our planet taken from far out in space? How does it make you feel when you see that picture?

2. In what better ways in your home can you save water?

3. Have you ever taken a walk out in nature and felt all the ways she enriches, sustains and nurtures you?

4. When you eat a meal, have you ever given thought to where the bread, produce and grains come from? Mother Earth provides everything for us.

5. Look through your home-cleaning products and see if you can use only those that are nontoxic and biodegradable.

6. One simple thing you can do to help make your environment a nicer place is to pick up litter.

7. Bring more plants into your home; they provide oxygen.

8. Give trees as gifts. Another nice gift is a cloth carry-all bag that your friends can use for all types of shopping.

9. Look within yourself and ask for guidance on how you can help save the planet. Be still. Listen. Act on what you hear.

10. Live in the presence of God.

Today's Affirmation

Planet Earth is my home. She provides for and takes care of all her children. I dedicate myself to living in complete harmony with Mother Earth.

CHAPTER 38

Living in the Presence of God

The most important discovery of my whole life is
that one can take a little rough cabin and transform it
into a palace just by flooding it with God. When one
has spent many months in a little house like this in
daily thoughts about God, the very entering of the
house, the very sight of it as one approaches,
starts associations which set the heart
tingling and the mind flowing.

Brother Lawrence, *Practicing His Presence*

P*racticing His Presence*, a book
that is more than three hundred years old, began to have a
profound effect on my spiritual life when I received my first copy
in 1976. Brother Lawrence, the author, is little known beyond the
words he left us. We do know that he was born Nicholas Herman
in French Lorraine in 1611. He was a soldier and then a footman.
In 1666, he entered a religious community called the Carmelites,
located in Paris. He became a lay brother among the devotees to
Christ, and he took the name Brother Lawrence.

He spent the rest of his years in this community, dying there at
the age of approximately eighty. He was known within the community, and later outside it, for his quiet and serene faith, and for
his simple experience of the presence of God. He dedicated his
time in the community to being aware of God's presence as much
as possible — no matter what he was doing. His book includes
some of his letters about his experience and some of his diary
writings. It inspires me to live the way he describes and to
cultivate the habit of being aware of God's presence.

This has been my goal during this forty-day spiritual rejuvenation program. I have tried to be in communion with God during all my waking hours. When I wash my hair, I think of God's hands washing my hair. When I write or work in my garden, I believe that God's hands are doing the work. Trying always to focus on God hasn't been easy. In the beginning, at least half of the time, I would be distracted from my purpose. After much practice, I can now stay focused on God about seventy percent of my waking hours.

I have learned so much from this experience. I see God everywhere — in nature, in other people, in the little things that occupy my everyday activities. I've discovered a joyous, profound peace in this. Brother Lawrence's words, better than mine, can describe the joy that comes from practicing His presence.

This concentration upon God is strenuous, but everything else has ceased to be so. I think more clearly, I forget less frequently. Things which I did with a strain before, I now do easily and with no effort whatever . . . I no longer feel in a hurry about anything. Everything goes right. Each minute I meet calmly as though it were not important. Nothing can go wrong excepting one thing. That is that God may slip from my mind if I do not keep on my guard. If He is there, the universe is with me. My task is simple and clear.

How much do you commune with God during the day? Or do you just leave that for a few minutes before you go to sleep or for an hour on Sundays? This one thing I know for sure. When you choose to put God first and you talk with God about everything, your life will be transformed. You will become healthier, happier, more joyful and peaceful than you ever imagined. When we hold Him constantly in our thoughts, we then feel Him uplifting, supporting and guiding us in our times of need and we see His light adorning all of our perceptions.

What about those times when we turn to God and we don't feel His presence? Don't be discouraged, for He is always there. Paramahansa Yogananda said, " Every word you have whispered to Him He has written in His heart, and someday He will answer you." And Sri Daya Mata offers this:

Think of it: Not a thought goes unheeded! Whatever you ask for will be fulfilled, when the time is right, and in the manner that is best for your ultimate good. What joyous expectancy this promise lends to prayer. Above all, the love that you offer to Him will be gathered in the chalice of His heart and multiplied with infinite generosity, hence to be poured back into your life, bestowing fulfillment beyond your dreams.

Meditation is a regular part of my life and during these forty days, I have devoted a minimum of three hours a day to meditation — oftentimes more. After I meditate, I hold on to the inner peace, which is really God's presence, and allow that to permeate everything I see, say, feel and do. I realize that everything in my life is God and that whatever comes to me comes from Him — to guide me, to teach me, to free and bless me eternally. I have felt God's radiance and am intoxicated by His love. Why should I drink from a teacup when I can drink from the river? Even when I make mistakes and have placed myself in difficult or challenging situations, I know I can turn to God and find solace in His presence. His grace and guidance will open before me the way to peace and happiness.

When we live in the presence of God, His love will guide us and heal all disharmony and conflict. This was made evident to me two months ago. I was traveling around the country on a three-week lecture/workshop/television tour, and I had two days to go. This particular night I was in a New York hotel giving a keynote address to approximately seven hundred people. The lights were up so I could see everyone's face. As I began to speak, I noticed that a woman in the front row kept talking to the person next to her. I could tell that she wasn't agreeing with or liking anything I was saying. Half way through my talk, she got up and left, walking brusquely down the center aisle and momentarily taking the rest of the audience's attention with her. Five minutes later she walked back in and sat down in the front row again. At this point, I talked to God. As I was still giving my presentation, I asked Him what to do. He told me, plain and simple, to send her love. So I proceeded to send love from my heart to her heart. Within a few seconds, she actually started paying attention. When

I finished, she was the first person to stand and applaud. I must admit, I was baffled by her abrupt change in attitude.

After my presentation at the banquet dinner, she came to me and asked if she could sit at my table. I invited her to sit down. Through most of the dinner, she hardly said a word. I did find out her name was Shirley and she lived in New York. After dinner when we were saying our good-byes, Shirley asked if she could talk to me privately. This is what she told me. She had been abused as a child and also by her ex-husband. Her life had been very difficult and she could barely afford to take care of her four children, all of whom were under ten years old. She used to pray to God but never felt that He listened or heard her prayers. When she heard me talking about taking responsibility for your life and working as co-creator with God to live your highest vision, she figured she didn't want to hear any more. She just didn't believe it was possible. That's when Shirley decided to walk out.

As Shirley was leaving the front door of the hotel, for the first time in her life, she thought she heard a voice inside her that said, "Go back and listen to Susan. She can help transform your life. Pay attention to what she is saying and listen with your heart and not your head." She tried to deny this inner guidance and asked the valet to get her car. As her car arrived, she realized that this wasn't just an ordinary voice; this was something special. She told the valet to park her car again and she walked back in and sat down. She said she instantly felt some warmth around her heart; a feeling that she had not felt before. She now felt that God could be part of her life, and she was open to making some changes.

I was thrilled to hear all this and agreed to meet her the following day. We visited for about three hours and I guided her gently on a new program of health, fitness, meditation and living more from inner guidance.

What I learned from this experience is that when you live in the presence of God, love lights your path and shows you what to do and how to be. Love unites all things; it's the essence of all life. Jesus was not only a great religious leader, but a brilliant light in a dark world of human separateness and alienation. He opened people's hearts. "Love one another," he taught. And "Love your neighbor as yourself," and "God is love."

Be steadfast in your desire to know God. Don't wait for others to love you. Love them first, for you are loving God at the same time. Choose to see God in everyone you meet, in everything you see. God is always there for us. "God is at home. It is we who have gone out for a walk," suggests Meister Eckhart. With God's love, all things are possible. Realize, as my friend Shirley did, that in every problem lies the solution if we just unite with God. Aspire to think God's thoughts about you and your life.

You can keep your mind on your work while you keep your heart connected to God. From time to time, talk to God silently in your heart and let Him know your needs, questions and desires. This is what I do all the time. In work situations, nobody else knows what I'm doing. What a wonderful feeling to know that you have this constant friend and companion who loves you unconditionally and is there for you every second of the day or night.

Through God's love, we make ourselves instruments through which God can love. To be God's instruments of love, we must be established in the consciousness of divine love. Devote your life to putting God first. This is the only way to create lasting peace, joy and fulfillment.

Choose to live peacefully and in the presence of God.

> When you learn to practice the presence of God in every moment that you are free to think of Him, then even in the midst of work you will be aware of divine communion.
>
> Paramahansa Yogananda, *Spiritual Diary*

Taking Inventory and Action

1. At what times during the day do you usually think of God?
2. Do you feel you can call upon God within you at any hour of the day or night?
3. Is God your closest friend?
4. Do you ever think of God as the tangible, physical things in your world?
5. With everyone you meet, connect your hearts and silently acknowledge your oneness with God.

6. Strive to make all of your life the expression of your worship of God.

7. Don't wait for others to love you. Love them first. Don't wait for the difficult times to cultivate a relationship with God. Start right now.

8. Take a walk in nature and with your spiritual eyes and heart, see God everywhere.

9. Look into the eyes of your family and friends and see God loving you back.

10. Live in the presence of God.

Today's Affirmation

I behold God in my marvelous body. I feel God in my heart and soul. I see God in all the beauty around me. I worship God in everything I do. We are one. I fill myself with the glory of God's love now and carry it with me through this day. This day I choose to live in the presence of God.

CHAPTER 39

Meditation

First things must come first. When you awaken in
the morning, meditate. If you don't, the whole world
will crowd in to claim you, and you will forget God. At
night, meditate before sleep claims you. I am so
strongly established in the habit of meditation that
even after I lie down to sleep at night, I find I am
meditating. I can't sleep in the ordinary way.
The habit of being with God comes first.

Paramahansa Yogananda, *Man's Eternal Quest*

Meditation provides numerous
benefits for your body; it releases tension, reduces stress and high
blood pressure, boosts immune functioning, improves concentration, increases awareness and brings about a more positive attitude.
But there is so much more to meditation than this. Meditation
restores calmness to the mind, so that we can perceive God's
reflection in our souls.

The more regularly you meditate, the easier it becomes. Eventually, after years of practicing meditation, you become one with
the rhythm of universal life; then every moment of your life
becomes a meditation, a love communion with God. This takes
self-discipline and commitment.

In prayer, I talk to God. In meditation, I listen to God. It is not
a passive exercise; I remain alert since I am in meditation for
inspiration and spiritual unfoldment. During meditation, I rise in
consciousness into an atmosphere of receptivity, into a consciousness where I feel God and all life becomes one. To become
centered in God consciousness, to me, is the first essential of a

fulfilling and peaceful life. As I rest in the Divine, in quiet meditation, I feel God's energy flowing through my mind, brain and nervous system. I am radiant with light. My mind is purified, my body is glorified, and my life is filled with peace and joy.

Meditation brings deep peace, joy, humility, patience, gratefulness and caring the way nothing else does. Through meditation, I celebrate that special oneness with my source; it's my strength, guiding light and my life. I am very disciplined about this part of my life. I arise early (before sunrise) each morning to meditate. Then before I sleep at night, I meditate again. In addition, once a week, one weekend a month for several consecutive days with each change of season, I practice extended periods of meditation and solitude.

I encourage everyone to meditate twice a day, beginning with twenty minutes each session. If more people meditate, the effect on the planet will be profound — we will create a peaceful world. World peace is a function of our inner peace. For the whole world to be elevated to a higher level of awareness, all of us must participate. In *Spiritual Nutrition and the Rainbow Diet*, Gabriel Cousens offers this:

> I believe this mission of world peace is becoming a planetary expression of God's will. By building a spiritual sanctuary out of the world, everyone's spiritual evolution will be quickened. We will be brought closer to the quantum leap in consciousness that we, as all of God's children, will someday make. By serving world peace, we are serving the development of inner peace for everyone. By giving our love to the world, we become that love. As love we become the spiritual sanctuary that we seek.

Meditation is a natural process of turning within. There is nothing to be afraid of, and of course, it takes practice — disciplined practice. We must be gentle with ourselves and let go of fear. Through regular meditation, we begin to experience our world through new senses, we start to see beyond our old reality, as defined by appearances, and we enter a state of clarity where we share a common self. We find that inner peace and unconditional love are, in fact, real and in our hearts.

If you are a beginner, I suggest you read about meditation to get a better understanding of its practice, purpose and benefits. The book that sparked my interest in meditation twenty years ago was *Autobiography of a Yogi,* by Paramahansa Yogananda. For complete instruction in the theory and practice of scientific meditation techniques, I highly recommend the Self-Realization Fellowship lessons. I also recommend the following books: *An Easy Guide to Meditation* by Roy Eugene Davis; *Peace Pilgrim*; *Metaphysical Meditations* by Paramahansa Yogananda; and *Your Maximum Mind* and *The Relaxation Response*, both by Herbert Benson, M.D. Also, in my book *Choose To Be Healthy*, I offer a step-by-step description of how to meditate.

By reading, you can gain some insight, but reading should never take the place of meditation. Meditation harmonizes the mind and the heart and fosters a positive attitude about yourself, others and life in general. It brings a softness and gentleness to life. It gets you in touch with your Higher Self, that part of you which is one with God and all life.

Here's a special meditation that I read in *Peace Pilgrim*. I incorporate this into my meditation session a couple of times a week. (Daily, I do a meditation technique called Kriya Yoga, which I learned through the Self-Realization Fellowship Lessons and books.) Here is what Peace Pilgrim writes:

> First, could we agree that God's protection surrounds us? Know that you are God's beautiful child, always in God's hands. Accept God . . . accept God's protection . . . there is really no problem to fear. Know that you are not the clay garment. Know that you are not the self-centered nature which governs your life needlessly. Know that you are the God-centered nature. The Kingdom of God within. The Indwelling Christ. Eternal and indestructible. Identify with the real you.

Say the following to yourself either out loud or silently. When I say it, I do it slowly and with feeling and it always makes me feel peaceful.

> Peace . . . be still . . . and know . . . that I am God.
> Peace . . . be still . . . and know . . . that I am.

Peace . . . be still . . . and know.
Peace . . . be still.
Peace . . . be.
Peace . . .
Peace . . .
Peace.

One of the greatest benefits of meditation for me is that I have become very peaceful and, most of the time, can live in a center of peace and serenity regardless of what is going on outside me. In that calmness, I feel my connection with God and know that with this type of partnership, anything is possible. My life has become an unfolding, great adventure and has taken on a richness and profundity that nothing in my outside world could ever provide me. With God as my closest friend and guiding light, I am living life to its fullest — healthfully, joyfully and peacefully. I salute your great adventure.

Choose to live peacefully, meditate and commune with God every day.

Human conduct is ever unreliable until man is anchored in the Divine. Everything in the future will improve if you are making a spiritual effort now.

Swami Sri Yukteswar

Taking Inventory and Action

1. Would you like to experience peace, love, gentleness, compassion, joy and serenity no matter what is going on in your life? Meditation will cultivate those qualities.

2. What area of your home can you devote to meditation? I use the corner of my bedroom.

3. Have you ever meditated while out in nature?

4. What excuses do you usually come up with as to why you don't have time to commune with God in meditation?

5. Do you live in a family environment and find it difficult to find time alone and in silence?

6. Get up early in the morning and devote your first waking minutes to God.

7. Walk in silence in nature and feel the healing power of the earth as you reconnect with your spirit and the beauty of nature.

8. In meditation, experience the power of being alive and in the present moment.

9. Your indwelling Christ will guide you to the light, love and peace. Listen, be still, and open your heart to God.

10. Live in the presence of God.

Today's Affirmation

The most important thing in my life is to remember God. In quiet meditation, the Indwelling Presence shows me the way to live in love and peace. My life has become a great adventure and I'm living fully — healthfully, joyfully and peacefully.

CHAPTER 40

Spiritual Unfoldment: Quest for Peace

The real voyage of discovery consists not in seeking
new landscapes, but in having new eyes.

Marcel Proust

Do you look at your life as a
quest for spirituality? You can when you know that God is your
guide, for then life can be a meaningful and fulfilling adventure of
unfoldment. My journey to the mountaintop has had many ups
and downs, sprinkled with a variety of side trips. Through it all,
I've learned so much about myself and this wonderful gift we call
life. I'd like to share some of my thoughts, lessons and experiences
with you in a way that summarizes the book and, I hope, motivates
and inspires you to choose a more peaceful life.

Take a moment to close your eyes, breathe deeply and look
closely at all areas of your life. Examine your self-image, your
relationships, your career or business, your level of health, your
income and your peace of mind. Is your life a celebration, lived as
a great adventure? Are you enjoying each day fully for what it
brings to you, grateful for your life experience, eager to learn,
grow and change? Or are you usually feeling that there must be
more to life, that there must be a higher level of fulfillment "out
there" somewhere? By virtue of being human, we all have the
capacity to embrace whatever thoughts we'd like and to become
anything we'd like to become. Around the world I see people
becoming masters of their own lives and taking a more active role
in transforming their beliefs. They are discarding the negative
beliefs — that life is meant to be a struggle, punctuated with fear,
lack and limitation; that we are mere victims — in favor of

positive beliefs — there is more to life than what we experience; our limitations are self-imposed; we all have a responsibility to reach our highest potential.

Making your life a great adventure begins by recognizing that we don't have to continue repeating our pasts. For much of my life, I felt as if I were on a treadmill and didn't know where, how or when to get off. Patterns repeated themselves; only the faces changed. It wasn't until I chose to let go, to surrender to the spirit of life, that I began to discover what living fully is all about. It's about being filled with God's love and giving your life to His service. It's up to you to create a charmed, fulfilling life.

To make every little thing in your life special is to grant a magical quality to your life and make it more spiritual. Once your life becomes charmed in such a way, whatever blocks or self-imposed limitations you may have experienced in the past or present, melt in the light of peace and love flowing from your heart.

So much of my spiritual awakening and awareness I owe to Paramahansa Yogananda, whose teachings and writings I have been studying for many years. Through him I learned the most important lesson of my life: to always put God first. Since making that commitment, I've also made lots of mistakes, but I'm realizing that the more I surrender to God, the more my life is filled with a peace and joy beyond my grandest imagination.

The turning point in my spiritual life came almost twenty years ago when I read Yogananda's book, *The Autobiography of a Yogi* (and started receiving the Self-Realization Fellowship Lessons), which showed me that perhaps there was a different way to live — that it was possible to control my thoughts, emotions and live a spirit-filled (hence peaceful, joyful, happy) life. My growing as a "holistic being" is a continual process of unfoldment. Yogananda founded Self-Realization Fellowship (SRF) in 1920 in order to teach the scientific principles of meditation. SRF believes in the brotherhood of man, that we have one common Father, and that all true paths lead to the same God. All religions are respected.

Through study, meditation and surrender, I am able to travel my path with more clarity and freedom. We are free to be whatever we decide we want to be as long as we believe it's possible and are willing to put in discipline and effort to bring it about. Thus, we are not victims of circumstance, but rather architects of our lives. We must be absolutely sure of the results we desire, and we must remain in constant control of our thoughts and mind. The best way to do this is to be with God all the time and to make peace and friends with your own company and divinity.

If you are going to realize and manifest your best desires, your life must be a harmonious expression of the insights and values of your Higher Self.

Being healthy goes hand in hand with being peaceful. There's more to health than a strong body, toned muscles, a clear mind and a disease- and pain-free existence. There is a divine nature and purpose to all life, and this is to prepare a way for spiritual growth and perfection. All of my endeavors towards attaining better health would be futile if I did not use my healthy body as the temple of God. "God's temple is holy, and that temple you are," we read in 1 Corinthians 3:17. And it's because of this view that a great deal of my work is on physical exercise, positive thinking and wholesome nutrition. This is what's right for me. Of course, attaining health requires time and discipline, but I wouldn't have it any other way. If we don't take time for health, we will have to take time for sickness. This is just the law of the universe.

My inner experiences of the past few years, and particularly the last forty days, have changed my perception of the daily events of my life. I experience a wholeness of being. Each moment is now permeated with peace, equanimity and joy. Of course, I didn't wake up one morning and all of a sudden feel this way. For a long time, I was confused about so much, had many questions that were unanswered and discovered through many difficult times that the answers cannot be found in the outside world. The answers are within.

A spiritual journey will naturally have many different levels and stages. At each stage you will see different changes: At one point you may change your diet; at another, your friends or job or what's on your walls or what books you read or movies you see or where and how you sit to meditate. All these factors contribute to the depth and freedom that you can know through knowing yourself, looking more within.

I have found that as I gradually develop a quiet and clear awareness, my living habits are naturally coming into harmony with my total environment, with my past involvements, present interests and future concerns. When you are in touch with your innermost self and really begin to discover who you are, the changes in your life come naturally.

My decision to fast for forty days came from inner direction, and my intention was to spend these days in communion with God, to be open to God's thoughts on how we can all live our lives more fully. I wanted to take my peacefulness to a higher level — to experience my oneness with God more consciously than ever before. It has been a time, essentially, of doing without my worldly activities in favor of aligning with my inner world. I haven't looked at this in a religious sense; rather it has been a spiritual discipline or consecration.

There are as many different definitions for religious as there are religions and people. I see myself as being religious or spiritual by the way I choose to look at life and living. As a child, I grew up believing that being religious meant going to church every Sunday, saying my prayers before going to sleep and singing in the choir. My awareness is different now. Spirituality for me today is more than perfunctory devotion to performing sacraments and reciting memorized Bible passages. I express my faith by the way I live, by ardently revering nature and nurturing humanity and respecting all living creatures. Being religious to me means being honest, truthful and sincere in human relations and practicing self-discipline in every aspect of life.

Thoreau said it best when he said, "Our religion is where our love is." I am deeply in love with all people, all creation and life. I also used to believe that God was this strange and inscrutable yet magnanimous force that lived up in Heaven and watched over us. Now I realize that God is strange only to the degree that we remain distant from Him. God is everywhere in this universe, and most assuredly this includes within you and me. For this reason, the universe within is a beautiful place. Because people don't take or make the time to visit this beautiful place, they are not aware of it and they remain distant from the infinite wellspring of peace, love, light, wisdom and happiness. God, as well as being my guiding light, strength and inspiration, is also my best friend. Christ is my prince of peace and my constant companion.

I'm not implying that you must lead a reclusive life or fast forty days to feel this way. Not at all. This was the path I chose to experience and was guided to follow. But, whatever way you choose to develop your spiritual nature, you should strive to get more in touch with yourself and spend some time alone each day in meditation. Then you will move quickly toward your goal. Whether you're sitting at your desk or in your car, whether in front of your meditation altar or out in nature, bring meditation to the forefront of your life. It will bring about an incredible wholeness, balance, harmony and peace, which will enable you to go out into the world knowing that you can handle any situation with aplomb and equanimity. I'm not saying that meditation, fasting or a more natural lifestyle will take all of your problems away. Rather when complications do arise, you'll be able to handle them. Things that used to appear as serious difficulties will now seem wonderful opportunities to grow, change and live closer to God.

Thoreau said: "How prompt we are to satisfy the hunger and thirst of our bodies: how slow to satisfy the hunger and thirst of our souls."

Don't ever consider your body a mere lump of flesh. It is a noble instrument; within is the source of all extraordinary powers in the world. We carry our own Heaven or Hell within every moment, for these are but the results of mental and emotional states that we have created. I see Heaven as a state of awareness and Hell as a state of not knowing, a separation from God. Through meditation — turning inward to God — we turn to the light. When you turn to that perfection that is within you, and as you become transformed and renewed, all fear will dissolve. We read in the Bible "Peace, be still, and know that I am God." (Psalms 46:10) When calm and still, we can feel that oneness.

We are all intimately connected to each other and to God — this oneness of all life. The biggest problem we face is the erroneous belief in a separation from the source. When that one is solved, all others will vanish. We must be honest with ourselves, forgive ourselves, get back in touch with the source. The answers are not out in the world somewhere; they are all within us. Through silence and meditation, we light up our lives and our world. In meditation, we go home. It is there we can transcend our differences, embrace our divinity, and remember who we are — thus enriching the quality of life on this magnificent planet. We can experience profound peace and take it with us wherever we go. We all want a more peaceful world; but first we must start with living peacefully ourselves. Let go of all unpeaceful thoughts. We develop according to that upon which our minds dwell. If we express positive thoughts, then health, harmony, peace, and love will all come back to us, magnified.

The best tip I can give you to be healthy and peaceful — one in which there is the most real profit — is to take care of your own body in such a way that your body is naturally able to take care of itself. God equipped us with the most remarkable, powerful and efficient healing system known to medical science. The body is designed to be self-cleansing, self-healing and self-rejuvenating. Treat your body with reverence and respect. Make the time to meditate and ask for inner guidance. Your guidance might recommend different foods, exercise, fasting or books to study. You might feel the need to spend more time out in nature. Or perhaps you might be led to simplify your lifestyle so that you can have more time to celebrate and enjoy life. We all need to spend more time *being* instead of constantly *doing*. We are *human beings*, not *human doings*.

Choose to live peacefully and in the presence of God. I salute your great adventure.

Fix your mind inwardly between the eyebrows (as in meditation) on the shoreless lake of peace. Watch the eternal circle of rippling peace around you. The more you watch intently, the more you will feel the wavelets of peace spreading from the eyebrows to the forehead, from the forehead to the heart, and on to every cell in your body. Now the waters of peace are overflowing on the banks of your body and inundating the vast territory of your mind. The flood of peace flows over the boundaries of your mind and moves on in infinite directions.

Paramahansa Yogananda, *Spiritual Diary*

Peace be with you,

Susan S. Jones

Afterword

*Delight yourself in the Lord and He will give
you the desires of your heart.*

Psalm 37:4

It's now been a month since I fin-
ished my forty-day consecration fast. It was the most challenging,
and at the same time, most enlightening time of my life. I succeeded
in taking only pure water for the entire forty days. Since I am used
to fasting, I didn't have any physical difficulty; remember, I took a
year to prepare my body. I did have several dreams and thoughts
about food, especially during the first half of the fast. Now, after
a gradual reintroduction to food, I am just about back to my
normal healthy eating program.

For those of you who are interested in the finer details, I ended
up reading fifty books (I was hoping to read forty); organized
every closet, cupboard and drawer of my home; gave away twelve
huge trashbags of "stuff" I cleaned out as part of my simplification process.

The challenging part was trying to keep my heart and mind
focused on God all my waking hours. I found that very difficult to
do. In the beginning, sometimes more than an hour would go by
before I realized my thoughts were not focused on God. As the
days and weeks went on, however, keeping my attention anchored
in the Divine became more second nature to me. I believe my
meditations helped immensely. Every day I meditated at least
three hours; early on I split that three hours among two or three
sessions. On Day Twenty, I increased my meditation time and,
towards the end, found myself desiring sometimes to meditate six
to eight hours at a stretch. I required much less sleep than usual,
sometimes only three to four hours each night. I occasionally took
cat naps during the day. I noticed that on the whole, my energy
level was high, although I went through a few days of feeling tired

and weak. For the most part, I did no strenuous, vigorous exercise. Every day I made it a point to get some fresh air, to take a ten- to fifteen-minute sun bath and to spend time outdoors. I think it's important to point out that the results of my fast are probably much related to years of spiritual discipline, fasting and meditation. I don't want to suggest that by fasting for forty days, everyone will share my same experiences.

As I opened myself up to God's peace and God's presence in my life, I learned so much. Now I feel as though God is walking with me all the time, no matter what I may be doing. Whether I'm washing the dishes or putting away the groceries, I sense God's wonderful Light in and around me. It never leaves me. Just imagine, if you can, the first time you fell in love. You could feel something wonderful happening inside you, and you were often bubbling over with joy and happiness. That new feeling of love colored your entire world. Well, that's how I feel. I feel this love for God bubbling up inside me and radiating out to everything. I've learned what it means to live by faith and trust. I know that I'll always be taken care of, and there is nothing to fear. Peace is now an integral part of my life. There is a union between my heart and my mind, between my soul and the presence of God. And more than ever before, I understand what it means to say, "Not my will, but Thy will be done on earth as it is in Heaven."

Having peace as my constant companion doesn't mean that I'll never have a challenge, feel upset or experience sadness. But now I find that when these things occur, they don't last very long and I see clearly that I always have a choice about how I respond. I can choose peace and can put God first instead of focusing on an appearance or emotion.

Not much in my outer life has changed. What has changed, however, is my perspective. My vision is unimpeded by past experience or compulsive attachment. My sensitivity is heightened, and so is my awareness. I see the colors, textures and shapes of things with greater clarity and recognize the underlying principles of harmony and order in everything. It's almost as though I've grown new eyes, new ears and a new heart. In connecting with my true nature — my indwelling Christ — I now recognize and experience my oneness to all people and all life.

All life is sacred. The joy of living comes to those who live together in peace and harmony. The challenge before us is not to try to transform the world or even to change others. We must all reawaken ourselves and find the peace in our own hearts so that we can radiate the light of God and touch everyone we meet. If we alter our own lives, we alter the world. Each one of us is like a drop or a wave in the ocean of life — of God. We are the world, so as we choose to live our own lives, we will influence the world. It is only through inner transformation that we can live more fully, experiencing our highest potential, and move toward a new world of harmony and peace.

Now is the right time for each of us to rethink our lives, our priorities, our vision. Are we living in the presence of God or in the absence of God? It is my hope that this book has inspired you to take a close look at your life and your way of being in this world. Do you want to live more peacefully? Within each one of you is a wellspring of peace just waiting to be tapped. By opening up to the peace that you are, you become peaceful. Peace comes from loving yourself and honoring your Divinity. Peace comes from living your life to the fullest with God in your heart and by your side. Peace is a result of living more from inner guidance and putting God first in your life.

Do you need to sequester yourself from the world and fast to experience living peacefully? Of course not! Seek your own way and be open to the gentle stirrings of your heart. All the answers are within you right now if you just take the time to be still, listen, in quiet and solitude, and then act on what you hear. Jesus said, "Ask, and it will be given to you; seek, and you will find; knock, and it will be opened to you." (Matthew 7:7)

Choose to live peacefully, live fully, celebrate yourself and your oneness with God. It's your choice. Peace be with you.

I'd like to end with one of my favorite poems, which so beautifully expresses how to live peacefully.

DESIDERATA

Go placidly amid the noise and haste,
and remember what peace there may be in silence.
As far as possible without surrender
be on good terms with all persons.
Speak your truth quietly and clearly;
and listen to others, even the dull and ignorant;

they too have their story.
Avoid loud and aggressive persons,
they are vexatious to the spirit.
If you compare yourself with others,
you may become vain and bitter; for always
there will be greater and lesser persons than yourself.
Enjoy your achievements as well as your plans.
Keep interested in your own career, however humble;
it is a real possession in the changing fortunes of time.
Exercise caution in your business affairs;
for the world is full of trickery.
But let this not blind you to what virtue there is;
many persons strive for high ideals;
and everywhere life is full of heroism.
Be yourself. Especially, do not feign affection.
Neither be cynical about love;
for in the face of all aridity and disenchantment
it is perennial as the grass.
Take kindly the counsel of the years,
gracefully surrendering the things of youth.
Nurture strength of spirit to shield you in sudden misfortune.
But do not distress yourself with imaginings.
Many fears are born of fatigue and loneliness.
Beyond a wholesome discipline, be gentle with yourself.
You are a child of the universe,
no less than the trees and the stars;
you have a right to be here.
And whether or not it is clear to you,
no doubt the universe is unfolding as it should.
Therefore be at peace with God,
whatever you conceive Him to be,
and whatever your labors and aspirations,
in the noisy confusion of life keep peace with your soul.
With all its sham, drudgery and broken dreams,
it is still a beautiful world.
Be careful. Strive to be happy.

Found in Old Saint Paul's Church, Baltimore
Dated 1692

May the Lord bless His people with peace.

Psalm 29:11

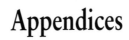

Appendices

One Solitary Life

He was born in an obscure village. He worked in a carpenter shop until he was thirty. He then became an itinerant preacher. He never held an office. He never had a family or owned a house. He didn't go to college. He had no credentials but himself. He was only thirty-three when the public turned against him. His friends ran away. He was turned over to his enemies and went through the mockery of a trial. He was nailed to a cross between two thieves. While he lay dying, his executioners gambled for his clothing, the only property he had on earth. He was laid in a borrowed grave.

Nineteen centuries have come and gone, and today he is the central figure of the human race. All the armies that ever marched, all the navies that ever sailed, all the parliaments that ever sat, and all the kings that ever reigned have not affected the life of man as much as that one solitary life.

Anonymous

Peace in the World

When there is wellness on the mind,
There will be wholeness in the person.

When there is wholeness in the person,
There will be harmony in the home.

When there is harmony in the home,
There will be forgiveness in the nation.

When there is forgiveness in the nation,
There will be peace in the world.

Susan Smith Jones

The Signs and Symptoms of Inner Peace

A tendency to think and act spontaneously rather than on fears based on past experiences.

An unmistakable ability to enjoy each moment.

A loss of interest in judging other people.

A loss of interest in interpreting the actions of others.

A loss of interest in conflict.

A loss of ability to worry.

Frequent, overwhelming episodes of appreciation.

Contented feelings of connectedness with others and frequent attacks of smiling.

An increasing susceptibility to the love extended by others as an uncontrollable urge to extend it.

Anonymous

For My Friend

I surround you with light as you grow through the challenges of this world. I have faith in you to make right decisions for your life.

If, in my humanness, I sometimes forget and make demands on you or judge you, please forgive me. At such times, you have my permission to ask me to stop, to step back, and let go my judgements. My highest and best self loves you just the way you are.

Sometimes, when I give in to my fears, I feel that I have a need to control others and to try to make them be like me. But when I am attuned to Spirit, I remember that I love you not only for the ways you are like me, but also for the ways you are not like me. Then, my only need is to give unconditional love.

I trust you enough to be myself around you. Thank you for being you and for loving me just the way I am — when I am radiant, gentle, supportive, fun, happy, kind, and generous, and when I seem to be less than these qualities.

I care about you. I believe in you. I love you. My world is better because you are in it. Thank you for being here for me.

Rev. John Strickland
Unity Church of Hawaii

Choose To Be Healthy

(Sing to the tune of "He's Got The Whole World in His Hands)

We've got the power to be healthy — in our hands.
We've got the power to be healthy — in our hands.
We've got the power to be healthy — in our hands.
We've got the power in our hands.

We've got a little child inside us — let him out.
We've got a little child inside us — let her out.
We've got a little child inside us — let them shout!
We've got the power in our hands.

We've got some new friends here at (your group, church,
    company) — let's hold hands.
We've got some new friends here at ( ) — let's hold hands.
We've got some new friends here at ( ) — let's hold hands.
We've got the power in our hands.

So let's choose to be healthy — everyday.
Let's choose to be healthy — everyday.
Let's choose to be healthy — in every way.
We've got the power in our hands.

repeat: We've got the power in our hands.

by Gary L. Brink
Educational Services Director
Bay Area Hospital
Coos Bay, Oregon

Decide To Be Happy

Decide to be happy
render others happy
proclaim your joy
love passionately your miraculous life
do not listen to promises
do not wait for a better world
be grateful for every moment of life

switch on and keep on the positive buttons in yourself, those
    marked optimism, serenity, confidence, positive thinking, love
pray and thank God every day
meditate — smile — laugh
whistle — sing — dance
look with fascination at everything
fill your lungs and heart with liberty
be yourself fully and immensely
act like a king or queen unto death
feel God in your body, mind, heart, and soul
and be convinced of eternal life and resurrection.

Robert Muller
Chancellor of the University of Peace, Costa Rica
Former Assistant Secretary-General of the United Nations

A Prayer For World Peace

I know there is but One Mind, which is the Mind of God, in which all people live and move and have their being.

I know there is a Divine Pattern for humanity and within this pattern there is Infinite harmony and peace, cooperation, unity and mutual helpfulness.

I know that the mind of each person, being one with the Mind of God, shall discover the method, the way and the means best fitted to permit the flow of Divine Love between individuals and nations.

I know there shall be a free interchange of ideas, of cultures, of spiritual concepts, of ethics, of educational systems and scientific discoveries — for all good belongs to all alike.

I know that, because the Divine Mind has created us all, we are bound together in one Infinite and perfect unity.

In bringing about World Peace, I know that all people and all nations will remain individual, but unified for the common purpose of promoting peace, happiness, harmony and prosperity.

I know that deep within every person the Divine Pattern of perfect peace is already implanted.

I now declare that in each person and in leaders of thought everywhere this Divine Pattern moves into action and form, to the end that all nations and all people shall live together in peace, harmony, and prosperity forever.

So it is now.

by Ernest Holmes
Founder of Science of Mind

I am There

Do you need Me?
I am there.
You cannot see Me, yet I am the light you see by.
You cannot hear Me, yet I speak through your voice.
You cannot feel Me, yet I am the power at work in your hands.
I am at work, through you do not understand My ways.
I am at work, though you do not recognize My works.
I am not strange visions. I am not mysteries.
Only in absolute stillness, beyond self, can you know Me as I
   am, and then but as a feeling and a faith.
Yet I am there. Yet I hear. Yet I answer.
When you need Me, I am there.
Even if you deny Me, I am there.
Even when you feel most alone, I am there.
Even in your fears, I am there.
Even in your pain, I am there.
I am there when you pray and when you do not pray.
I am in you, and you are in Me.
Only in your mind can you feel separate from Me, for only in
   your mind are the mists of "yours" and "mine".
Yet only with your mind can you know Me and experience Me.
Empty your heart of empty fears.
When you get yourself out of the way, I am there.
You can of yourself do nothing, but I can do all.
And I am in all.
Though you may not see the good, good is there, for I am there.
I am there because I have to be, because I am.
Only in Me does the world have meaning; only out of Me does
   the world take form; only because of Me does the world go
   forward.

I am the love that is the law's fulfilling. I am assurance. I am
peace. I am oneness. I am the law that you can live by. I am
the love that you can cling to. I am your assurance. I am your
peace. I am one with you. I am.
Though you fail to find Me, I do not fail you.
Though your faith in Me is unsure, My faith in you never
wavers, because I know you, because I love you.
Beloved, I am there.

James Dillet Freeman

Peace Prayer

God's infinite Love flows into me (us),
And shines forth from me (us) as a
brilliant spiritual Light of Love.

The spiritual light of Love grows and grows in intensity,
Covering the entire world,
And arousing in the hearts of all mankind,
Thoughts only of love, peace, order,
and the Truth of oneness under God.

Dr. Masaharu Taniguchi

Unity's Prayer of Protection

The light of God surrounds me;
The love of God enfolds me;
The power of God protects me;
The presence of God watches over me;
Wherever I am, God is.

New Beginning Affirmation

Today is a new beginning for me. My world is made fresh and
new. Today I go forward to do my best, committed to being
healthy, happy, peaceful, prosperous and in love with all life.
Today is a new beginning for me for as I change my consciousness,

release the past and choose to embrace each moment, allowing light and love to flow through me. I know I can be all I was created to be.

As an expression of God, I now choose to live each day with joy and enthusiasm. I go forward each day determined to do my best. I give thanks that old limitations are now gone forever. Today I lay hold of new ideas, new faith and new positive thoughts about myself and my life. Each day finds me refreshed, encouraged, inspired and enlightened.

Today I am made new.

(I use this affirmation at the end of many of my workshops, seminars and lectures.)

Healing Meditation

You can record the following meditation yourself, or ask someone you love and trust to speak the words in a calm, gentle voice. If you desire, you can put some relaxing music on in the background. Before you begin, get comfortable, take a few moments to do some deep breathing, and relax.

I use this meditation in many of my workshops.

It's now time to relax and be comfortable. Gently close your eyes and feel the magic of what happens to you when you take in a long, slow, deep breath and allow the light of God's presence to fill and surround you. Breathe in peace and love. Breathe out any tension you may be feeling. Sense the light of God's love and let it encompass you.

Let's take this affirmation deep . . . deep within our being: "The light of Christ is the head of my life. I follow this light in the healing of my body and the lifting of my soul in unity with God." Repeat this silently to yourself.

Your body is the temple of the loving, light-filled spirit. Take in a long, slow deep breath and know that your mind and body are perfect expressions of harmony and peace.

As you rest . . . rest in the Christ . . . allow your mind to be in perfect peace. In that peace, take another deep breath . . . knowing that breath is . . . the holy breath of God, the universal outpouring of life. Continue to breathe in this holy breath of God and consciously allow it to move in and through your lungs on vibrations of love. The holy breath of God is so calming and relaxing. Feel the wonders that this breath has awakened in you. Feel the breath within you that heals, blesses, and uplifts you. Know that God's energy, life and intelligence are moving in and through every part of your body, doing a perfect healing for you. This power of life moves through every atom and cell of your being and your body is singing: *I am light. I am the light of the world. In this light, there can be no darkness. There is nothing to fear for I am light.*

Oh, holy one within me, I know that we are one. I acknowledge your presence and your power and I let my body temple bathe in your healing light. As I feel waves of light and love flowing over me, I trust and I believe. I know that I am centered in love, surrounded with beauty and filled with joy.

Heavenly Father-Divine Mother, I am ready to let your healing light flow in and through me — cleansing, healing and renewing me. And so I invite you to focus this light into the area of my mind, body, emotions or activity where healing is needed and let it flow. Let the mighty healing of God be done. Let go. Let go and let waves of healing love and light purify your mind, body, emotions and activities.

Now feel the life of God flow in and through you. Experience peace. Be peace. You are a radiant being of light. Give thanks with all your mind and heart that the healing, harmonizing power of God is now active in your life.

Now take a long, slow, deep breath and repeat silently to yourself:

Peace . . . be still . . . and know . . . that I am God.
Peace . . . be still . . . and know . . . that I am.
Peace . . . be still . . . and know.
Peace . . . be still.
Peace . . .
   Peace . . .
   Peace . . .

And when you desire to do so, ever so gently bring your awareness back to this time and place, back to this room (or wherever you are) where we are. Begin to feel the blood flow through your arms and legs. Stretch a little bit now. And when you feel like it, let yourself gently open your eyes, take in your environment and feel good about yourself. Feel thankful and joyful and peaceful. And so it is. Amen.

The Dilemma

To laugh is to risk appearing a fool.
To weep is to risk appearing sentimental.
To reach out for another is to risk
involvement.
To expose feelings is to risk rejection.
To place your dreams before the crowd is to
risk ridicule.
To love is to risk not being loved in return.
To go forward in the face of overwhelming
odds is to risk failure.

But risks must be taken because the greatest hazard in life is to risk nothing. The person who risks nothing does nothing, has nothing, is nothing. He may avoid suffering and sorrow, but he cannot learn, feel, change, grow or love. Chained by his certitudes, he is a slave. He has forfeited his freedom. Only a person who takes risks is free.

Anonymous

Full Moon Ritual

The full moon (bright with light and full of energy) is a time of honoring God's abundance and omnipotence and Mother Earth's love and generosity. Some full moon rituals acknowledge this with lighted white candles. The color white contains all the other colors, invoking the abundance of spirit and the planet. For my last full moon ritual I did the following, as suggested to me by my special friend, Kathy Martelli, who teaches and conducts special rituals honoring ourselves and Mother Earth.

My focus was on the theme of abundance. I lit a white candle, surrounded myself with some white roses and focused my attention on the abundance of Mother Earth and all God's blessings in my life. Then, on a white piece of paper, I wrote down and accepted for myself abundance in specific areas of my life, i.e., an abundance of ideas for writing, an abundance of love for sharing, an abundance of health, an abundance of money, etc. The writing was followed by a guided visualization in which I found myself in a clearing in a forest surrounded by trees and seated before a campfire. I felt the earth under my feet. I noticed the full moon above me in the night sky and called down her energy to fill my being. I then embarked on a journey, in my mind's eye, to a place of personal power, a sacred place for me. I went into the mountains. I visualized that I was carrying with me on this journey both a lighted white candle and my piece of white paper. I explored the place, paying attention to the sounds, smells, sights, animals and anything that I was feeling. I sat quietly and asked for God's guidance and greater understanding. When I left this sacred place, I left behind my candle and paper as a symbol of my devotion and intention.

Through this ritual, I felt empowered. Each month I learn more about myself through my writing. As I repeat this ritual (or something similar) month after month and peruse my writings, I can see my awareness changing and my understanding and connection to the oneness of life expanding.

Spring Equinox Ritual — March 21–23

The spring equinox celebrates the rebirth of the planet and marks the change in light and dark, for it is the day when there is an equal number of daylight and nighttime hours. Spring is the time when the planet moves into a new cycle of life and, metaphysically, we can use this special time to renew and re-balance our energies, aligning again with the natural order of the planet. For this ritual, I often use the theme of acknowledging the child within. I might use bright yellow candles and focus on the renewal of hope, dreams and goals; these I surround in the warm, protective glow of the early spring sun. I write down my thoughts, dreams, expectations, goals on a yellow piece of paper and surround myself with bright yellow flowers and balloons, ribbons and teddy bears.

Be creative. You want to feel safe and relaxed. This ritual is very uplifting and freeing. Sometimes I sing and dance, skip or blow bubbles; last spring equinox I flew a kite, swam in the ocean, played on the swings and celebrated my inner child and God's ever-present renewing power. With God, all things are made new.

Summer Solstice Ritual — June 21–23

The summer solstice is a celebration of relaxation and the ease of being surrounded by abundance. I decorate my surroundings with summer flowers and bright colors. Just opposite of the winter solstice, the summer solstice marks the day when we have the most daylight hours. I usually do this ritual outdoors, in the mountains or by the ocean. I acknowledge and give thanks for all the abundance around me, all of God's love and blessings in my life. There is a very different, noticeable energy on this day compared with the other changes of season. The energy is light and playful. As with all season changes, this is a time of re-balancing energy and feeling our connectedness with Mother Earth.

Fall Equinox Ritual — September 21–23

Like the spring equinox, this marks the day when the number of daylight hours equals the number of nighttime hours. In ritual, we can use this day to honor Mother Earth for all of our abundance, for this is the time of harvest. This is the time of reaping what we have sown and storing away for the winter season ahead. The ritual is one of Thanksgiving. Surround yourself with fall colors in candles and flowers, corn, nuts, seeds and grains. It's a wonderful time to acknowledge and give thanks for all the blessings in your life. Notice all the bounty of goodness around you, all of Mother Earth's blessings. On this day, I usually write down all the things in my life for which I'm grateful. God the good, the omnipotent, is flowing through me, blessing me with love and abundance. I give thanks and acknowledge God as my only source.

Winter Solstice Ritual — December 21–23

This day has the shortest amount of daylight hours, thus the longest night of the year. For my last winter solstice, I celebrated with Kathy Martelli and a small group of friends. Our visualization was done almost totally in silence. Only one candle was lit in the room. This is the Native American time to go to the place within in the medicine wheel of life. It is represented by the totem animal of the bear and by the color black. The theme is introspection.

The meditation began with visualizing going out into a cold, dark night. Everyone went individually. In our mind's eyes, each of us saw ourselves taking a lit candle and going out and feeling the aloneness and the coldness of the night air. Sometimes Kathy plays music during the ritual; this last time, she had on some Native American flute music. Because the ritual is a solitary time for meditation, she kept talking and directions to a minimum. We were asked to find a cave or dark shelter to visit. Upon entering the cave, we sensed the darkness and the feelings that began to surface. Some people cried; some were afraid. This ritual is the connection to the subconscious, the underworld, the hidden within ourselves. We're asked not to judge our feelings but to simply allow them to surface. Just as nature has a darker side, so do we all. We can feel afraid, isolated, alone, disconnected and uncertain. During this ritual, we honor and reflect on those times and feelings we have experienced in the year up until now. Recognizing their higher purpose, we bless them and then let them go.

We left our candles in the cave to remind us that we can always bring light into the darkness. When everyone was finished with the journey, we all lit candles from the one white candle that was originally lit. The room filled with light. There was a sharing of experiences and food, symbolizing our understanding that darkness is a phase of the planet and we are now moving into longer days of daylight as the wheel turns. We're moving from the darkness to light, from winter to spring, to renewing and new beginnings . . . endings and beginnings and so the cycle goes — renewed hope, renewed balance and energy.

Bath Ritual

There are so many variations you can do with a shower or bath ritual. Here's just one example. Feel free to change anything to fit your needs, mood, goals and desire. Be creative.

First, I create a temple or sanctuary in my bathroom. I make sure it is clean, and I bring in fresh flowers and candles. I sometimes play music or burn incense. As the water is running in the bath, I light the candle(s), pour in some bath oil or gel, enter the bath and begin to breathe deeply and relax. Upon entering, I close my eyes and rest for a few minutes, in quiet meditation and prayer. I usually prefer to have the candles as the main source of light. I enjoy the peacefulness and solitude.

When I feel ready, I begin to run handfuls of water over each part of my body — blessing each. I bless my hands, my arms, my shoulders, my head, my face and so on. Sometimes I add flowers to the bathwater, taking petals and letting them float on the water. I acknowledge the four elements — the water, the earth (flowers), the fire (candles) and the air (visually symbolized by the smoke you see after you blow out the candle).

I talk to God and ask for guidance. For me, it's usually a time of surrender, a time of giving all that I am to God to cleanse and purify. I acknowledge my connection with Mother Earth and give thanks for all her abundance. I accept healing in my body and life and also let the bath water wash away my disharmony and blockages to the awareness of God's presence. After more prayer and meditation, I simply sit back, relax and rejoice. Sometimes I drink some water or sip tea. Often I have a theme of color, i.e., pink (flowers, bath oil, candles) for healing, blue for relaxing, purple for spiritual awakening. If the water cools down too much, I let some hot water run in so I stay comfortable. If I want to be energized, I use the colors of red, orange or yellow and use cool water in the bath. The color of the candles, flowers, bathwater and drink will change with the intention of the ritual.

When ready, I let the water drain out, affirming that my body, mind and spirit are cleansed and renewed. Before leaving the room, I always end my ritual with a prayer of acceptance and thanksgiving, knowing that God is my source.

Affirmations

1. I am in perfect health.
2. I love my body and treat it with respect.
3. I love and accept myself completely, just as I am.
4. I am healthy, happy and radiant.
5. God's love heals me and makes me whole.
6. I radiate optimum health.
7. My body is healed, renewed and filled with energy.
8. When grocery shopping, I read labels and select foods with healthy ingredients.
9. My body is trim, fit and beautifully shaped.
10. My muscles are firm and strong.
11. I weigh exactly what I desire, easily and effortlessly.
12. I know and accept that I can shape my body as I want.
13. I exercise regularly and vigorously and I love it!
14. I give thanks for increasing energy, confidence and well-being.
15. My body is created to express health and wholeness. I hold this picture in my mind.
16. I am created to be healthy. I claim health and peace for myself now.
17. I take responsibility for my well-being.
18. I am confident and self-assured.
19. I treat myself to the very best because I deserve it.
20. I draw to myself my ideal friends and lovers.
21. I am attracting supportive, loving relationships.
22. I radiate love to everyone I meet.
23. God is guiding me to fulfilling work.
24. My work is love in action.
25. I am doing what I love and getting paid for it.
26. In everything I do, I prosper.
27. Money flows to me easily and effortlessly.
28. I always have an abundance of money.

29. I deserve to prosper.

30. I invest wisely and responsibly.

31. God is my source.

32. I share my prosperity with others.

33. Always the best for me.

34. I dwell in love, peace and confidence, with God as my source. I am now becoming all I was created to be.

35. This day I choose to spend in perfect peace.

36. The peace within permeates my entire being. I am joyously serene.

37. I live in the heart of God.

38. I give myself permission to be healthy, happy, prosperous and at peace.

39. I let God's light shine through me in everything I think, feel, say and do.

40. Spirit is peace, the truth of my being.

Blessed are the peacemakers for they will be called the children of God.

Matthew 5:9

References and Recommended Reading

Adams, Richard. *Watership Down*. New York: McMillan, 1972.

* Airola, Paavo, Ph.D. *Cancer. Causes, Prevention and Treatment: The Total Approach*. Phoenix: Health Plus Publishers, 1963.

* Airola, Paavo, Ph.D. *Every Woman's Book*. Phoenix: Health Plus Publishers, 1979.

* ———. *How to Get Well*. Phoenix: Health Plus Publishers, 1974.

* ———. *How To Keep Slim, Healthy and Young with Juice Fasting*. Phoenix: Health Plus Publishers, 1971.

* Airola, Paavo, Ph.D. *There Is A Cure For Arthritis*. West Nyack, NY: Parker Publishing Co., Inc. 1968.

Alexander, Thea. *2150 A.D.* New York: Warner Books, Inc., 1971.

Allen, Gay Wilson. *Waldo Emerson*. New York: Penguin Books, Ltd., 1981.

* Allen, Hannah. *Fasting: Fastest Way to Superb Health and Rejuvenation*. Pearsall, TX: Healthway Publications, 1975.

Amos, Wally "Famous." *The Power in You*. New York: Donald I. Fine, Inc., 1988.

* Anderson, Andy. *Fasting Changed My Life*. Nashville, TN: Broadman Press, 1977.

Anderson, Bob. *Stretching*. Bolinas, CA: Shelter Publications, 1980.

Anderson, Walter. *Courage Is a Three-letter Word*. New York: Random House, 1986.

André, Rae, Ph.D. *Positive Solitude*. New York: Harper & Row, 1991.

Armor, Reginald. *Ernest Holmes THE MAN*. Los Angeles: Science of Mind Publications, 1977.

* Arndt, Rev. Herman. *Why Did Jesus Fast?*. Mokelumne Hill, CA: Health Research, 1962.

Bach, Marcus. *I, Monty*. Norfolk Island, Australia: Island Heritage Limited, 1977.

Bach, Richard. *Illusions*. New York: Delacorte Press, 1977.

———. *Jonathan Livingston Seagull*. New York: Avon Books, 1970.

Bailey, Covert. *Fit or Fat?*. Boston: Houghton Mifflin Co., 1977.

———. *The Fit-or-Fat Woman*. Boston: Houghton Mifflin Co., 1989.

Baldwin, Bruce. *It's All in Your Head: Lifestyle Management Strategies for Busy People*. Wilmington, NC: Direction Dynamics, 1985.

Barksdale, L.S. *Essays on Self-Esteem*. Idyllwild, CA: Barksdale Foundation, 1977.

Beck, Renee and Metrick, Sydney Barbara. *The Art of Ritual*. Berkeley, CA: Celestial Arts, 1990.

* *These books contain information on fasting.*

Benson, Herbert. *The Relaxation Response*. New York: Avon Books, 1976.

——. *Your Maximum Mind*. New York: Avon Books, 1987.

* Bidwell, Victoria. *The Health Seekers' Yearbook*. Fremont, CA: Getwell, Stay well, America, 1990.

Block, Douglas. *Words That Heal*. New York: Bantam, 1990.

Bloomfield, Harold H. *Making Peace With Your Parents*. New York: Random House, 1983.

Boone, J. Allen. *Kinship With All Life*. New York: Harper, 1954.

Bradshaw, John. *Bradshaw On: The Family*. Deerfield Beach, FL: Health Communications, Inc., 1988.

——. *Healing the Shame That Binds You*. Deerfield Beach, FL: Health Communications, Inc., 1988.

——. *Homecoming — Reclaiming and Championing Your Inner Child*. New York: Bantam Books, 1990.

* Bragg, Paul and Bragg, Patricia. *The Miracle of Fasting*. Santa Barbara, CA: Health Science, 1990.

Braunstein, Mark Matthew. *Radical Vegetarianism*. Los Angeles: Panjandrum Books, 1981.

Brazelton, T. Berry. *Families: Crisis and Caring*. New York: Ballantine Books, 1990.

Brown, Gabrielle. *The New Celibacy*. New York: Ballantine Books, 1980.

Brown, Melanie. *Attaining Personal Greatness*. New York: William Morrow and Company, 1987.

Browning, Peter. *John Muir in His Own Words*. Lafayette, CA: Great West Books, 1988.

Brunton, Paul. *Advanced Contemplation — The Peace Within You*, Vol. 15. Burdett, NY: Larson Publications, 1988.

* Buchinger, Otto H.F. *Everything You Want to Know About Fasting*. New York: Pyramid Books, 1972.

Bucke, Richard Maurice. *Cosmic Consciousness*. Secaucus, NJ: Citadel Press, 1961.

* Bueno, Lee. *Fast Your Way to Health*. Springdale, PA: Whitaker House, 1991. (Obtained through Born Again Body, Inc., P.O. Box 969, Calistoga, CA 94515)

Burnham, Sophy. *A Book of Angels*. New York: Ballantine, 1990.

Buscaglia, Leo. *Bus 9 to Paradise*. Thorofare, NJ: Slack, 1986.

——. *Living, Loving and Learning*. Thorofare, NJ: Slack, 1982.

——. *Loving Each Other*. Thorofare, NJ: Slack, 1984.

——. *The Fall of Freddie the Leaf*. Thorofare, NJ: Slack, 1982.

Butterworth, Eric. *Discover the Power Within You*. San Francisco: Harper and Row, 1989.

---

* *These books contain information on fasting.*

———. *The Concentric Perspective.* Unity Village, MO: Unity Books, 1989.

Cady, H. Emile. *Lessons in Truth.* Unity Village, MO: Unity Books, no date.

Capra, Fritjof. *The Tao of Physics.* New York: Bantam Books, 1975.

Carey, Ken. *Return of the Bird Tribes.* Kansas City, MO: A Uni*Sun Book, 1988.

Carper, Jean. *The Food Pharmacy.* New York: Bantam Books, 1988.

Carter, Forrest. *The Education of Little Tree.* New York: Delacorte Press, 1976.

Carter, Jimmy. (Foreword) *The Words of Peace.* (Selections from the speeches of the winners of the Nobel Peace Prize.) New York: New Market Press, 1990.

Castaneda, Carlos. *Journey to Ixtlan.* New York: Pocket Books, 1972.

Chernin, Kim. *The Hungry Self.* New York: Harper and Row, 1985.

Chopra, Deepak. *Quantum Healing: Exploring the Frontiers of Mind/ Body Medicine.* New York: Bantam Books, 1989.

Cinque, Ralph C. *Quit for Good: How to Break a Bad Habit.* Fremont, CA: Getwell, Stay well, America, 1991.

Cohen, Alan. *Joy Is My Compass.* Somerset, NJ: Alan Cohen Publications, 1990.

———. *The Healing of the Planet Earth.* Atlanta: New Leaf Distributors, 1987.

———. *Dare to Be Yourself.* Somerset, NJ: Alan Cohen Publications, 1991.

Cole-Whittaker, Terry. *Love and Power in a World Without Limits: A Woman's Guide to the Goddess Within.* San Francisco: Harper and Row, 1989.

Colton, Helen. *The Gift of Touch.* New York: Seaview/Putnam, 1983.

* Cott, Allan. *Fasting: The Ultimate Diet.* New York: Bantam Books, 1975.

Coudert, Jo. *Advice From a Failure.* Chelsea, MI: Scarborough House, 1965.

* Cousens, Gabriel, M.D. *Sevenfold Peace.* Tiburon, CA: H.J. Kramer Inc., 1990.

———. *Spiritual Nutrition and the Rainbow Diet.* Boulder, CO: Cassandra Press, 1986.

Cousins, Norman. *Head First.* New York: Penguin, 1990.

Covey, Stephen. *The 7 Habits of Highly Effective People.* New York: Simon & Schuster, 1989.

Cox, Connie, and Evatt, Cris. *Simply Organized!.* New York: Perigee Books, 1986.

---

* *These books contain information on fasting.*

Curtis, Donald. *40 Steps to Self Mastery.* Lakemont, GA: CSA Press, 1985.

Dadd, Debra Lynn. *Nontoxic and Natural.* New York: St. Martin's Press, 1990.

Dass, Ram. *Be Here Now.* New York: Crown Publishers, 1971.

Davis, Roy Eugene. *An Easy Guide to Meditation.* Lakemont, GA: CSA Press, 1988.

———. *God Has Given Us Every Good Thing.* Lakemont, GA: CSA Press, 1986.

———. *How to Have the Courage to Live and to Prosper.* Lakemont, GA: CSA Press, 1989.

———. *How You Can Use the Technique of Creative Imagination.* Lakemont, GA: CSA Press, 1988.

———. *Life Surrendered in God.* Lakemont, GA: CSA Press, 1990.

———. *The Responsibilities of Discipline.* Lakemont, GA: CSA Press, 1986.

———. *The Science of Kriya Yoga.* Lakemont, GA: CSA Press, 1984.

DeAngelis, Barbara. *How to Make Love All the Time.* New York: Dell Publishing, 1987.

———. *Secrets About Men Every Woman Should Know.* New York: Delacorte, 1990.

Dees, Morris. *A Season for Justice.* New York: Charles Scribner's & Sons, 1991.

* De Vries, Arnold. *Therapeutic Fasting.* Los Angeles: Chandler Book Company, 1963.

Diamond, Harvey. *Your Heart, Your Planet.* Santa Monica, CA: Hay House, 1990.

Diamond, Harvey, and Diamond, Marilyn. *Fit for Life.* New York: Warner Books, 1985.

———. *Fit for Life II: Living Health.* New York: Warner Books, 1987.

Diamond, Marilyn. *A New Way of Eating.* New York: Warner Books, 1987.

———. *The American Vegetarian Cookbook.* New York: Warner Books, 1990.

Dravecky, Dave, with Stafford, Tim. *Comeback.* New York: Harper and Row, 1990.

Dyer, Wayne W. *Gifts From Eykis.* New York: Simon and Schuster, 1983.

———. *What Do You Really Want for Your Children?.* New York: William Morrow and Company, Inc., 1985.

———. *You'll See It When You Believe It.* New York: William Morrow and Company, Inc., 1989.

---

* *These books contain information on fasting.*

Easwaran, Eknath. *Conquest of Mind.* Petaluma, CA: Nilgiri Press, 1988.

——. *Gandhi the Man.* Petaluma, CA: Nilgiri Press, 1978.

——. *The Compassionate Universe.* Petaluma, CA: Nilgiri Press, 1989.

* Ehret, Arnold. *Mucusless Diet Healing System.* Beaumont, CA: Ehret Literature Publishing Co., 1972.

Eisler, Riane. *The Chalice and the Blade.* San Francisco: Harper & Row, 1988.

* ——. *Rational Fasting.* New York: Benedict Lust Publications, 1971.

Felder, Leonard. *A Fresh Start.* New York: New American Library, 1987.

Ferguson, Marilyn. *The Aquarian Conspiracy.* Los Angeles: Jeremy P. Tarcher, Inc., 1980.

Fields, Rick. *Chop Wood, Carry Water.* Los Angeles: Jeremy P. Tarcher, Inc., 1984.

Fillmore, Charles. *Christian Healing.* Unity Village, MO: Unity Books, 1906.

——. *Jesus Christ Heals.* Unity Village, MO: Unity Books, 1939.

——. *Mysteries of Genesis.* Unity Village, MO: Unity Books, 1936.

——. *Prosperity.* Unity Village, MO: Unity Books, 1936.

——. *The Twelve Powers of Man.* Unity Village, MO: Unity Books, no date.

Finegold, Julius J., and Thetford, William N., eds. *Choose Once Again.* Berkeley, CA: Celestial Arts, 1981.

Fisher, Robert. *The Knight in Rusty Armor.* North Hollywood, CA: Wilshire Publishing, 1987.

Flynn. *Mister God, This is Anna.* New York: Ballantine Books, 1974.

Forward, Susan, with Buck, Craig. *Toxic Parents.* New York: Bantam Books, 1989.

Foster, Richard J. *Celebration of Discipline.* San Francisco: Harper and Row, 1978.

Fox, Arnold, M.D. and Fox, Barry, Ph.D. *Beyond Positive Thinking.* Santa Monica, CA: Hay House, 1991.

Fox, Emmet. *Power Through Constructive Thinking.* New York: Harper and Row, 1932.

Frankl, Viktor. *Man's Search for Meaning.* New York: Washington Square Press, 1963.

Free, Ann C. (Editing and Commentary) *Animals, Nature and Albert Schweitzer.* Bethesda, Maryland: Flying Fox Press, 1989.

Fulghum, Robert. *All I Really Need to Know I Learned in Kindergarten.* New York: Villard Books, 1988.

---

* *These books contain information on fasting.*

Fuller, R. Buckminster. *Critical Path*. New York: St. Martin's Press, 1981.

———. *Intuition*. San Luis Obispo, CA: Impact Publishers, 1970.

Gawain, Shakti. *Creative Visualization*. Mill Valley, CA: Whatever Publishing, 1978.

Gibran, Kahlil. *Jesus The Son of Man*. New York: Alfred A. Knopf, 1928.

———. *The Prophet*. New York: Alfred A. Knopf, 1923.

* Goldstein, Jack. *Triumph Over Disease by Fasting*. New York: Arco Publishing, 1977.

Goldsmith, Joel S. *Invisible Supply*. San Francisco: Harper Collins Publishers, 1991.

* Gross, Joy. *Raising Your Child Naturally*. Secaucus, NJ: Lyle Stuart Inc., 1983.

* ———. *Thin Again!*. Secaucus, NJ: Citadel Press, 1978.

* Haas, Elson, *Staying Healthy With Nutrition*. Berkeley, CA: Celestial Arts, 1992.

* ———. *Staying Healthy With the Seasons*. Berkeley, CA: Celestial Arts, 1981.

Halpern, Steven. *Sound Health*. New York: Harper and Row, 1985.

Hanh, Thich Nhat. *Peace Is Every Step*. New York: Bantam Books, 1991.

Hay, Louise L. *You Can Heal Your Life*. Santa Monica, CA: Hay House, 1984.

———. *Heart Thoughts*. Santa Monica, CA: Hay House, 1990.

———. *The Power is Within You*. Santa Monica, CA: Hay House, 1991.

* Hazzard, Linda Burfield. *Scientific Fasting*. Mokelumne Hill, CA: Health Research, 1963.

Hill, Napoleon. *The Master-key to Riches*. New York: Fawcett Crest, 1965.

Hoff, Benjamin. *The Tao of Pooh*. New York: E.P. Dutton, Inc., 1982.

Holmes, Ernest. *Sermon by the Sea*. Los Angeles: Science of Mind Publications, 1967.

———. *The Science of Mind*. New York: Dodd, Mead and Co., 1938.

———. *This Thing Called Life*. New York: Dodd, Mead and Co., 1943.

———. *This Thing Called You*. New York: Dodd, Mead and Co., 1948.

———. *Words That Heal Today*. New York: Dodd, Mead and Co., 1949.

Houston, Jean. *The Possible Human*. Los Angeles: Jeremy P. Tarcher, Inc., 1982.

———. *The Search for the Beloved*. Los Angeles: Jeremy P. Tarcher, Inc. 1987.

---

* These books contain information on fasting.

Huxley, Laura A. *Between Heaven & Earth*. Santa Monica, CA: Hay House, 1975.

——. and Ferrucci, Piero. *The Child of Your Dreams*. Minneapolis: CompCare Publishers, 1987.

* Immerman, Alan M., D.C. *Health Unlimited*. Happy Camp, CA: Naturegraph Publishers, 1989.

Jafolla, Mary Alice. *The Simple Truth*. Unity Village, MO: Unity Books, 1982.

Jampolsky, Gerald G., M.D. *Love Is Letting Go of Fear*. New York: Bantam Books, 1970.

——. *One Person Can Make A Difference*. New York: Bantam Books, 1990.

——. *Out of Darkness Into the Light*. New York: Bantam Books, 1989.

——. and Cirincione, Diane V. *Love Is The Answer: Creating Positive Relationships*. New York: Bantam, 1990.

Jastrow, Robert. *God and the Astronomers*. New York: Norton, 1978.

Jeffers, Susan., Ph.D. *Feel the Fear and Do It Anyway*. New York: Fawcett Columbia, 1987.

——. *Opening Our Hearts to Men*. New York: Fawcett Columbia, 1990.

Jensen, Bernard. *A New Slant on Health and Beauty*. Escondido, CA: Jensen Publishing, 1976.

* ——. *Chlorella: Gem of the Orient*. Escondido, CA: Bernard Jensen, 1987.

* ——. *Empty Harvest*. New York: Avon, 1990.

——. *Tissue Cleansing Through Bowel Management*. Escondido, CA: Bernard Jensen, 1980.

——. *Vibrant Health from Your Kitchen*. Escondido, CA: Bernard Jensen, 1986.

Johnson, Spencer. *The Precious Present*. New York: Doubleday and Co., 1984.

Jones, Susan Smith. *Choose To Be Healthy*. Berkeley, CA: Celestial Arts, 1987.

Juline, Kathleen, ed. *Beyond Appearances*. Los Angeles: Science of Mind Communications, 1990.

Jung, Carl G. *Man and His Symbols*. New York: Dell, 1968.

Keyes, Ken, Jr. *The Hundredth Monkey*. Coos Bay, OR: Love Line Books, 1985.

——. *Handbook to Higher Consciousness*. Coos Bay, OR: Love Line Books, 1975.

——. *Your Life is a Gift*. Coos Bay, OR: Love Line Books, 1987.

---

* *These books contain information on fasting.*

Kilham, Christopher S. *The Bread & Circus Whole Food Bible*. New York: Addison-Wesley Publishing Company, Inc., 1991.

Kime, Zane R. M.D., M.S. *Sunlight*. Penryn, CA: World Health Publications, 1980.

Klaper, Michael, M.D. *Pregnancy, Children and the Vegan Diet*. Umatilla, FL: Gentle World Press, 1988.

——. *Vegan Nutrition: Pure & Simple*. Umatilla, FL: Gentle World Press, 1987.

——. *The Power of Unconditional Love*. Coos Bay, OR: Love Line Books, 1990.

* Krakovitz, Rob. *High Energy*. Los Angeles: Jeremy P. Tarcher, Inc., 1986.

Kubler-Ross, Elisabeth. *On Life After Death*. Berkeley CA: Celestial Arts, 1991.

Kulvinskas, Viktoras. *Survival Into the 21st Century*. Wethersfield, CT: Omangod Press, 1975.

Lawrence, Brother, and Laubach, Frank. *Practicing His Presence*. Portland, ME: Christian Books, 1976.

Lehrman, Fredric. *The Sacred Landscape*. Berkeley, CA: Celestial Arts, 1988.

Leslie, Sharlin. *Slanting*. Washington Mills, NY: Starlight, 1985.

Lindbergh, Anne Morrow. *Gift from the Sea*. New York: Pantheon Books, 1975.

MacEachern, Diane. *Save Our Planet*. New York: Dell Publishing, 1990.

Mandino, Og. *The Greatest Miracle in the World*. New York: Bantam Books, 1975.

——. *The Greatest Salesman In the World*. New York: Bantam Books, 1968.

Mary. *All That You Are*. Marina del Rey, CA: DeVorss and Co., 1959.

——. *You Are God*. Marina del Rey, CA: Devorss and Co., 1955.

Maslow, Abraham. *Toward A Psychology of Being*. Princeton, NJ: Van Nostrand, 1968.

Mata, Sri Daya. *Only Love*. Los Angeles: Self-Realization Fellowship, 1971.

——. *Finding the Joy Within You*. Los Angeles: Self-Realization Fellowship, 1990.

McDougall, John, *McDougall's Medicine*. Piscataway, NJ: New Century, 1986.

——. *The McDougall Plan*. Piscataway, NJ: New Century, 1984.

Mendelsohn, Robert S., M.D. *Confessions of a Medical Heretic*. New York: Warner Books, 1979.

---

* *These books contain information on fasting.*

Millman, Dan. *The Warrior Athlete: Body, Mind and Spirit*. Walpole, NH: Stillpoint Publishing, 1979.

———. *Way of the Peaceful Warrior*. Tiburon, CA: H.J. Kramer, 1984.

———. *Sacred Journey of a Peaceful Warrior*. Tiburon, CA: H.J. Kramer, 1991.

Montagu, Ashley. *Growing Young*. Westport, CT: Bergin and Garvey Publishers, Inc., 1989.

Muggeridge, Malcolm. *Something Beautiful for God*. New York: Harper and Row, 1971.

Muller, Robert. *Most of All, They Taught Me Happiness*. New York: Doubleday, 1978.

———. *New Genesis, Shaping a Global Spirituality*. New York: Doubleday, 1984.

———. *The Birth of Global Civilization*. Anacortes, WA: World Happiness and Cooperation, 1991.

Murray, Michael, N.D. Pizzorno, Joseph, N.D. *Encyclopedia of Natural Medicine*. Rocklin, CA: Prima Publishing, 1990.

Nearing, Helen. *Simple Food for the Good Life*. Walpole, NH: Stillpoint Publishing, 1980.

* Nelson, Dennis. *Maximizing Your Nutrition*. (Obtained through Box 2302, Santa Cruz, CA 95063, $4.50.)

Null, Gary. *The Vegetarian Handbook*. New York: St. Martin's Press, 1987.

Oaklander, Violet. *Windows to Our Children*. Highland, NY: Gestalt Journal, 1989.

Ornish, Dean, M.D. *Reversing Heart Disease*. New York: Random House, 1990.

* Oswald, Jean A., and Shelton, Herbert. *Fasting for the Health of It*. Pueblo, CO: Nationwide Press, 1983.

———. *Yours for Health: The Life and Times of Herbert A. Shelton*. Franklin, WI: Franklin Books, 1989.

* Owen, Bob. *Roger's Recovery From AIDS*. Malibu, CA: DAVAR, 1987.

Peale, Norman Vincent. *The Power of Positive Living*. New York: Doubleday, 1990.

Peck, M. Scott. *The Road Less Traveled*. New York: Touchstone/ Simon and Schuster, 1980.

Perkins-Reed, Marcia A. *When 9–5 Isn't Enough*. Santa Monica, CA: Hay House, 1990.

Peterson, Wilfred A. *The Art of Creative Thinking*. Santa Monica, CA: Hay House, 1991.

* Pilcher, Joseph. *Fast Health*. New York: Berkeley Publishing Corp., 1977.

---

* *These books contain information on fasting.*

* Pilgrim, Peace. *Peace Pilgrim*. Santa Fe, NM: Ocean Tree Books, 1983.

———. *Steps Toward Inner Peace*. Hemet, CA: Friends of Peace Pilgrim, 1989.

Ponder, Catherine. *Open Your Mind to Receive*. Marina del Rey, CA: DeVorss and Company, 1983.

Price, John Randolph. *A Spiritual Philosophy for the New World*. Boerne, TX: Quartus Books, 1990.

———. *Mastering Money*. Boerne, TX: Quartus Books, 1990.

———. *Superbeings*. Boerne, TX: Quartus Books, 1981.

———. *The Abundance Book*. Boerne, TX: Quartus Books, 1987.

———. *The Planetary Commission*. Boerne, TX: The Quartus Foundation, 1984.

Prigogine, Ilya. *Order Out of Chaos*. New York: Bantam Books, 1984.

Proctor, Bob. *You Were Born Rich*. Willowdale, Ontario: McCrary Publishing, 1984.

Rama, Swami; Ballantine, Rudolph; and Hymes, Alan. *Science of Breath*. Honesdale, PA: The Himalayan International Institute of Yoga Science and Philosophy, 1979.

Ray, Sandra. *I Deserve Love*. Berkeley, CA: Celestial Arts, 1976.

———. *The Only Diet There Is*. Berkeley, CA: Celestial Arts, 1981.

Reid, Clyde. *Celebrate the Temporary*. New York: Harper and Row, 1972.

Robbins, Anthony. *Unlimited Power*. New York: Simon and Schuster, 1986.

Robbins, John. *Diet for a New America*. Walpole, NH: Stillpoint Publishing, 1987.

———. and Mortifee, Ann. *In Search of Balance*. Tiburon, CA: H.J. Kramer, Inc., 1991.

Rosanoff, Nancy. *Intuition Workout*. Boulder Creek, CA: Aslan Publisher, 1988.

* Ross, Shirley. *Fasting*. New York: St. Martin's Press, 1976.

Roth, Geneen. *Breaking Free from Compulsive Eating*. New York: Penguin Books, 1986.

Saint-Exupery, Antoine de. *The Little Prince*. New York: Harcourt, Brace and World, 1943.

Schaef, Anne Wilson. *Meditations For Women Who Do Too Much*. New York: Harper and Row, 1990.

Schutz, Will. *Profound Simplicity*. New York: Bantam Books, 1979.

Shain, Merle. *Hearts That We Broke Long Ago*. New York: Bantam Books, 1983.

Sheldrake, Rupert. *A New Science of Life*. Los Angeles: Jeremy P. Tarcher, 1981.

---

* *These books contain information on fasting.*

* Shelton, Herbert M. *Fasting Can Save Your Life*. Chicago: Natural Hygiene Press, 1964.

* ———. *Fasting for Renewal of Life*. Chicago: Natural Hygiene Press, 1978.

* ———. *Human Life, Its Philosophy and Laws*. Oklahama City: How to Live Publishing Co., 1928.

* ———. *Superior Nutrition*. San Antonio, TX: Dr. Shelton's Health School, 1951.

* ———. *Food Combining Made Easy*. San Antonio, TX: Willow Publishing Inc., 1982.

* ———. *The Science and Fine Art of Fasting*. Chicago: Natural Hygiene Press, 1978.

* ———; Willard, Jo; and Oswald, Jean A. *The Original Natural Hygiene Weight Loss Diet Book*. New Canaan, CT: Keats Publishing, 1986.

Siegel, Bernie S. *Love, Medicine and Miracles*. New York: Harper and Row, 1986.

———. *Peace, Love and Healing*. New York: Harper and Row, 1989.

Sidhwa, Keki R. *Medical Drugs on Trial? Verdict: "Guilty!"* Chicago: Natural Hygiene Press, 1976.

* Sinclair, Upton. *The Fasting Cure*. Mokelumne Hill, CA: Health Research, 1955.

Sinetar, Marsha. *Do What You Love, the Money Will Follow*. New York: Dell Publishing, 1987.

———. *Living Happily Ever After*. New York: Dell Publishing, 1990.

Singer, Peter. *Animal Liberation*. New York: Avon, 1991.

———. *Ordinary People As Monks and Mystics*. New York: Paulist Press, 1986.

———. *Animal Rights*. New York: The New York Review, 1975.

* Smith, David R. *Fasting: A Neglected Discipline*. Fort Washington, PA: Christian Literature Crusade, 1969.

Smith, Manuel J. *When I Say No, I Feel Guilty*. New York: Bantam Books, 1985.

Stark, Harold Richter. *A Doctor Goes to Heaven*. Littlerock, CA: High Mountain Estate, 1982.

Stevens, John. *The Marathon Monks of Mount Hiei*. Boston: Shambhala, 1988.

Steward-Wallace, Sir John. ed. *Women Saints East and West*. Hollywood, CA: Vedanta Press, 1955.

Stone, Hal, and Winkelman, Sidra. *Embracing Our Selves*. Marina del Ray, CA: DeVorss and Co., 1985.

Szekely, Edmond Bordeaux. *From Enoch to the Dead Sea Scrolls*. Matsqui, BC, Canada: I.B.S. Internacional, 1978. (The Essence

---

* *These books contain information on fasting.*

books by Szekely can be ordered through The International Biogenic Society (IBS), Box 205, Matsqui, British Columbia, Canada V0X 150.)

* ——. *The Essenes by Josephus and His Contemporaries*. Matsqui, BC, Canada: I.B.S. Internacional, 1981.

* ——. *The Essene Gospel of Peace*, Book One. Matsqui, BC, Canada: I.B.S. Internacional, 1981.

* ——. *The Essene Jesus*. Matsqui, BC, Canada: I.B.S. Internacional, 1977.

Talbot, Michael. *The Holographic Universe*. New York: Harper Collins, 1991.

Taniguchi, Masaharu. *The Taniguchi Commentary on the Gospel According to St. John*. Gardena, CA: SEICHO-NO-IE, INC., 1988.

——. *365 Golden Keys to a Completely Free Life*. Gardena, CA: SEICHO-NO-IE, INC., 1990.

Taub, Edward A. *Voyage to Wellness*. Orange, CA: Wellness America, 1988.

The Bible.

The Earth Works Group. *50 Simple Things Kids Can Do To Save The Earth*. Kansas City, MO: Andrews & McMeel, 1990.

——. *50 Simple Things You Can Do To Save The Earth*. Whittier, CA: Green Leaf Publishers, 1990.

Thoreau, Henry David. *Works of Henry David Thoreau*. New York: Crown Publishers, 1981.

* Tilden, John H., M.D. *Toxemia: The Basic Cause of Disease*. Chicago: Natural Hygiene Press, 1974.

——. *Toxemia Explained, Revised Edition*. Mokelumne Hill, CA: Health Research, 1981.

* Treece, Patricia. *The Santified Body*. New York: Doubleday, 1987.

Veary, Nana. *Change We Must*. Vancouver, BC, Canada: Water Margin Press, 1989.

Venolia, Carol. *Healing Environments*. Berkeley, CA: Celestial Arts, 1988.

* Wade, Carlson. *Slim Fasting*. West Nyack, NY: Parker Publishing, 1977.

Wagner, Lindsay and Spade Ariane. *The High Road to Health*. New York: Prentice Hall Press, 1990.

Wagner, Lindsay and Klein Robert. *New Beauty: The Accupressure Face Life*. New York: Prentice Hall Press, 1987.

* Walford, Roy L. *Maximum Life Span*. New York: W.W. Norton and Co., 1983.

---

* *These books contain information on fasting.*

* Walford, Roy L., M.D. *The 120 Year Diet*. New York: Simon and Schuster, 1986.

* Walker, Norman W. *Become Younger*. Prescott, AZ: Norwalk Press, 1978.

* ———. *Colon Health*. Prescott, AZ: Norwalk Press, 1979.

* ———. *Fresh Vegetable and Fruit Juices*. Prescott, AZ: Norwalk Press, 1970.

* Wallis, Arthur. *God's Chosen Fast*. Fort Washington, PA: Christian Literature Crusade, 1971.

Wapnick, Kennick. *The Fifty Miracle Principles of a Course In Miracles*. Crompond, NY: Foundation for A Course In Miracles, 1985.

Weil, Andrew. *The Natural Mind, Health and Healing*. New York: Houghton Mifflin, 1986.

Wesley, John. *Sermons on Several Occasions*. London, England: Epworth Press, 1971.

* ———. *The Journal of the Reverend John Wesley*. London: The Epworth Press, 1938.

Wigmore, Ann. *The Sprouting Book*. Wayne, NJ: Avery Publishing Group Inc., 1986.

Wilbur, Ken. *The Holographic Paradigm*. Boulder, CO: Shambhala, 1982.

Wilde, Stuart. *Miracles*. Taos, NM: White Dove, Intl., 1983.

———. *The Secret of Life*. Taos, NM: White Dove, Intl., 1990.

———. *The Trick to Money is Having Some!* Taos, NM: White Dove, Intl., 1989.

Yogananda, Paramahansa. *Man's Eternal Quest*. Los Angeles: Self-Realization Fellowship, 1976.

———. *Metaphysical Meditations*. Los Angeles: Self-Realization Fellowship, 1984.

———. *Spiritual Diary*. Los Angeles: Self-Realization Fellowship, 1968.

———. *The Autobiography of a Yogi*. Los Angeles: Self-Realization Fellowship, 1974.

———. *Scientific Healing Affirmations*. Los Angeles: Self-Realization Fellowship, 1974.

———. *The Divine Romance*. Los Angeles: Self-Realization Fellowship, 1986.

———. *The Law of Success*. Los Angeles: Self-Realization Fellowship, 1972.

———. *Where There Is Light*. Los Angeles: Self-Realization Fellowship, 1988.

Yukteswar, Swami Sri. *The Holy Science*. Los Angeles: Self-Realization Fellowship, 1972.

---

* *These books contain information on fasting.*

Zinn, Rebecca. *On the Wings of Spirit*. Kansas City, MO: Uni-Sun, 1988.

——. *Stardust*. Walpole, NH: Uni-Sun, 1986.

Resource Directory

Aloe Falls®, Yerba Prima®, Inc., 740 Jefferson Avenue, Ashland, OR 97520-3743.

Aloe Falls® by Yerba Prima® is preservative-free, great tasting and Certified Active™, which means that Aloe Falls® is lab-verified to provide the health benefits of aloe. Found in your health food store, their Aloe Juice Formula contains 50% aloe vera and a powerful herbal blend of peppermint, chamomile, and parsley to boost its soothing properties in your digestive system. They also have Hawaiian ginger Aloe, 100% Whole Leaf Aloe, and light and refreshing tea and juice beverages. Write for more information.

American Natural Hygiene Society, *Health Science* magazine, James M. Lennon, P.O. Box 30630, Tampa, FL 33630, (813) 855-6607.

This wonderful organization publishes the award-winning *Health Science* magazine. Annual membership dues are $25.00 which includes a subscription to *Health Science* to which I contribute articles regularly. Members also receive discounts on health books, videos, cassette programs, seminars, lectures, and more. I encourage you to write and become a member.

Bio-Strath, distributed by Bioforce of America, 122 Smith Road Extension, Kinderhook, NY 12106, (800) 645-7198.

Bio-Strath is an excellent liquid herbal food supplement. It's based on plasmolysed yeast and wild herbs and has been available for decades in over 40 countries around the world—a result of accurate, scientifically-based work. I've included Bio-Strath in my health program for over a decade and highly recommend it. It has been found to combat fatigue, lethargy and nervousness, increase physical and mental efficiency, reinforce the immune defense system and restore vitality. It's available in health food stores or you can call the number above to order.

BodySlant & Body Lift, P.O. Box 1667, Newport Beach, CA 92663, (800) 443-3917.

A superb slant board that also functions as a bed and ottoman. I recommend using it daily. The Body Lift is a simple and comfortable way to stand your body upside down so that your shoulders rest on a thick cushion, your head dangles off the floor, and your neck naturally stretches. I use the BodySlant and Body Lift daily and highly recommend them for better health, vitality, and rejuvenation. For more information or to order, write or call them.

CamoCare, Abkit, Inc., 207 East 94th Street, New York, NY 10128, (800) CAMOCARE.

CamoCare is a marvelous line of natural skincare based on a special chamomile flower from Europe. Clinical studies show CamoCare has a dramatic soothing and smoothing effect on the skin; visually reducing fine lines and wrinkles caused by sun damage. I recommend CamoCare highly, particularly their Under-Eye Therapy and Facial Therapy. CamoCare's new alpha+beta hydroxy products, called Face Lift, are a real breakthrough because, thanks to the soothing chamomile, they reveal beautiful new skin without sting or burn.

Celebrate Life! Audiocassette series by Susan Smith Jones, Ph.D. Includes 7 tapes, 14 different programs, and 6 guided meditations.

1A. *The Main Ingredients: Positive Thinking & The Mind*
1B. *The Main Ingredients: Exercise, Nutrition & Relaxation*
2A. *Get High on Life through Exercise*
2B. *Make Your Exercise Program a Great Adventure*
3A. *Nutrition for Aliveness*
3B. *Superlative Dining*
4A. *Your Thoughts May Be Fattening*
4B. *Living Lightly, Naturally Trim*
5A. *Experience Aliveness*
5B. *Learn from Children How to Celebrate Life*
6A. *The Joy of Solitude & The Art of Serenity*
6B. *Relaxation & Meditation: Natural & Easy*
7A. *Celebrate Your Magnificence*
7B. *Affirm a Beautiful Life*

To order the entire 7-tape album, send $80.00 (or $15.00 per tape), U.S. check or money order only, payable to: Health Unlimited, P.O. Box 49396, Los Angeles, CA 90049. For more information on these tapes, send a business size, stamped, self-addressed envelope to the above address. For credit card orders, call (800) 220-ROSE.

Center for Chiropractic and Conservative Therapy, Inc., 4310 Lichau Road, Penngrove, CA 94951, (707) 792-2325.

Co-founded by Dr. Alan Goldhamer and Dr. Jennifer Marono, this center offers an alternative approach to the restoration and maintenance of optimum health. The focus is on helping people make diet and lifestyle changes and certified supervising fasting.

DeSouza Chlorophyll Products, P.O. Box 395, Dept. SJ, Beaumont, CA 92220, (800) 373-5171.

DeSouza's liquid chlorophyll (also in tablets and capsules) and other personal care products are very beneficial for enhancing health. I highly recommend their entire line of products. For additional information, a catalog, or to order, please write or call the company.

Dr. Cinque's Health Resort, 305 Verdin Drive, Buda, TX 78610, (512) 295-4256.

This is a small, quiet place where you can relax and rejuvenate your body at affordable prices. Dr. Cinque offers water and juice fasting programs for those seeking detoxification or weight loss. Dr. Ralph Cinque is certified by the International Association of Hygienic Physicians (IAHP) as a qualified and experienced fasting supervisor. There is no better way to promptly break bad habits and switch to a health-supporting lifestyle than by fasting as I describe in that chapter.

EarthSave, 706 Frederick Street, Santa Cruz, CA 95062-2205, (408) 423-4069.

Founded by John Robbins, author of *Diet for a New America* and *May All Be Fed,* EarthSave is a nonprofit organization providing education and leadership for transition to more healthful and environmentally sound food choices, non-polluting energy supplies and a wiser use of natural resources. Write for their catalog of books, audio and videotapes, and other products.   ·

Ester-C, Inter-Cal Corporation, 533 Madison Avenue, Prescott, AZ 86301, (520) 445-8063.

Inter-Cal is the manufacturer of Ester-C calcium ascorbate. Ester-C is formulated in a wide variety of nutritional supplements by many different distributors and can be found on the shelves of health food stores, drug stores, and supermarkets. Look for labels with the Ester-C logo (a small "e" enclosed in a big "C"). If you can't find a source, call or write Inter-Cal.

Fortified Flax, Omega-Life, Inc., P.O. Box 208, Brookfield, WI 53008-0208, (414) 786-2070, (800) 328-3529.

Fortified Flax is one of the best sources of Omega-3 fatty acids, along with soluble and insoluble fiber, plus a great source of lignans. This brand is fortified with the proper vitamins and minerals to help the essential fatty acids in flax metabolize properly, as well as keep the ground seed fresh. Write for more information.

Good Medicine, Physicians Committee for Responsible Medicine, 5100 Wisconsin Avenue NW, Suite 404, Washington, DC, 20016.

An excellent quarterly newsletter on health and living a vegetarian lifestyle. A year's subscription and annual membership costs $20.00 and is tax deductible.

How To Achieve Any Goal: The Magic of Creative Visualization— Living Your Vision/Commitment.

A one-and-a-half-hour audiocassette by Susan Smith Jones. Includes a twenty-minute meditation you can use every day to help you realize your goals and dreams. To order, please send $15.00, U.S. check or money order only, payable to: Health Unlimited, P.O. Box 49396, Los Angeles, CA 90049.

Jones, Susan Smith, Health Unlimited, P.O. Box 49396, Los Angeles, CA 90049.

Lectures, seminars, workshops, retreats, and keynote addresses for your corporation, community, or church group. For information, write to the above address, attention: Director.

Kyo-Chrome, Kyo-Green, Kyolic Aged Garlic Extract, and Gingko Biloba Plus, Wakunaga of America Co., Ltd., 23501 Madero, Mission Viejo, CA 92691, (800) 825-7888.

These are all excellent nutritional supplements available in your health food store that I write about in detail in my books *Choose To Live Each Day Fully* and *The Main Ingredients of Health & Happiness.* For more information or free samples of these products, write or call.

Nutrition Action Health Letter, Center for Science in the Public Interest, 1875 Connecticut Avenue NW, Washington, DC 20009.

This is an excellent newsletter on nutrition and health topics. Subscriptions are available for $24.00 for one year (ten issues).

Peace Pilgrim, Friends of Peace Pilgrim, 43480 Cedar Avenue, Hemet, CA 92544, (909) 927-7678.

To receive a free, 32-page booklet, *Steps Toward Inner Peace;* a free, 216-page book, *Peace Pilgrim;* a marvelous free video documentary titled "The Spirit of Peace"; or an inspiring newsletter, write to the above address. Friends of Peace Pilgrim is a nonprofit, tax-exempt, all-volunteer organization.

PMRI Residential Retreats, 900 Bridgeway, Suite One, Sausalito, CA 94965, (800) 775-PMRI, Ext. 221.

PMRI stands for Preventive Medicine Research Institute. This non-profit public institute offers Dr. Dean Ornish's week-long residential retreats to teach comprehensive lifestyle changes to individuals. Dr. Ornish attends each of the retreats, giving lectures and answering questions about his program. Gourmet, low fat, low cholesterol meals and cooking instruction are also provided.

Self-Realization Fellowship, 3880 San Rafael Avenue, Los Angeles, CA 90065, (213) 225-2471.

Write for more information on Paramahansa Yogananda, his books, meditation, home study lessons, the locations of the Self-Realization Fellowship Centers, or a catalog of their books, tapes, quarterly magazine and other products.

Soft Health Sauna, 1561 South Congress Avenue, Suite 272, Delray Beach, FL 33445, (800) SOFT-HEAT.

Taking saunas has been an important part of my health program for more than twenty years. Soft Health Sauna makes a top quality, unique sauna that I highly recommend (for your home or office) for optimum health. It is excellent for weight contol, skin cleansing, pain relief, stress reduction, stiff joints and cardiovascular fitness. Call or write for their detailed information packet or to order. It's one of the best investments you can make for radiant health and vitality.

Spectrum Naturals, Inc., 133 Copeland Street, Petaluma, CA 94952, (800) 995-2705.

Producers of Veg Omega-3 Organic Flax Seed Oil, Spectrum Spread, Wheat Germ Oil, natural vegetable oils pure-pressed without chemicals, and a variety of natural, delicious condiments. Write for their information and consumer education series on healthy oils.

Super Blue Green Algae, Cell Tech, 1300 Main Street, Klamath Falls, OR 97601-5941, (800) 883-8848.

Founded in 1982 by Daryl and Marta Kollman, Cell Tech pro-duces the best blue-green algae in Upper Klamath Lake, known for its pure water which provides a unique growth medium for blue-green micro-algae. Their super blue-green algae is a rich source of natural nutrition which helps heal and rejuvenate the body. It's an important part of my "whole foods" nutrition program and I highly recommend it. The Cell Tech Network is composed of thousands of men and women throughout the United States and Canada who are committed to make positive changes in themselves and in the world. Cell Tech is a company with heart, redefining what it means to be in business. Please call the above number for more information on the company, how to order, or how to become a distributor.

Tree of Life Seminars & Rejuvenation Center, P.O. Box 1080, Patagonia, AZ 85624, (520) 394-2520.

Tree of Life is a metaphor for a way of being in the world which supports one's own spiritual evolution in an integrated, balanced, and harmonious way. There are a variety of seminars (including rejuvenation retreats) conducted by Nora and Gabriel Cousens, M.D. Write for a brochure.

Vita-Mix, Vita-Mix Corporation, 8615 Usher Road, Cleveland, OH 44138, (800) VITAMIX.

For seventy years, the Vita-Mix Corporation has been dedicated to improving lives with quality products. Substituting health-building, whole food nutrition in place of devitalized, packaged food is fast and convenient with the Vita-Mix Total Nutrition Center. Turn fruits and vegetables into "whole food" juices in less than four minutes. Freeze a half gallon of all-fruit ice cream in less than 60 seconds. The machine performs 35 processes in all. The Vita-Mix TNC delivers to your body the balanced nutrition found only in whole foods, which ultimately can improve the way you look and feel. Please refer to this book when calling for further information or to order.

Westbrae Natural/Westsoy, 1065 E. Walnut Avenue, Carson, CA 90746, (310) 886-8200, (800) SOY-MILK.

Westbrae makes a complete line of delicious, non-dairy, vegetarian, all natural, organic milk alternatives made from rice and soy, in addition to a variety of healthy food items (soups, beans, snacks, etc), all available in natural food stores. For more information on their soy beverages and other products, or for samples or product coupons, call (800) SOY-MILK.

Y.S. HoneyBee Farms, RR1, Sheridan, IL 60551, (800) 654-4593.

Their bee pollen, propolis, and royal jelly help to increase energy, boost the immune system, rejuvenate and detoxify the body, promote longevity, and reverse the aging process. Their products are pure, harvested by healthy bees, quality controlled, and organic—meaning pesticide, herbicide, and pollutant-free. Y.S. Bee Farms bee products are available at your local health food store but I encourage you to call for more information.

About the Author

Susan Smith Jones is a leading voice for health, fitness, and peaceful living in America today. She not only teaches wellness, she lives it—dynamically. In 1985, Susan was selected as one of ten *Healthy American Fitness Leaders* by The President's Council on Physical Fitness and Sports,* and in 1988, the President's Council designated Susan as National Master in weight training. Susan enjoys hiking, ocean-swimming, jogging, stretching, weight training, cycling, yoga, in-line skating and walking. Looking for more of a challenge, she completed a 100-mile run from Santa Barbara to Los Angeles and has participated in several triathalons.

Susan speaks with authority. Her credentials include a doctorate in health sciences, a Master's degree in kinesiology, (specializing in exercise physiology) and a Bachelor's in psychology. She has been a fitness instructor to students, staff, and faculty at UCLA for over 20 years. But she is probably best known as an advocate of healthy, peaceful living, and positive thinking. She is the author of eight books, appears regularly on radio and television talk shows, and has written more than 500 magazine articles (many award-winning) with her picture on several covers.

Susan also travels internationally as a health and fitness consultant and motivational speaker for community, corporate, and church groups. Her inspiring keynote presentations and workshops are often scheduled one to two years in advance. As a health and fitness trainer, she develops personalized wellness programs for individuals and families.

Susan is founder and president of Health Unlimited, a Los Angeles-based consulting firm dedicated to the advancement of human potential, health education, and peaceful living. She has acquired the nickname of "Sunny" and lives in Brentwood, Los Angeles.

*Other honorees have included Jack LaLanne, Richard Simmons, Kathy Smith, Denise Austin, Coach John Wooden, Senator Richard Lugar, Gold-medalist John Nabers, George Allen, Astronaut James Lovell, and Ronald Reagan.

Other Books by Susan Smith Jones

Choose To Be Healthy
Choose To Live Each Day Fully
The Main Ingredients of Health & Happiness

Audiocassettes

Celebrate Life! (7-tape album)
Choose To Live a Balanced Life*
A Fresh Start: Rejuvenate Your Body*
Making Your Life a Great Adventure*

**If you wish more information on Susan's audiocassette programs or would like to purchase her books and tapes, please call anytime:
(800) 220-ROSE**

*2-tape albums recorded "live" from her popular seminars.

Other Celestial Arts books you may enjoy

Choose to be Healthy
By Susan Smith Jones, Ph.D.
The choices we make in life can greatly increase our health and happiness—this book details how to analyze one's choices about food, exercise, thought, work and play, and then use this information to create a better, healthier life. Paper, 252 pages.

Staying Healthy with Nutrition
By Elson Haas, M.D.
The long-awaited examination of how what we eat determines our health and well-being. A truly complete reference work, it details every aspect of nutrition from drinking water to medicinal foods to the latest biochemical research. Paper, 1,200 pages.

Staying Healthy with the Seasons
By Elson Haas, M.D.
One of the most popular of the new health books, this is a blend of Eastern and Western medicines, nutrition, herbology, exercise, and preventive healthcare. Paper, 252 pages.

The Family Health Guide to Homeopathy
By Dr. Barry Rose, Forward by Sir Yehudi Menuhin
This book offers guidelines for diagnosing and treating over 200 common ailments. Each area of the body is covered in detail with separate sections on first aid, dealing with emergencies, pregnancy, health problems in children, and infectious diseases. Paper, 310 pages.

Love is Letting Go of Fear
By Gerald Jampolsky, M.D.
One of the most popular New Age books ever. The lessons in this extremely popular little book, based on *A Course in Miracles,* will teach you to let go of fear and remember that our true essence is love. Includes daily exercises. Over 1,000,000 copies in print. Paper, 144 pages.

Gentle Yoga
By Lorna Bell, R.N. and Eudora Seyfer
This book is especially designed for people with arthritis, stroke damage, multiple scleroses, those in wheelchairs, or anyone who needs a gentle, practical way to improve their health through exercise. The book is spiral bound to stay open while you work and includes over 135 helpful illustration. Paper or spiral,144 pages.

Recovery from Addiction
By John Finnegan and Daphne Grey
Alternative herbal and nutritional therapies for a wide range of addictions, from cigarettes to sugar to caffeine to hard drugs. Includes first-person accounts of how these treatments have worked for a variety of specific problems. Paper, 192 pages.

Self Esteem
By Virginia Satir
A simple and succinct declaration of self-worth for the individual in modern society who is looking for new hope, new possibilities, and new, positive feelings about themselves. Paper, 64 pages.

Moosewood Cookbook (expanded edition)
By Mollie Katzen
This top-to-bottom revision of our bestselling cookbook retains all the old favorites and adds twenty-five all-new recipes. All recipes are as delicious as ever, and the lowered amounts of high-fat dairy products and eggs now reflect today's lighter tastes. "One of the most attractive, least dogmatic meatless cookbooks printed . . . an engaging blend of hand-lettered care and solid food information." —*The New York Post*. Paper or cloth, 256 pages.

Healing Environments
By Carol Venolia
This holistic approach to "indoor well-being" examines healing, awareness, and empowerment, and how they are affected by various aspects of our environment. Its principles can be applied to homes, workplaces, and healthcare centers to bring greater peace and harmony into our lives. Paper, 240 pages.

Available from your local bookstore, or order direct from the publisher.

CELESTIAL ARTS, P.O. Box 7123, Berkeley, CA 94707
For VISA, Mastercard or American Express orders, call **(800) 841-BOOK**

"Her writing and presence continuously inspires me and reminds me that health, inner peace, and a joyful heart are available to me if I choose them. She is a master teacher of a balanced path of strength and heart."

ALAN COHEN
Motivational speaker and author of *Dare to be Yourself*

"During my 15 years of medical educational experience in a hospital setting, it has become very clear that complete patient treatment involves physical, mental, emotional, and spiritual healing...I am also convinced that many illnesses, diseases, and surgical procedures could be prevented by choosing to live a healthy lifestyle as described so beautifully in her latest book...CHOOSE TO LIVE PEACEFULLY. I am highly recommending [Susan Smith Jones's] work to physicians, nurses, other hospital personnel, and all my friends."

GARY L. BRINK, MSW
Director of Educational Services, Bay Area Hospital, Coos Bay, Oregon

"If you would like some practical effective ways to deal with stress; if you desire to be healthier, happier, or more peaceful; if you want some insightful guidance on how to live a more balanced life; or if you simply want to enrich your experience of living, making your life a great adventure and celebration, then Susan's [CHOOSE TO LIVE PEACEFULLY] is just for you."

GEORGE C. MARKS
Assistant minister, Founder's Church, Los Angeles, California

"Books that I love become more than ink on paper; they become good friends. Long after they are read, even sitting on the shelf, their vibrations continue to bless, heal, enrich, and nurture me. Susan's latest book, CHOOSE TO LIVE PEACEFULLY, is destined to be such a friend."

JOHN STRICKLAND
Minister, Unity Church of Hawaii, Honolulu

"CHOOSE TO LIVE PEACEFULLY clearly reveals the author's extensive research and personal application of everything she writes about. Here are guidelines to a lifestyle fully supportive of the reader's highest aspirations and spiritual growth."

ROY EUGENE DAVIS
President and founder of the Center for Spiritual Awareness